AF538915

ROLE OF EVALUATION IN EDUCATION

ROLE OF EVALUATION IN EDUCATION

Edited by

S.P. NAIK

ANMOL PUBLICATIONS PVT. LTD.

NEW DELHI - 110 002 (INDIA)

ANMOL PUBLICATIONS PVT. LTD.
4374/4B, Ansari Road, Daryaganj
New Delhi - 110 002
Ph.: 23261597, 23278000
Visit us at: www.anmolpublications.com

Role of Evaluation in Education

ISBN 81-261-0162-8

PRINTED IN INDIA

Published by J.L. Kumar for Anmol Publications Pvt. Ltd., New Delhi - 110 002 and Printed at Mehra Offset Press, Delhi.

Contents

Contents

PREFACE

This book is primarily designed to serve as an authoritative reference work on Role of Evaluation in Education. The material is compiled from diverse authentic sources.

Role of Evaluation in educational technology; Approach to evaluation; Evaluation for revision; Evaluation resources and assessment techniques; Evaluation proceses and strategies etc. are the major themes, discussed in this book.

I am thankful to all the scholars and authors whose writings are cited or substantially made use of in this book. I am also grateful to Mr. J. L. Kumar for agreeing to publish this book.

—Editor

1

THE ROLE OF EVALUATION IN EDUCATIONAL TECHNOLOGY

EVALUATION AND EDUCATIONAL TECHNOLOGY

Introduction

The two components in title—evaluation, and educational technology—will be familiar enough in the present setting to need to definition. However, they share one major disadvantage when one attempts to use them as elements in a general discussion, as this is intended to be. Each is a very broad concept, embracing a variety of different but interconnected meanings, and designating a miscellany of diverse but interrelated activities. In endeavouring to make some sense of this complexity, it may be useful to begin with a modest venture in logical mapping. By this we mean no more than the drawing of a few internal boundaries within each concept. The outcome should be at least a minimal frame of reference within which to organise our subsequent observations.

Accordingly, in the first part of this paper we shall set out to distinguish three main forms of educational technology. In the second part, we shall similarly aim to delineate three main forms of educational evaluation. These exercises, in what we earlier denoted as logical mapping, can then be followed by an attempt to identify matches and mismatches in the superimposition of the two patterns. That is, we shall the various types of evaluation, and the various forms of educational technology, and ask what does and does not seem to make a useful fit. In the final part of the paper, I shall follow up some of the implications of this analysis.

Varieties of Educational Technology

My first self-imposed task is to mark some distinctions—intended to be useful of subsequent discussion—within the overall notion of educational technology. I have opted for three broad categories, partly because these seem to be based on fairly obvious logical boundaries, and partly because I am reluctant to go into finer detail. To make may more demarcations would involve a more complex mapping exercise than it seems useful to undertake within the constraints of a relatively brief analysis.

The three groups of activities will be labelled—for reasons which I hope will soon become evident—as *product-oriented, process-oriented* and *organisation-oriented* forms of educational technology. I have no intention of suggesting that the frontiers between the three are in practice clear-cut and precise, or that borderline cases cannot be found. The distinctions I am making are conceptual, in rather the same way that the equator is. Although many countries are either north or south of it, there are a number through the middle of which it passes. The existence of these equatorial countries does not render less useful our references, for purposes of classification, to the northern and southern hemispheres. I am not, then, claiming that any application of educational technology must belong to only one of the three categories. All I want to suggest is that each of the groups marks off distinguishably different sets of properties, some or all of which may be possessed by any particular case in point.

One way to visualise the three groups is to think of a set of three concentric circles, marking off three identifiable domains. It is to the innermost of these—what might be called the hard core of educational technology—that the first of my distinctions refers. By *product-oriented* educational technology I mean that cluster of activities which is centred on pre-defined objectives. What is often called the 'objective model' of learning or training (Tyler, 1949) is central to so many developments that it scarcely merits further description. The whole notion of a systems approach in education is predicated on the idea that intended learner outcomes can be specified in advance, in behavioural terms, that their degree of achievement can thus be measured, and that any deficiencies identified in practice can be compensated by suitable remedial action.

Hard-core approaches in educational technology, then, take the characteristic form of basic training systems (sequences, for example, on how to check the electrical circuit of a car); or straightforward learning systems (eg how to solve algebraic equations); or even 'off-the-peg' testing systems (eg batteries of tests of reading proficiency). In all such cases, the acceptable responses at each stage are clearly determined in advance, and are amenable to direct measurement of a kind which aspires to be neutral and non-subjective.

In this category of activities, the emphasis is on the acquisition of fairly straightforward skills or factual information which does not allow any ambiguity or room for interpretation. The label 'product-oriented' seems appropriate because attention is focused on the product of the exercise—the success of the training or the learning or the testing sequence—rather than on the process by which that outcome is attained in any given case. Allowing that the desired outcome is achieved, no questions need be asked about the nature or the means of its achievement. To that extent, the quality of any individual participant's learning experience is regarded as a 'black box' whose contents are inaccessible to legitimate inquiry.

If we turn to the next of our three concentric circles, we

see this hard-core domain of product-oriented developments as surrounded by an atmospheric layer of *process-oriented* approaches (Bruner, 1966; Stenhouse, 1975). These comprise instances of educational technology in which the outcomes are neither very specific nor clearly pre-determined. In other words, they do not subscribe to the philosophy of behavioural objectives, and are not usually categorised as educational or training systems. Their concern is rather with the promotion of improved teaching or learning techniques, the enhancement of motivation and the enrichment of the context of learning.

Examples of the process approach in educational technology would include a wide range of non-traditional modes of presentation, including television and other visual media; simulations, ranging from the sophistication of the flight trainer to the simplicity of role play exercises; learning games; and the use of the computer both for modelling hypothetical situations and for heuristics of the kinds pioneered by, for example, Seymour Pappert (Pappert, 1980) and Gordon Pask. What these very diverse examples have in common is a readiness to cope with the uncertainties and unpredictabilities associated with exploratory learning, despite the lack of definition of outcomes and the associated difficulty of measuring achievements.

Developments within process-oriented educational technology tend, understandably, to justify their effectiveness in terms of the positive experiences to which they give rise, as well as of the complex, high-level competences which they help to develop. Their emphasis is on understanding and adaptable skills, rather than on factual knowledge and routine techniques. In contrast within product-oriented activities, developments in this second category are directly concerned with what actually goes on in the process of teaching and learning. Indeed, they are designed to contribute positively to that process, in the expectation that if only its quality can be improved, the end-products will take care of themselves.

Now for the third and final category—the outermost of the three concentric circles, which might be thought of as a stratosphere enveloping the process-oriented atmosphere and the product-oriented core. I chose the label *organisation-oriented* educational technology because the strategies I have in mind are all concerned to promote fairly generalised developments at the level of major institutions, local authorities or the education service as a whole. Their concern, in other words, is not so much with helping the individual in a specific learning of training context as with the management of the larger enterprise in which acts of individual learning are intended to take place (Schramm, 1967; Mackenzie *et al,* 1975).

Illustrations of an organisation-oriented approach might include mechanisms for distributing information (such as television satellites and CEEFAX); computer-managed learning networks; the use of testing techniques for student diagnosis and allocation; and system-wide procedures for accountability. None of these examples can be comfortably accommodated within the categories of product-oriented or process-oriented developments, though it would I think, be generally agreed that they constitute legitimate instances of educational technology.

The main emphasis of developments in this category is on promoting system-wide efficiency, or effecting substantial cost savings, or enhancing existing forms of quality control. Organisation-oriented schemes address themselves to a different, more generalised, set of questions from those we have previously considered. Their validity is established neither in terms of individually measurable learning products, nor in terms of the quality of individual learning processes, but rather in terms of the net financial gain or aggregated performance statistics.

These categories, could of course be elaborated in considerably greater detail. I hope, however, that the very brief thumb-nail sketches I have offered are adequate for the present purpose. As I have already emphasised, although I hope that the distinctions may be useful for the purpose of analysis, they are not intended to be mutually exclusive in practice. Indeed, a number of significant developments—perhaps most noticeably the Open University—can be seen to encompass elements of all three domains.

Varieties of Evaluation

In looking next at the concept of evaluation, I shall continue the attempt to identify some useful internal boundaries. Again, my distinctions will be threefold. There is no particular magic in the number three, but, as previously mentioned, it provides a conveniently small framework of analysis, and happens to match the main distinctions I propose to draw. That is scarcely surprising, in that the categories of evaluation I would like to explore happen to correspond exactly with those already marked out for educational technology.

In other words, I want to argue that the broad field of educational evaluation can be divided into the three groups of *product-oriented, process-oriented* and *organisation-oriented* activities. Again, the notion of three concentric circles may be helpful in picturing the different domains of evaluation.

The inner core comprises *product-oriented* approaches. The intellectual tradition behind such forms of evaluation is that of psychometrics. The effectiveness of any educational enterprise is determined, on this approach, solely in terms of students' terminal scores on some appropriate (and properly standardised) objective test. The reliance on predetermined outcomes is obvious. In every instance, the evaluation measure has to be defined in terms of the anticipated end-point of the learning process (Glaser, 1970).

Product-oriented evaluation can appear in a number of different guises. Perhaps the most familiar is based on the notion of matched experimental and control groups, where the experimental group of learners is given a special educational diet, as against the control group's normal fare. Here the difference in educational performance is taken as a measure of the success or otherwise of the experimental programme. This approach, which has rather unkindly been labelled 'the agricultural-botany model' (Parlett and Hamilton, 1976) has tended to fall out of favour in a climate in which innovative developments no longer share many common aims with traditional ones. An alternative which meets this difficulty of incommensurable end-products is the input-output approach, in which an innovative programme is assessed in terms of its own stated (and behaviourally measurable) objectives, its success being gauged by the mean student gains between pre-test and post-test performance. A further variant is 'factor evaluation', in which one element in a complex situation is isolated for scrutiny, and its contribution to the eventual learning outcome appraised. An example of this approach is a recent study by Elihu Katz (Katz, 1977) of the comprehension of broadcast information, in which 'half of a random sample was asked to sit with their backs to the television screen in order to see what difference the picture makes for recall, understanding and emotional arousal'.

The salient features of evaluations of this type are, first, that they tend to concentrate on straightforward quantifiable gains in factual knowledge or performance skills; and, second, that they do not attempt to take into account the quality of the actual process of learning or the broader context in which it takes place. That is to say, they share the characteristics which were earlier attributed to product-oriented educational technology.

The same correspondence holds, broadly speaking, between *process-oriented* evaluation and its counterpart in educational technology. The type of study in question here is anthropological rather than psychometric, with an emphasis on qualitative factors relating to learning experiences and the environment in which they occur (Hamilton *et al,* 1977). There is no particular concern with pre-defined quantifiable outcomes, since the most significant elements in the educational process are considered to be both unpredictable and unamenable to measurement.

Investigations in this category may be found under a variety of brand-names—illuminative, naturalistic, and responsive perhaps being the best-known. Some process-oriented evaluations are virtually indistinguishable from ethnographic case studies, and have helped to prompt a resurgence of interest in case study research (Stake, 1978). The typical methods employed are observation and loosely-structured or unstructured interviews, as against the performance tests which feature largely in product-oriented evaluation. The emphasis is on the appraisal of the attitudes and concerns of participants in the teaching-learning process, on the characterisation of key events, and on the depiction of the wider setting in which that process is embedded.

Organisation-oriented evaluations are concerned with developments at a higher level of generality than the product-oriented assessments in our first domain, or the process-oriented exercises in our second domain. Their emphasis is on studies of managerial policy at the level of the system as a whole, or one of its sub-systems. The concern here is not so much with assessing the learning process of individuals or groups as with gauging the overall effectiveness of broad educational policies and programmes (Fielden and Pearson, 1978).

Examples of evaluation techniques in this genre include cost-benefit and cost-effectiveness studies, programme-analysis review, and other comparable procedures introduced sporadically into departments of central and local government since the late 1960s. The aim of such techniques is to evaluate priorities and monitor and control the implementation of policy decisions on a systematic basis. The main data for organisation-oriented studies are economics, statistics and quantitative information based on indicators of performance.

As before, in emphasising the differences between these conceptual categories of evaluation, I have no intention of implying that every actual instance must fall neatly into one and only one of them. Real life is not as tidy as logic. The point is amply proved by the evaluative component in the National Development Programme for Computer Assisted Learning, which shared features of all three.

Matches and Mismatches between Categories

It may be useful at this point briefly to review the two parallel sets of distinctions I have drawn within the concepts of educational technology and evaluation. The first category, labelled in each case as *product-oriented*, has to do primarily with measurable objectives. It emphasises the need for predictability and objectivity. It also reflects an analytic approach, based on the principle that any complex situation can be disaggregated into separate, relatively simpler, components which—once they are satisfactorily dealt with—can be recombined to help make sense of the whole.

The second, *process-oriented*, classification differs from the first in a variety of ways. It is not much concerned with outcomes, whether or not these are defined in behavioural and measurable terms. The emphasis is on means rather than ends, and on the wider context in which learning is intended to take place. Behind this approach lies a belief in holism rather than analysis—that is, a view that reality cannot be dissected into separate elements without a serious cost to both meaning and validity.

The third, *organisation-oriented*, element is different again. It might be described as the application, at a more global level, of the systems thinking which lies behind the product-oriented approach. It, too, is concerned with objectives and with the measurement of performance. However, its ends tend towards the needs of managers rather than of teachers and trainers; and, its predominant emphases are on the techniques of large-scale resource provision and distribution.

The purpose of making such distinctions is, as I suggested at the outset, to clarify the relationships between evaluation and educational technology. It is now time to put them to work by exploring the matches and mismatches between categories. To do the job exhaustively would require nine distinct comparisons—an exercise likely to provoke more tedium than enlightenment. Instead, I shall select only a few examples to illustrate my conclusions.

One might begin by asking what happens when non-corresponding elements are paired. What, for instance, can be said about product-oriented evaluation as applied to process-oriented educational technology? The answer is, in this case, straightforward enough. The evaluation is doomed to failure, because the activity being evaluated is not defined in terms of measurable objectives. It is indeed not concerned with the promotion of the kinds of knowledge, or the acquisition of the kinds of skills, which can be identified in advance and quantified at the point of achievement. So the product-oriented evaluator has no definable products on which to exercise his psychometric techniques, and must therefore find it virtually impossible to come to any clear conclusions.

It might be argued that the same difficulties need not arise in applying process-oriented evaluation techniques to product-oriented educational technology. Evaluators in the illuminative tradition would maintain that context is no less important in the case of such developments than it is in those which directly stress the process of learning. One well-known case is the study by Smith and Pohland of a computer-assisted instruction (CAI) programme in the rural Appalachian highlands (Smith and Pohland, 1974). Their evaluation report is particularly informative about the difficulties of communicating the developers' intentions; the multiplicity of agents involved; effects of cuts in funding; problems of the location of terminals; erratic functioning of hardware; difficulty of integration with the rest of the curriculum; and the wide variability of practice between participating teachers. None of this important information would have emerged in a purely product-oriented evaluation. But with this said, one is left with a sense of a task which remains incomplete. Although some attention is given to pupils' reactions to the CAI programme, there is no indication at all in the evaluation report whether or not the children in question learnt any mathematics, and, if so, whether they were in any way better off than children given conventional teaching. Since this was the central purpose of the whole exercise, an evaluation report which makes no mention of it must be judged oddly deficient.

Perhaps, then, the ideal match is one of direct correspondence between evaluation strategy and style of educational technology. If, as we have seen, a process-oriented evaluation of a product-oriented scheme is liable to leave out of account the crucial question of learning gains, would it not be better simply to concentrate in such a case on a matching product-oriented evaluation? Before one leaps too hastily to any conclusion on this point, it many be worth considering the case of IMU, the Swedish individualised mathematics project for secondary schools (Becher and Maclure, 1978). This was in its time—the late 1960s—a remarkably sophisticated learning system in the best product-oriented style. It provided a common core of mathematical content for pupils at three distinct levels of aptitude, and a series of diagnostic tests which allowed periodic transfer from one level to another. The evaluation study which accompanied it was designed with considerable care, providing formative information which helped with the revision of materials and summative information which recorded, for potential adopters, pupils' learning gains relative to those following traditional courses. Because they were based firmly on the product-oriented tradition, the IMU evaluators deliberately excluded and consideration of what teachers and pupils thought about the new scheme or the political context in which trials were taking place. As it happened, the teachers soon became restive with their changed role from dispensers of knowledge to managers of learning, and the pupils became bored with long periods spent working at mathematics on their own. The project developers, realising this, wanted to alter radically the pattern of presentation. The evaluators, whose whole elaborate design was based on the existing structure, resisted any such change, claiming that their initial data would then become valueless. The stalemate was eventually resolved by the appearance of a rival scheme devised on more flexible lines, and the IMU programme itself was quietly abandoned by its official sponsors.

What this cautionary tale suggests is that contextual data, of a kind that process-oriented evaluations specifically set out to provide, are indispensable in any attempt to appraise even the most emphatically product-oriented developments in educational technology. Put alongside this, the Smith and Pohland case study serves to emphasise that such an approach, though necessary, is not sufficient to constitute a complete evaluation. It begins to look as if the best answer might be a combination of product-oriented and process-oriented inquiries, the first evaluating the success of the development in its own terms, and the second checking its impact on the people, institutions and policies it most directly affects.

Arguing along much the same lines, I would want to suggest that organisation-oriented developments are best appraised by a combination of organisation-oriented and process-oriented studies. First, simply to get the question out of the way, it may be remarked that he frames of reference of product-oriented and organisation-oriented styles, whether of development or of evaluation, are so far apart from one another that there is little possibility of fruitful interaction. That is, it is difficult to conceive of an organisation-oriented evaluation, couched at a very general level and seeking gross cost and performance data, being applied to the very specific and down-to-earth setting of a product-oriented application of educational technology. Equally, it is hard to see how a product-oriented evaluation, designed to quantify a limited range of measurable learning gains in a closely-defined context, could be of much relevance in assessing the overall effectiveness of an organisation-oriented educational technology programme.

But if we consider such a programme—an educational television satellite, let us say—it seems to make good sense to evaluate it in a matching style, by employing the techniques of organisation-oriented investigation. In considering whether the service deserved to be continued, any policy-maker would be likely to ask not only about overall costs, but about the comparative economics of alternative systems. He or she would also clearly want to know about the generalised impact of the development on the educational levels of the target audience, as indicated (for example) by changes in national examination results over a period of time. Evaluation data at this global level seems more appropriate than other types of evidence in the appraisal of organisation-oriented educational technology. Once again, however, a niggling doubt suggests itself. Whatever the broad social indicators show, and whatever the economic calculations indicate, there must remain the question of whether what is happening on the ground bears any relation to what was originally envisaged. Are the resources provided by the scheme being used as intended? Are the local managers of the scheme in touch with its developers, or with its recipients? Are the teachers enthusiastic or hostile? What is the pupils' conception of what is happening? Such contextual questions need to be asked, and answered, if the evaluation is to be anything other than narrowly and dangerously blinkered. As in the case of product-oriented developments, the best buy seems to be a matching—that is, an organisation-oriented—evaluation, supplemented by a process-oriented one.

When it comes to process-oriented developments in

educational technology—the group typified by non-traditional presentation media, simulations, computer modelling and the like—we have already seem that product-oriented evaluations are inapplicable. So, in general, are organisation-oriented ones—how could cost-effectiveness techniques be applied to business games, or computer modelling be assessed in terms of performance indicators? Here the matching evaluation strategy is the only one which seems appropriate. That is to say, process-oriented developments are best assessed by process-oriented evaluation, alone rather than in conjunction with other strategies.

Concluding Comments

To sum up, this analysis, based on three broad categories of educational technology and three parallel categories of evaluation, suggests that process-oriented evaluation is in something of a privileged position as against its counterparts. In each case, we have seen that a particular type of development in educational technology seems to call for a matching type of evaluation. But product-oriented and organisation-oriented developments, so the earlier arguments suggest, appear to call for a complementary process-oriented study as well. Thus process-oriented evaluation figures against all three broad types of educational technology, while the other two forms of evaluation appear only once, in matching their counterpart styles of development.

One the face of it, this lack of symmetry is peculiar. However, the reason for it becomes, after further consideration, clear enough. The acquisition of definable knowledge and measurable skills does not occur in total isolation from other human activities. No more does the development of high-level adaptive techniques, or the distribution or monitoring of educational facilities through sophisticated management systems. That is to say, within the field of educational technology, product-oriented, process-oriented and organisation-oriented developments cannot in practice be confined within the tidily aseptic atmosphere of a psychology laboratory, a design studio or a planning office. All such activities have to be played out in a complex and largely uncontrollable social environment. Sometimes as in home-based learning systems—the contextual factors may become less obtrusive, though by the same token the demands on individual motivation may be greatly increased. In the main, however, what people learn at any given time is affected, for better or worse, by what is happening in the rest of their learning context. Considerations related to other aspects of the curriculum, to one's relationships with one's teachers, to external expectations, to one's level of self-esteem—all these and more can assume an important place in educational performance.

It follows that educational technology, whatever style it adopts, cannot simply be plugged in and expected unfailingly to meet its designer's specification. The main implication, as I see it, of the arguments developed in this paper is that evaluation should help to bridge the gulf between the ideal and the actual. One of its central purposes might be to unravel the contextual complexities which are an inevitable consequence of putting ideas into practice. Another key task might be to enhance the educational technologist's understanding of what does and does not seem likely to function harmoniously in a particular range of settings.

In advancing these conclusions, I have to demonstrate a final paradox. I have put forward a largely theoretical argument: to be consistent, I must acknowledge that the real world of evaluation is of necessity far less tidy than the conceptual world I have here created for it.

2

THE APPROACH TO EVALUATION

The Decision to Integrate Evaluation

The main reasons for evaluating the training were to check the soundness of the scheme's design, to assess the extent of the achievement of the training objectives, and to be able to report to senior management about training effectiveness. It was also deemed advantageous to be able to use both informal and formal methods to maximise data collection, to make appropriate changes as early as possible during the operation of the scheme, and to use evaluation to diversify training staff skills. For all these reasons, and taking into account the lack of data from earlier training arrangements and the impracticability of setting up control groups, an integrated approach to evaluation was chosen.

Models for Evaluation

Much of the evaluatory literature deals either with a specific course or fails to provide practical guidelines by concentrating on such as arguing the need for evaluation, providing an overview of specific evaluatory exercises, or making theoretical observations about conducting an evaluation. This criticism does not apply, however, to evaluatory models, notably those advocated by Moors (1979) and Stake (1976) which have been of considerable assistance in designing the evaluation exercise.

Moors' model level I, notwithstanding its emphasis on

formal evaluation, was especially helpful in clarifying purposes by its systematic analysis of evaluatory interests. After slight modification its principles were used for:

- ❑ briefing the Trustees of the Bank of our intention;
- ❑ obtaining evaluatory interests from all parties concerned;
- ❑ checking each stage of the procedure before going on to the next by applying the model as a 'route map'.

Stake's model, on the other hand, deals with informal as well as formal evaluation, directing attention to the need to be sensitive to unintended circumstances, activities or outcomes, and to the importance of their 'lack of congruence' with that intended. Similarly, Parlett and Hamilton (1972), in emphasising the importance of the total 'learning milieu', influenced the adoption of a holistic approach by urging the seeking out and inclusion in the evaluation of informal comments and observations of all parties concerned (supervising staff, trainees and instructors) so that a complete record of influences is made.

Opportunities for and Constraints to Action

Evaluation activities of the kind described in this paper are extensive and, whilst every opportunity is taken to derive benefit from the data obtained, it is accepted, for the moment, that it is relatively easy to change such things as:

- ❑ course objectives;
- ❑ the time each trainee spends on each programme to cater for individual needs;
- ❑ learning methods and materials;
- ❑ the location for learning particular topics;
- ❑ the deployment of Education and Training Department staff and, to a lesser extent, branch staff.

However, it is difficult, if not impossible, to:

- make significant changes to the intake pattern;
- expand the resources of the department in accordance with any increase in the number of entrants;
- control the quality of entrants;
- alter the flow pattern of trainees through the scheme (it being assumed that the failure rate would be negligible).

The Evaluation Exercise

The first step was to elaborate the main evaluatory interests into a series of more detailed questions:

- What is the actual usage of taught abilities at (i) the counter; (ii) the inquiry position; (iii) the office?
- What is the difference between management's expectations and cashiers' performance?
- Are the scheme's methods—courses, workbook, visits, assignments—the most appropriate in relation to its aims?
- What difficulties do trainees have in modifying their learning style to the requirements of the scheme?
- What is the extent and effects of deviations from the planned operation of the scheme?
- How does (9) the branch environment, and (ii) movement between branches, influence the trainee's progress?
- Is the documentation adequate?

Thus a starting point for the preparation of the evaluation plan was established.

The Evaluation Plan

The evaluatory interests outline the evaluation plan, within which the questions posed by Cranton and Legge (1978) were re-expressed and extended to describe the generation and collection of data. With such a highly structured scheme it was then easy to identify each of these processes within its operation.

The resulting evaluation plan collects data by:

- ❑ interviews at branches;
- ❑ questionnaires with a combination of open-ended and scaled questions, used during course reviews and by branch staff at pre-determined stages in the scheme;
- ❑ recording trainee profiles (Hills, 1980) of pre-course readiness;
- ❑ attainment tests prior to and during courses;
- ❑ observations and comments received by training staff;

so as to form a composite picture of each trainee's progress.

Those tests relating to in-branch training are marked by branch staff. The branch thereby obtains direct feedback on the trainee's progress, becoming more closely involved with the training and encouraged to comment on its relevance and effectiveness. Branch staff were also best placed to complete trainee profiles. The regular visits to branches by training officers to monitor progress and counsel trainees and supervising staff were also used for both formal and informal evaluatory activities.

Practical Problems

Instrumentation

With the evaluation plan finalised came the task of instrument design (Oppenheim, 1966; Edwards, 1951; Yorke *et al*, 1980). Whilst these were quickly developed, unfortunately it was not possible to pilot their use. To maximise opportunities for learning, all appropriate training staff were involved as each instrument was designed. Despite the considerable pressure this policy put on the training team, confidence and motivation grew as skills developed.

Data Collection

It soon became evident that the collection of informal data was fraught with problems. Whilst willing to co-operate, staff experienced difficulties with recognising relevant data and appreciating its significance and value. Regular coaching and review meetings developed their observational skills and clarified the ways data entered the records.

Data Collection

The amount of data to be handled is large and it is crucial that the important points are identified quickly. To this end, indicators of course performance were charted in tabular form. These, together with observations made by instructors in later problem analysis sessions, were used to improve both the tuition and the evaluation procedure.

The collection and collation of formal data is relatively straightforward. Informal data, by virtue of its unstructured nature and unpredictable timing, is much more difficult, particularly in the case of opinions expressed by branch staff. A simple, but effective, solution to this problem was to list opinions from the interview schedules from which a category system was developed, which allowed frequency of opinions to be recorded with tally marks. Also, in this way, a comparison of comments from supervisors and trainees can be made.

Miscellaneous Problems

Training courses last three or five days, and commence weekly. Sometimes courses are duplicated to match an increase in intake. It was impractical, therefore, to make changes on a weekly basis so major reviews were carried out at five week intervals. This provided feedback from 30 per cent of the estimated total annual intake on which to base modifications of courses for the remaining 70 per cent.

Although alerted to the unexpected dimensions, via Stake (1976), the bank's need to increase staff to service business expansion threatened to upset the operation of the scheme during its inaugural year. This change in recruitment increased trainees from an expected 150 to an actual 275. Rather than restructure the whole of the scheme, whenever possible, both group size and the number of courses were increased. This solution unfortunately reduced the available resources for evaluation, research, material design, branch visits and computer terminal practice.

Review

Over 260 recruits have entered the training scheme to date, at a varying rate up to a maximum of 20 per week. Although a complete review will not be possible for some considerable time, the initial indications are that the basic structure of the scheme is sound and that appropriate evaluation techniques are being employed. Apart from expected teething troubles, the scheme has been introduced successfully. These early problems stemmed mainly from staff shortages in branches, rather than from non-co-operation. Unsolicited comments by branch staff to visit training officers tend to be supportive with critical views being in the minority. Some examples, with the number of contributors in brackets, are:

- The scheme helps trainees to learn more quickly than in the past (14).
- the scheme is properly thought out (10).
- The scheme is not as good as previous methods (3).
- The training undertaken in the Training Centre and partly in-branch is the only way to train staff (29).

The evaluation exercise has been incorporated into the operation of the scheme largely as planned, although the data recording systems needed urgent and early revision to cope with the volume of data. Whilst it has provided a broad overview of the effectiveness of the scheme, particularly with regard to the thin sandwich patterns of centre and in-branch training, it has also facilitated staff development quantified the additional work-load, and identified specific areas of training on which to focus evaluation in the future.

Acknowledgments

The authors are grateful to Don Moors and Jim Hills for their help with the design of the evaluation exercise and trainee profiles. They would also like to thank the Trustees of the Trustee Savings Bank of Birmingham and the Midlands for their permission to publish this paper.

3

EVALUATION FOR REVISION: A CASE STUDY OF A TRAINING PROGRAMME

Introduction

The effectiveness of any training programme is determined, to a large extent, by the procedures employed to collect and make use of evaluation data. If provisions have been made for continuous evaluation during the design, development and implementation phases, the training will have greater likelihood for success in meeting the needs of the target population.

This paper presents a case study of the evaluation of a training programme which is based upon several key evaluation concepts. First, evaluation is viewed as decision-oriented, that is, data are collected and analysed in order to answer specific questions and/or to assist in making particular decisions. Second, for programmes in which the outcomes, target population, content or organisational context are subject to change, the focus of evaluation is of a formative nature. Although a programme has been summatively proven to be effective, subsequent data may reveal the need for modifications. Third, multiple evaluation methods should be used to obtain information on which to base decisions regarding revisions. In this respect, both product and process can be evaluated through the use of expert appraisal and trainee performance data collection techniques. Finally, evaluation is seen as an ongoing, iterative process with data being collected during all phases of programme development and implementation. These data are obtained through measures administered before, during and after training.

Workshop Description

The Dawson and Hebein 'Train and Trainer' workshop is designed to provide trainers and training supervisors with the knowledge, skills and attitudes needed to prepare, conduct, evaluate and manage performance-oriented training. Instruction within the workshop is performance-oriented, thereby demonstrating the training principles being presented and providing participants with direct experience in performance-oriented training.

The workshop consists of ten four-hour modules, each focusing on one aspect of applying the systems approach to training. Within each module, several performance objectives are accomplished. The topics addressed in the module are:

(a) Introduction to Performance Oriented Training
(b) Managing and Communicating in Training
(c) Determining Training Status
(d) Developing Performance Objectives
(e) Preparing to Conduct Training
(f) Selecting and Developing Training Media
(g) Evaluating Training
(h) Conducting Performance-Oriented Training
(i) Gaining Acceptance for New Training Ideas
(j) Implementing New Training Ideas.

The workshop is sequential in that the activities of one module build upon the knowledge and products developed in previous modules. This enhances the application of the systems approach to training and provides continuity to the activities of the workshop.

The topics included in the course are presented through a variety of media and techniques. The participants acquire knowledge and skills related to the use of these media and techniques in training through 'learning by doing'. Their direct experiences give them insights they would not acquire by reading or listening to formal presentations about these methods.

Evaluation is an ongoing activity throughout the workshop. Data are collected and analysed in order to fulfil several purposes.

Evaluation Methods

In order to determine the effectiveness of the training programme, to evaluate the performance of the participants, and to make revision decisions, several evaluation methods are used in the Dawson and Hebein 'Train the Trainer' workshop. The data from the evaluation instruments indicate training needs related to performance-oriented training before and after the workshop; participants' attitudes toward performance-oriented training; participants reactions to the information and presentation methods of the workshop; and transfer of skills and knowledge to real-world training situations. The evaluation methods used include:

- Self-assessment
- Value assessment
- Content assessment
- Performance assessment
- Transfer assessment

Pre-testing of trainees to obtain entry level data on all objectives of the workshop is not practical, given the time and resource constraints of this programme. Therefore, a Participant Self-Assessment Survey is administered to determine the trainees' perceptions of their levels of expertise, as well as their attitudes and values about the topics of the workshop. This information is later compared with data from the same questionnaire, obtained upon completion of the course. The post workshop questionnaire also requests participants to list the three topics that will be of greatest value to them on the job. Thus, this self assessment form provides data to assess changes in perceived levels of expertise on workshop topics and in the importance of the topics to the trainees' own interests and job-related duties.

During the workshop, performance data for each participant on all objectives of the course are obtained and recorded in individual Job Books. The Job Books list all tasks required in the workshop. Participants record a 'Go' or 'No Go' upon completion of a task, based on minimum performance criteria established in the objectives.

In addition to performance data, participants also provide content assessment data during the course. The Workshop Rating Scale is completed by each participant at the end of every module of the workshop. The individual items require the trainees to react to the characteristics and elements of each module, including the objectives, activities, informational content and co-ordinators' performance. They also list any strong and weak features of the module. This form allows the participants an active part in the evaluation for revision process. This is effective not only from the perspective of the valuable data obtained but also because of the sense of influence and involvement participants feel in providing this type of feedback.

The last type of evaluation information obtained is related to the transfer of skills and knowledge acquired in the course to the real-world training environment. To determine whether transfer occurs, a follow-up Training Questionnaire is sent to participants six to eight weeks after completion of the workshop. Responses to this questionnaire are compared with pre-workshop responses to the same items. Changes in the responses indicate areas in which the workshop may have been responsible for improved training.

Using Evaluation Data for Revisions

The approach used to analyse the evaluation data in order to determine where modifications are needed in the workshop is an adaptation of Robert Stake's matrix method (Stake, 1976). Figure 3.1 presents a six-cell matrix in which the two columns are labelled *intents* and *observations*, while the three rows are designated *entry conditions*, *training* and *outcomes*. After information is recorded in each cell of the matrix, a number of comparisons can be made which, in turn, may suggest revisions in one or more aspects of the training programme. These comparisons are of two main types. First, any one cell in the intents column can be compared with another cell in the intents column, in order to determine the match or degree of appropriateness among the intended trainees, the intended training programme, and the intended outcomes. These comparisons are qualitative in nature and are made through expert appraisal of the data during early stages of programme development. Second, the two cells in each row of the matrix can be compared in order to determine the congruence between what was intended and what actually was observed during the training programme. For example, Did the trainees exhibit the expected entry conditions? Was the training workshop implemented as planned? Were the specified outcomes achieved? Objective observational data and trainee performance and attitudinal information are needed to answer these questions. The instruments described in the previous section provide the required data.

Several specific uses of this approach, as it has been applied to the 'Train the Trainer' workshop, will serve to illustrative how revisions are suggested through an analysis of the matrix data.

During the initial design of the programme, the intended trainees were described in terms of duty titles, job responsibilities, general aptitudes and abilities, and training needs. Precise performance objectives were developed which specified the task, conditions and standards to be accomplished as a result of the training. A proposed programme of instruction which included the specific content, methods and media of instruction was also developed. The workshop developers reviewed this information for contingencies among the entry conditions, the training, and the outcomes. Additionally, several categories of experts appraised the data, among them decision-makers within the organisation for which the programme was intended, subject-matter experts within the particular area of training, and individuals who were potential participants. These reviews were focused on the matches between the intended trainees and the planned training, between the intended trainees and the specified outcomes, and between the planned training and the specified outcomes. Some of the revisions which were suggested at a result of these reviews related to:

1. The addition or deletion of certain objectives.
2. The inclusion of training materials available from the organisation.
3. The simplification of some content and activities.
4. The incorporation of more opportunity for practice.

	Intents	Observations
Entry conditions		
Training		
Outcomes		

Figure 3.1. *Training Evaluation Matrix*

During the pilot test of the workshop, and as an ongoing process in subsequent iterations, a variety of data was recorded in the *observations* cells of the matrix. Mismatches have been noted across all three rows of cells in the matrix which, in turn, have led to modifications in various aspects of the workshop.

Looking first at the entry conditions, several mismatches have indicated a need for revisions in the programme. The workshop was originally designed for a heterogeneous group of participants representing trainers and training managers. Decision-makers within the organisation assign personnel to attend the workship. Over a period of time, the participant have become more homogenous in that they are almost exclusively trainers. The other major mismatch was related to the general ability level of the participants and their degree of motivation and attention span. It was observed that many trainees did not read as well as had been anticipated, that motivation was lacking in some, and that others had very short attention spans. These incongruencies between intended and observed entry conditions led to modifications in both outcomes and training. On the one hand, some of the original objectives were more relevant to managers than to trainers. These were substituted with outcomes more consistent with the needs of the novice trainer. On the other hand, activities within the workshop were revised, taking into account the observed ability, motivational and attention levels of the participants. For example, reading passages were shortened and simplified, oral presentations were limited, and more active participation with feedback was built into the workshop.

Mismatches between intended training and observed training were often related to incongruencies between intended and observed entry conditions. For example, a planned activity called for the participants to complete a self-instructional programmed booklet within an hour. It was observed that many trainees required assistance in completing the task, that some took much longer than an hour, and that others were not able to attend to the activity and were easily distracted. As a result, mismatches were evident between the two outcome cells; rather than being able to perform the specified objective as a result of completing the self-instructional programme, a large percentage of the trainees received 'No Go' on the task. It was obvious that changes were needed in the training activities. An audio-visual presentation, interspersed frequently with small group activities in which the task is taught in small sequential steps, is now used in place of the programmed text. The observations in terms of the trainees' performance during the activities and on the performance test are now consistent with expectations.

Discrepancies also occur between intended and observed outcomes. As previously noted, these often are related to mismatches between other cells of the matrix. A given person or group of people may not achieve the intended outcome because:

1. They do not possess the intended entry conditions.
2. The training was not implemented as planned.
3. The outcomes were not appropriate for the audience.
4. The training content, methods or media were not appropriate to teach the task.

Thus, when a mismatch occurs between the outcome cells, it is necessary to analyse the contingencies and congruencies among the other cells in order to pinpoint the reason for the difference between intended and observed outcomes and, as a result, to make needed revisions.

One example of the process used to pinpoint the reason(s) for a mismatch between intended and observed outcomes pertains to the objective which requires participants to conduct a critique of another participant's training session. Among the criteria to be met are that the critique must be positive and constructive and that it actively involves the participant trainer in the identification of his or her strengths and weaknesses. Repeated observations indicated that these criteria were not met, although opportunity to practice and feedback had been provided. Participant evaluators tended to focus on weaknesses, to be judgement and to bombard the participant-trainer with a barrage of negatively-toned criticisms. The participant-trainers tended to assume a passive role and avoid responsibility for identifying their own strengths and weaknesses.

Familiarity with the organisational climate in which the participants work provided insights into the reason for this mismatch. These appears to be an institutionalised emphasis on the negative which permeates all aspects of the work and training environment. A single presentation of the guidelines for an effective critique, followed by one practice session, was not sufficient to overcome the conditioned negative approach learned through experience on the job.

Revisions include:

1. Contrasting examples of an effective and an ineffective critique session.
2. Group discussion of personal reactions to positive and negative criticism.
3. Opportunity to role-play a critique, taking alternatively the part of the trainer and the evaluator.
4. Observation of the role-play critiques of other participants.
5. A constant stress, to the extent of saying the words several times during each module, on 'positive' and 'constructive'.

Summary

The Dawson and Hebein 'Train and Trainer' workshop is evaluated for several purposes using a variety of data collection techniques. The training evaluation matrix adapted from Stake (1976) has been a useful tool in analysing and interpreting the data. Its use, however, is limited to suggestions regarding revisions for improvement, because there are not hard and fast rules to apply in making revision decisions. The best modifications are based upon a combination of good evaluation data and creativity.

4

EVALUATION RESOURCES AND ASSESSMENT TECHNIQUES

4.1 An Evaluation Resource Pack: Issues and Implications

Introduction

Evaluation has always been problematic. With increasing interest being shown in institution-based evaluation and self-evaluation, both practical and theoretical issues need modifying from large-scale schemes. This paper examines these issues, and outlines attempts to overcome problems during the production of an evaluation resource pack.

Background

In May 1979, the Council for Educational Technology (CET) invited the University of Bath to develop:

> a workshop of self-help materials for those people running long courses in educational technology. Any examples are to focus on the projects which are carried out as part of the course work.

The full brief given by the Council for Educational Technology focused on the production of materials that would help long course organisers:

(a) improve their evaluation skills;
(b) develop schemes of evaluation.

The materials were developed in collaboration with those institutions preparing for, or providing, courses leading to qualifications in educational technology. The field testing was in these institutions, with the University of Bath acting as a co-ordinating agent.

Long courses in educational technology were defined as those courses listed in the directory *Courses Leading to Qualification in Educational Technology 1980-1981* (CET, 1979). In general, the courses run for a minimum of one year full-time or two years part-time. The audience was identified as those people who were named contacts in the annual CET *Directory on Courses in Educational Technology*. Many of these contacts also involved their colleagues. Altogether there are 30 institutions that run such courses, the courses being classified by qualifications and attendance. For the purpose of the needs assessment, the research degrees and the City and Guilds Certificate courses were not included: the research degree courses because they were not structured; the City and Guilds Certificate courses because of low student numbers. Some of the Master's degrees were taught courses and therefore retained.

The course organisers and tutors stated in interviews that they were concerned with their own skills and schemes of evaluation. In addition, they wanted resources to help them teach evaluation in their courses. A proposal was made for the structure of the materials and the way that the resources could be used, based on the information collected by interviews and discussions. Respondents were asked to react to the proposals by writing comments over their copy of the materials, or by comments on one side of A4 paper.

From the information collected, the decision was made to keep the dual purpose of the pack:

(a) to improve the skills of organisers and teachers;

(b) to allow its use as a resource pack for teaching.

More adjustments to detail were made during a small intensive weekend workshop help at Bath in December 1979. The workshop was attended by three course tutors from different types of institutions.

Further feedback was encouraged as follows:

1. *Individual comments* were made by anyone who was willing to read the resource materials in their draft form.
2. *A questionnaire* was used with 10 sets of materials which were sent to those institutions who were willing to read them. The questionnaire included closed questions with a scale and spaces for comments. Five of the 10 were returned.
3. *A workshop,* based on the materials, was organised with the aim of:
   (a) allowing formative evaluation data to be collected;
   (b) simulating the planning of a small-scale evaluation;
   (c) gaining some idea of what to put in a Users' Guide.

The first and last aims were adequately met. A wealth of constructive comment was collected which led to a revision of materials. The comments were collected by each of the three syndicates (six or seven participants) feeding back notes of their sessions, and a final plenary session during which detailed notes were made of the inter-syndicate discussion.

By this time, 21 institutions had been involved in the development in one way or another (see Harris and Bailey, 1980).

Qualification / *Attendance*	*Certificate: City and Guilds*	*Diploma: self-or locally validated**	*Diploma: CNAA*	*Post-experience: BA degree*	*Master's degree*	*Ph.D.*	*Total*
Full-time	0	5	2	0	4	1	12
Part-time	6	2	4	1	2	0	15
Full-time or part-time	0	2	0	1	4	2	9
Full-time and part-time	0	2	0	1	0	0	3
Total	6	11	6	3	10	3	39

* validated by local university or by the college.

Figure 4.1. Long Courses in Educational Technology Offered by 24 Institutions in England, Scotland and Wales.

Outline of the Product

Information collected from the formative evaluation was used to send to each user proposals outlining the changes needed to produce the final Resource Pack. The Evaluation Resource Pack (Harris and Bailey, 1980) can be used by course organisers to help them evaluate their own course and as training materials for their students.

The materials include a number of flexible units to allow the user to select materials to suit his or her own needs. The main components are:

1. *Users' Guide* combining:
   (a) outline of the materials;
   (b) suggestions for using the materials in different ways.
2. *Introduction to Evaluation* containing:
   (a) brief description of models;
   (b) brief description of techniques;
   (c) glossary of essential terms.
3. *Tool Kit* containing a number of guides to help the collection, analysing summarising and reporting of evaluations. The guides cover the writing of questionnaires, interview schedules, group meetings, observation schedules, resource analysis, using assessment data, and how to summarise, analyse and organise the information for a report.
4. *Planning an Evaluation* including a guide to help select suitable techniques of evaluation. The materials take a pragmatic approach, mainly in the form of checklists and examples. The Introduction to evaluation unit introduces some theoretical concepts and is supported by a bibliography to allow those who wish to follow up issues in depth.

A summary of the contents of the Evaluation Resource Pack is given in Figure 4.2.

Evaluation, Self-Evaluation and Educational Technology

Educational technologists as evaluators have tended to concentrate on products rather than processes. Strategies are based on a systems view of educational technology, represented by the objectives, methods, content and output model.

Users' Guide	**Introduction to Evaluation**
Planning an Evaluation	**Took Kit**
Purpose of evaluation	Pencil and paper
Identify sponsor and audience	Talking and listening
Choose evaluator	Observation
Available resources	Sociometric
Context information	Assessment
Focus evaluation	Resource analysis
Choose procedures (see Took Kit)	Curriculum analysis
Define responsibilities	Summarising and analysing
Timetable	Reporting
Report (see Took Kit)	

Figure 4.2. *Summary of the Evaluation Resource Pack Materials.*

Recently, increasing attention is being directed towards small-scale evaluations and self-evaluations which often favour study of the processes of education rather than the products. Reasons for this are varied, but generally centre on the need to provide information relevant to, and of practical use by, individual institutions. Such information may relate to a range of situations, from an individual teacher's professional practices to an institution's performance within the wider social context. When studying processes of education, the values and aspirations of individuals, and interactions between individuals, become important considerations. Methodologies of the systems approach, which are seen as having their roots in the 19th century view of the scientific method, are criticised for not considering these values and interactions.

Criticism has led towards a search for alternative methodologies. Such alternatives are often seem as being provided by social anthropologists, many claiming them to be in opposition to the quantitative systems approach (see Bell, 1980).

Methodologies of Evaluation

As an aid to understanding the range of methodologies available to educational evaluators, it may be useful to study, and to classify, ways in which those engaged in evaluation are seen to work and view their work. Any number of categories are possible, but a four-fold classification maintains a manageable system, whilst overcoming some of the problems of a dichotomy. The ideas behind the following schemes originate from theoretical classifications proposed by Argyris and Schon (1974), Mitroff and Kulmann (1978), and Harris and Bailey (1980).

Category One

This approach, based on the classical view of scientific method, strives for objectivity of results. The evaluator remains external to the situation being evaluated, and adopts a disinterested, a political approach. Strict boundaries to the range of inquiry are maintained, these boundaries often being agreed prior to commencing the evaluation. The evaluator is viewed as a an unbiased expert. To overcome the effects of an individual's personally held values, large numbers of people are often studied using statistical analysis of collected data.

Education is seen as the transmission of organised knowledge from the older to the younger generation. Attention is focused upon the *products*, rather than the *processes*, of this transmission.

Category Two

This approach, like the analytic, strives for an impersonal, disinterested description of the situation being evaluated. At the same time, it recognises that the values and aspirations of the evaluator may play an important part in the way the evaluation proceeds. Unlike the analytic approach, inquiry is not seen to have strict predefined boundaries. By viewing the situation being studied from a variety of perspectives, the evaluator produces multiple, often novel, explanations to describe that situation.

Although emphasis is placed on education as being the transmission of organised and accumulated knowledge, attention is focused upon large-scale differences in products. Education as a process and the individuality of the learners is taken into account.

Category Three

Education is seen as an essentially individual human process. It differs from the previous two approaches in certain basic assumptions:

1. It is impossible for the evaluator and those being studied to remain separate.
2. Value neutrality is improbable.
3. Those taking part have an interest in the results of the evaluation.

The main aim of an evaluation is not the production or ordering of knowledge, but the promotion of human development and growth on the widest possible scale. Individuals are helped to understand the processes in which they engage. The focus of the evaluation is on the generation of information relevant to those being studied, and to the evaluator.

The ideas of action research, and of illuminative, or problem-centred, evaluation where investigation is holistic, open-ended and accepts multiple explanations, fall within this category. As in the case of previous approaches, results of an evaluation are reported by the evaluator, and may, ultimately, be seen as judgemental.

Category Four

An 'evaluator' adopting this approach is acting in a different capacity from those previously described. Little interest is shown in formulating general theories; the concern is to understand the uniqueness of a particular situation. Analytical or theoretical sophistication is not seen as an acceptable substitute for the presence of a participating observer who has empathy for those being observed. The 'evaluator' acts as a facilitator for the evaluation, enabling participants to gain an in-depth understanding of themselves and their situation.

Education is viewed as the personal development of the individual young becoming educated by, interacting with, and learning from, their environment.

This approach encompasses the notions of self-evaluation (Elliott, 1979; Simons, 1980) and of participant observations (Delamont, 1976).

Implications

We do not suggest that any one approach is inherently better or worse than any other, or that the categories are mutually exclusive to an individual evaluator. Rather, we suggest an approach should be chosen to suit the situation encountered. In no way should the methodological tail be allowed to wag the evaluating dog!

The categories outlined above suggest a continuum of methodologies suited to a range of situations. Such a continuum is represented in Figure 4.3.

In addition certain methodologies being more applicable to certain situations, within one 'evaluation' a range of different approaches may be adopted.

The approaches of categories two and three may be useful when initially defining, and focusing on, the problem areas for evaluation.

Category One approach			Category Four approach
Analytic Survey	Field trials	Action research	Participation observation
Large-scale (product) evaluations			Small-scale (process) evaluations

Figure 4.3. Range of Methodologies.

The approaches of all categories may be useful to gather information which can subsequently be ordered and judged.

The approach of category four may be useful for the important step of increasing professional self-awareness, perhaps towards the end of an evaluation.

The Evaluation Resource Pack was designed for a specific audience, that is, organisers of long courses in educational technology. It was not designed with the view of promoting self-evaluation, but to support an individual in evaluating his or her course. As such, the Pack's philosophy falls into categories two and three of our framework of methodologies, whilst the materials offered will support those wishing to adopt the approach of categories one to three.

For those wishing to engage in institution-based self-evaluation, a new project, based at the University of Bath, funded jointly by the Council for Educational Technology and the Schools Council, is under way.

4.2 Evaluation Resources for Teachers

Organiser's Account

The workshop was based on new materials being produced for use by teachers in schools and other educational institutions who wish to evaluate their courses or practices. The project is funded jointly by the Council for Educational Technology and the Schools Council. [The materials are not related to the *Evaluation Resource Pack* (Harris and Bailey, 1989)].

Workshop participants were given a choice of activities, either:

(a) discussing the proposed contents of the materials; or
(b) discussing one section of the materials.

Participants chose to study contents, and then the section of materials if time permitted.

Each participant was asked to write comments about the contents. In pairs, participants identified similarities and differences in their comments, subsequently reporting to the whole group.

A number of issues were raised:

(a) Materials should be short and concise, using simple language and concepts.
(b) The need for, and utility of, evaluation and what is meant by evaluation should be made explicit.
(c) 'Accountability' and 'evaluation' should be distinguished.
(d) The materials which are being produced were thought to be applicable to training institutions. For this audience, some of the terms used may need changing.
(e) It was considered desirable that the names of the funding organisations, in particular the Schools Council, should not be too prominent on the materials.

In addition, many useful comments were made regarding specific items on the contents list and in the materials.

4.3 Answers at Distance

Introduction

An important feature of learning at a distance is the separation of teacher (tutor) from learner (Holmberg, 1981). Despite this separation it is important that a two-way communication is maintained between the learner and the tutor so that progress problems and attitudes can be discussed. It is not sufficient to send printed materials to the learner and expect him to learn. It has been shown (Skinner, 1954; Annett, 1969; Murray *et al.*, 1977) that participation on the part of the learner during the learning process makes for more effective learning.

If immediate and regular feedback is given to the learner, his retention and comprehension are tested and his subsequent ability to understand and solve problems is improved.

In distance learning programmes, it is important that an effective method of providing feedback is used as it is often the only communication the learner will have with the teacher for a period of time. Not only does a system of questions and answers help the learner to monitor his own learning, but the reinforcement gained during the process motivates him to continue learning (McGuire, 1967). A variety of techniques has been used to provide feedback in the educational setting. This paper describes:

(a) A number of techniques and some applications.
(b) The advantages and disadvantages of the methods with particular reference to distance learning.

Techniques and Applications

1. *Answers given at the back of the book or on another page.*

This is the method frequently used, for example, in school children's arithmetic books.

2. *Answers given on the same page at the bottom of the page.*

Another standard textbook method but less common than the previous example.

3. *Answers given on the same page but printed upside down.*

Used in the 'Do You Know' corner of the children's page in daily newspapers.

4. *Answers in frames covered by a mask.*

The text is divided into frames and the answer given at the beginning of the next frame further down in the page, in the traditional programmed learning manner. This involves the conscientious reader in covering later frames with a slip of paper which he slides down as he works through the questions.

5. *Programmed text with small page format.*

A variation of the previous method. A small amount of text appears on one page with a question. The answer is on the next page and the reader overtly answers the question before turning over.

6. *Scrambled book—branching frame.*

The reader is referred to various pages throughout the book to find answers, and again, depending on his answers, will be directed to another page in the book.

Number 4 to 6 are variations of the programmed learning theme, but bucking the system, either intentionally or unintentionally, becomes progressively more difficult.

7. *Answers appear at the back of the book but in random order.*

By this method, questions are posed in the text. Blanks are left for the student to complete answers and the blanks given random reference numbers. At the back of the book the answers are numbered in sequence. Using this method there is less likelihood of the student seeing the next answer when looking up the current one (Tucker, 1980).

8. *Answers are printed using a 'scrambled print' technique.*

In this method the answers are printed in one colour (eg blue) and then concealed by overprinting in a second colour (eg red). The reader places a transparent red plastic mask over the scrambled print to reveal the text underneath. This method is well-known in medical education.

9. *Answers are highlighted using a pre-cut transparent template.*

The reader places the template over a set of multiple-choice answers to indicate the correct one.

10. *Latent image printing of answers.*

This method, used extensively in medical education and now taken up by other educationalists, is an invisible ink printing technique. A message or answer is printed on paper, next to the question, and remains invisible until treated by a developing pen to reveal the message.

The technique has been around sine the 1940s, but the developments by A.B. Dick Co. in the United States have gone a long way to providing a method which is technically reliable.

It is available commercially in two forms—one designed for use on a spirit duplicator and the other for offset printing. Both methods use standard equipment.

Spirit Duplicating

The cheaper of the two methods, this requires a spirit duplicator, latent image transfer sheets and latent image developer pens.

The information that is to be visible is typed or written on a carbon spirit master. A latent image transfer sheet then replaces the carbon and the 'invisible' sections (the answers) are typed or written on the same master. Copies (between 100 and 150) and run off from the master on a standard spirit duplicator. The answer remain invisible until treated with the developer pen.

At Dundee College of Technology, in a distance learning course for firemen sitting statutory promotion exams, a development of this technique has been used (Tucker, 1980). The visible sections have been prepared by offset printing and only the 'invisible' sections have used the spirit duplication method for applying latent answers.

Offset Printing

In a similar way to the spirit duplicator process the visible information is printed by offset and then printed again with the 'invisible sections'. Large numbers can be run and multi-coloured printing can be used for the visible information. Adding the latent sections is no more expensive than adding another colour.

The latent image process by offset litho is not, as yet, available commercially in the UK. Printing must be done in the US by A.B. Dick Co.

It has been used at the centre for Medical Education, Dundee University in a series of self-assessment exercises for general practitioners (Rogers *et al.*, 1979; Harden *et al.*, 1980).

11. *Cholesteric liquid crystals.*

Another method where answers remain latent until specially treated by heat, from the hand.

12. *Scratch-off printing.*

This method is familiar in the form of instant lottery tickets where one scratches off a silver-coloured deposit with a coin or the fingernail.

13. *Audio method.*

There would seem to be three possibilities:

(a) The lesson is recorded on tape. A tone instructs the student to switch off and write the answer to a question on a paper response sheet. He then switches on again to receive the correct answer.

(b) The lesson is presented on paper with blanks for answers to be completed by the student. He switches on a tape to obtain the correct answer.

(c) The lesson is recorded on tape. Pauses are left for the student to record his answer on the tape, immediately followed by the correct answer on tape. This is the well-known language laboratory approach.

14. *Computer.*

Microcomputers have the facility not only to provide answers but also to do calculations, to generate problems, and to provide the learner with appropriate *personalised* feedback. Methods of use include the following:

(a) A choice of answers of the multiple choice type is given. The letter of the answer chosen is typed into the computers. If the answer is wrong then the computer can give further guidance and the student be asked to 'try again'.

(b) No choice of answers is given. The student writes his own answer in the blank space on the question paper and then types into the computer the number of the question. He is given the correct answer and asked if he would like any further explanation in case he is wrong.

Discussion

While all of the technique described are valid methods of providing instant feedback, they all have advantages and disadvantages. When selecting one for use in a particular distance learning programme, it is important to bear these in mind and to select the most appropriate, and therefore the most effective, method, taking into account the style of the material and the situation of the student.

Distance learning programmes will be more effective if:

(a) Answers are provided immediately so that there is no delay for the learner between recording his own answer and learning whether he is right or wrong.

(b) Answers are provided in a way that is fool-proof, so that the reader can use the material independently without recourse to his tutor.

(c) Answers are designed so that when the reader looks up a current answer he does not see the next half dozen answers at the same time.

(d) Answers are designed so that when put into the text a continuous narrative is produced which is useful for revision purposes.

Advantages and Disadvantages for Distance Learning of the Methods Described

1. *Answer given at the back of the book.*

This method is valid if the problem posed involves reasonably long work, e.g. calculations. The learner is then less likely to observe and remember the answers to the next question whilst looking up the current answer. The method can be extremely tiresome to use, however, if frequent answer checking is needed.

2. *Answer given at bottom of same page.*

This method is used as an alternative to the back of the book method and may be considered less irritating.

3. *Answers printed upside down on the same page.*

Really only a minor variation on 2, but there is less likelihood of seeing an answer beforehand. Again, it is irritating to use and not very useful as a permanent record.

The advantages of the three methods described so far are that all are reasonably easy to organise and so do not involve much extra cost. The major disadvantages are that all the methods are non-motivational and unpleasant to use. In most cases one has to be fairly blinkered to avoid seeing the next answer when looking at the current one.

4. *Answers is frames covered by a mask.*

Perhaps one of the reasons why programmed learning went out of vogue was that this method of feedback was tedious, physically cumbersome and non-motivational.

5. *Programmed text—small page format.*

This method is used particularly when simplicity is essential and motivation is necessary. The format, however, is somewhat odd.

6. *Scrambled book.*

The main disadvantage is that no permanent record is produced for revision purposes. It is irritating to use because of frequent hunting through the book.

7. *Answers at back of book in random order.*

This method is designed so that the reader does not see the answer to the next question each time he refers to the current answer. It is certainly neat and cheap to produce. It can, however, be a disadvantage in that no permanent answer appears in the next, thus providing no revision facility. The importance of the disadvantages depend on the content and uses to be made of the materials.

8. *Scrambled print.*

This method has been used extensively in medical journals. Undoubtedly the novelty wears off after a time. Unless printed very accurately the text is never completely obscured. Many people find this distracting as there is a tendency to concentrate on 'beating the system' rather than on the answer itself. As it involves two or three colour printing the method is expensive to produce. It is, however, possible to produce a crude do-it-yourself version using a typewriter and overprinting with rows of the letter 'x' typed in a second colour. The colour of the plastic must match as well as possible the second colour typing. A continuous text is provided with this method.

9. *Answers highlighted by template.*

The method can be effectively used in many learning situations where the multiple-choice question format is the preferred choice for knowledge testing. It has the disadvantage that the answers are checked one page at a time—thus there is not quite immediate feedback.

10. *Latent image printing of answers.*

A strong advantage of providing answers by latent image printing is that the method is quick and easy to use. It is well-recognised that any barriers set up between the learner and his materials will tend to decrease motivation and usage (McGuire, 1967). With latent image printing the answer is immediate and can be provided alongside the question, providing, once revealed, a permanent record. The likelihood of seeing the answer before attempting the question is less than in previous methods. As little or as much information as is appropriate in the particular learning situation can be (i) supplied by the author and (ii) revealed by the reader. This means that further explanation can be given other than the correct answer and that the reader can selectively reveal the information that is particularly relevant to him or her, and can keep a permanent record.

This method, with its flexibility and scope for individualisation, is very appropriate for use in distance learning programmes. Disadvantages of the technique are concerned with the technical aspects of the process. Copies may take longer to produce, and the cost may be somewhat higher than with conventional printing. The better quality offset process is probably not economical unless large print runs are required. This must be processed, as yet, in the United States.

For small print runs the duplicating process can be used. The method is not, however, fool-proof and accuracy of register can be a problem. These materials have a more limited shelf-life than the offset printed materials, especially once the message has been revealed.

11. *Liquid crystals.*

This new method, developed in Japan, is, as yet, unknown in this country for educational purposes. It employs, on paper, the same techniques as for visual display—for example, certain types of digital thermometers. Advantages are as for latent image, with the added one that the print is revealed only for a short time. The materials are therefore reusable but there is not a permanent visible record.

12. *Scratch-off printing.*

Both the advantages and disadvantages of this method are similar to the latent image type, except that there is no do-it-yourself method. It must be processed commercially, but can be done in the United Kingdom (Pegasus Print Ltd).

13. *Answers on audio-tape.*

(a) Lesson on tape—answers on paper—feedback on tape:

a permanent record is provided on tape but the method is not fool-proof.

(b) Lesson on paper—answers in blanks—feedback on tape: as there is no simple way of locating a particular answer on the tape it is very easy to lose the sequence of answers.

(c) Lesson on tape—student records answers—feedback: this is the only method described which is useful for non-readers. However, the method is mechanically difficult as there is the danger of erasing the programme.

14. *Microcomputers.*

With recent developments in microcomputer technology and the lowering of costs, the technique has come within the reach of most educators. Provided that the equipment is available, the immediate feedback possible on microcomputers can be used with great effect in distance learning programmes.

This is probably the most flexible of all the methods. Not only can the correct answer, but also remedial feedback, be provided if an incorrect answer is chosen. It is probably better to present the lesson on paper as this allows for better diagrams. photographs, etc.; also reading large sections of print from a VDU is tiring.

Disadvantages of the microcomputer method are:

1. No permanent record is provided.
2. The microcomputer is too expensive to provide for individual students to use in their own home. They would have to come to a local centre.

Summary

There is a large number of methods to be used to provide answers at a distance ranging from simple programmed learning to highly sophisticated and sometimes expensive techniques. The choice of methods is very much dependent on how important it is that the learner should not be able to see the next answers when looking at current answers, and whether or not it is important that answers inserted into the text can form a continuous narrative for revision purposes.

Conclusions

One of the most important features of distance learning is feedback. We conclude that if appropriate and immediate feedback to the learner is provided then distance learning materials will be more effective.

4.4 Answers at a Distance

Organisers' Account

The aim of this workshop was to provide participants with more details of some of the less common methods of providing feedback in distance learning materials described in the previous paper. This was to be achieved by demonstrations and by 'hands on' experience of both using and producing materials.

The feedback methods available were grouped into three categories.

1. Feedback via PET microcomputer
2. Latent image
3. Miscellaneous examples.

Feedback Via a PET Microcomputer

Two examples were provided for participants to try for themselves on two microcomputers.

(a) (Adapted from 'IF'—a course in continuing medical education for General Practitioners.)

Participants were given a leaflet which gave a patient's case history and then they presented a variety of possible diagnoses and courses of treatment.

The user studies the case details and then rates each diagnosis or treatment on a 1-5 scale, depending on the extent to which he agrees or disagrees with it. He enters his rating of each diagnoses or treatment into the computer, one at a time. The computer then shows him the ratings given by 100 fellow-GPs and also by a hospital specialist. If the user wishes, he can ask to see a short comment by the hospital specialist and also get a print-out (to take away) from a tractor printer connected to the PET. The print-out shows his rating, the ratings of the 100 GPs and the specialist together with the specialist's comments.

(b) (Adapted from a distance learning course in elementary chemistry for firemen sitting of the station officer examination.)

Participants were given a leaflet containing an extract from the response sheet for one of the lessons. The response sheet showed two worked examples of simple calculations involving calorific values, followed by several examples to be worked by the student.

The student enters his answer to each problem into the PET which then provides him with appropriate feedback, remedial if necessary. For example, common predictable errors, such as losing a zero, dividing instead of multiplying, and getting the division the wrong way up, are recognised and the student is told what he has done wrong and is asked to try again. There are also facilities for HINT if a start is needed and HELP if the student wants to be shown how to do the whole calculation.

Latent Image

Two types of ready-produced material were available for participants to examine and try.

In both, the visible print was by offset litho. In one, the latent image had been added by litho as well (printed in

Chicago). In the other, the latent image has been added by means of a spirit duplicator. In both cases the latent image was revealed by using a developer pen.

An opportunity was provided for participants to add latent image answers for themselves to ready-prepared xeroxed sheets of questions using the spirit duplicator method.

Spirit duplicator masters for the answers were prepared in the usual way but using the special latent image carbon. There were then run off on a spirit duplicator and tested with the developer pens provided.

Of very great interest was the demonstration by Mr. D. Mayho of A.B. Dick Company of a new method of printing latent image by means of a cut stencil duplicator. This was the first time that this system had been demonstrated in the UK. The latent image answers are typed on an ordinary cut stencil which is then fitted to an A.B. Dick single-cylinder duplicator loaded with the 'invisible' ink.

The superiority of this cut stencil method over the spirit duplicator method was very obvious. The reliability and quality of the latent image were vastly superior. The spirit duplicator has a run limit of about 100; the cut stencil duplicator can produce several thousand copies.

Miscellaneous Methods

On display were examples of scrambled print, scratch-off print, and cholesteric crystals.

The cholesteric crystals took the form of small black squares stuck on the response sheet beside the blank spaces for the answers. When warmed by the finger the blackness fades to green or blue and the correct answer becomes visible. As it cools down the answer becomes obscured as the blackness returns.

The cholesteric crystals are designed to reveal the answer

between 26°C and 33°C. Unfortunately, the ambient temperature in the room in which the workshop was held was very high (over 27°C) and the answers on the sample sheet were already revealed before applying the finger. (It had been found also that at ambient temperatures below about 18°C most people's fingers are too cold to cause the answers to be revealed).

Before this method can be put to practical use, a lot of further technical development work is clearly required.

5

EVALUATION PROCESSES AND STRATEGIES

5.1 Evaluating the Process of Learning

Any model of evaluation (and Eraut, 1972 identifies eleven) represents explicitly or implicitly a view of the nature of learning, what influences it, and how it can be investigated. The traditional 'test measurement' model has close links with the stimulus response approach of behaviourist psychology, while, at the other end of the scale, the 'illuminative' model (Parlett and Hamilton, 1972) represents a wider approach from the social sciences. By its very nature the basic information processing model of learning provided by cognitive psychology focuses attention on the actual process of learning, seeing 'the learner, and his cognitive stages and information processing strategies, as the primary determiner of learning with understanding and long-term memory' (Wittrock, 1974).

Figure 5.1 illustrates the features of a basic information processing system and the three basic stages into which it can be divided for the practical purpose of evaluation (see Lawless, 1979, and Lawless, 1980, for discussion of its implications for the design of instruction as a whole, and for assessing student performance). In this approach the learner actively processes information received through the senses, encodes it, and stores it. Effective application of knowledge depends on the way it is stored (or 'structured') and the quality of the individual's retrieving or problem-solving skills.

Even though supported by experimental evidence, such a representation of 'the complexities of human mental processes' (Neisser, 1967) is essentially an analogy or model in the sense used in the physical sciences 'to unify limited aspects of a particular reality' (Elton and Laurillard, 1979). This concept of a model has several advantages when used as a basis for the design of instruction, of which evaluation must be seen as an integral part. First, it allows essentially integrated and continuous processes to be divided into stages for practical investigation. Second, it allows other models with different emphases to be used alongside it. Third, it is not put forward as a definitive explanation of learning and covers both controversies and alternative approaches, e.g. Weil and Joyce (1978) identify six information processing models. Finally, the use of an approach as a model allows techniques from other, even rival, backgrounds, to be used where relevant.

If evaluation is broadly taken to mean investigating learning situations and materials with a view to improving them, then a cognitive approach appears to pose three basic questions. What are the stages of the learning process? How can they be evaluated? What types of changes is it likely to lead to? The main contrast with other approaches to evaluation is that investigations are carried out *during* learning, rather than just on the results of learning.

The first task of this approach to evaluation is to look into the purposes, stated or otherwise, of instructional situations and materials. Since the cognitive approach is concerned with knowledge and mental procedures, evaluation must be focused on the knowledge and skills that lie behind a specific performance. It is important that students should be right for the right reasons. A learner may give correctly 0.15 as the answer to 0.3 x 0.5, but reveal deficient knowledge if he goes on to give 0.9 for 0.3 x 0.3. Where purpose is stated in performance terms, as a 'behavioural objective', it needs to

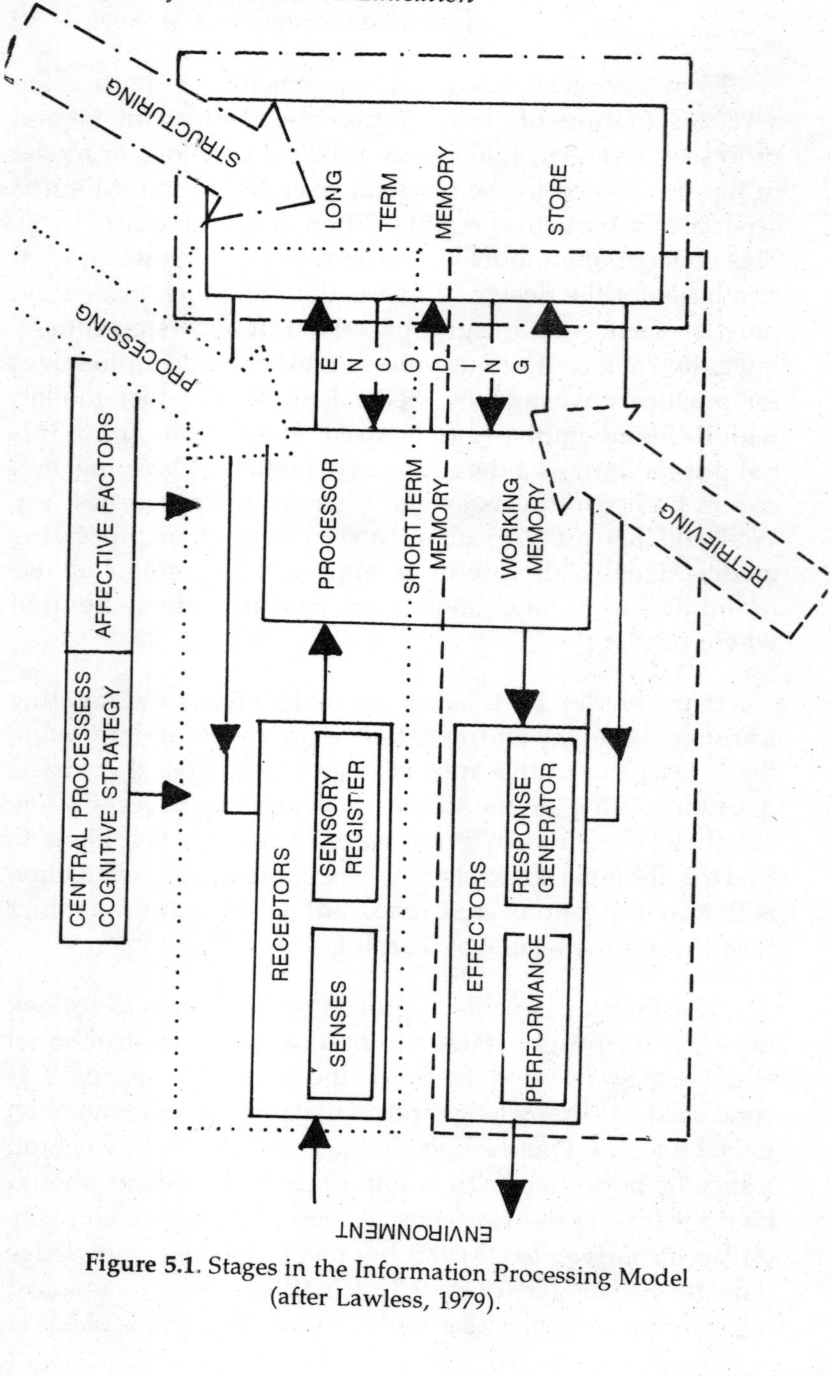

Figure 5.1. Stages in the Information Processing Model (after Lawless, 1979).

be asked whether the stated task or behaviour is in fact the objective of instruction or whether its function is rather to sample the student's knowledge. If the performance is the actual objective (e.g. 'to be able to solve quadratic equations') then the knowledge required to do it needs to be clearly set out. Even the most mundane and apparently repetitive task can require complex procedures for deciding when and when not to perform it. On the other hand if, as is usual in higher education, part, at least, of the purpose of instruction is that the student should acquire knowledge (usually allied, implicitly, to certain mental skills), then performance has a sampling function. The nature of the knowledge to be sampled needs to be probed to see if the performance really does sample what it is claimed to; that it involves using procedures, not just recalling facts. The contrast between these two (rather artificial) positions brings out the need to come to terms with variety in learning. There are different types of purpose, involving different types of learning often within a single course or unit of instruction, and to try to force them into the straightjacket of a single format like the behavioural objectives approach will be counterproductive.

The information processing model is concerned with meaningful learning in which the learner successfully incorporates new facts and skills into his existing cognitive structure. Hence the need to examine the knowledge component, the content, of instruction for potential meaningfulness (see Ausubel *et al.*, 1978, for a full discussion of meaningful learning). Where do the concepts or elements come from? What do they mean? How are they used? How do they interrelate? In what ways do they relate to other areas of knowledge? This is an aspect which, as Lewis (1974) has shown is usually totally neglected. Knowledge is not just made up of concepts, but of procedures for using them. Are these procedures set out. What is their origin? How are they applied? These are the sorts of question which need to be asked about statements of aims or purposes of instruction.

Where high level procedures are specified, e.g. that students should think and operate as physicists or historians, it is important to be clear about what exactly is expected of students who are operating in a 'second hand' situation. Are they expected to display the skills or to recall and demonstrate an expert's display of those skills? The results of analysis using these questions have direct implications for both the type of tasks set for assignments and, in some degree, to the sequencing of teaching itself.

Meaningful learning involves building up the cognitive structure, incorporating new concepts and developing richer patterns of relationships. This facilitates further learning particularly when allied to explicit development of learning skills. In evaluating the aims of instruction an important issue is whether the knowledge is really going to lead to further and better learning and, if so, whether it is the type of learning required.

Evaluating the nature of purpose in this way contrasts with the 'test-measurement' model which accepts specified objectives and then investigates the extent to which students have achieved them. The illuminative approach goes in the opposite direction and purposely ignores objectives completely.

Although the working of the information processing system is essentially integrated and continuous it is useful to divide it into stages. In the 'input' stage, attention, selection, and perception prepare the material for encoding and then storing in the structure of the long-term memory. It is usual, though misleading, to refer to this part of the whole system as 'processing'. What this means in practice is well summed up in this description of a particular processing deficiency.

> Most students entering an introductory college physics course do not possess the learning skill of gaining an understanding of a new relation presented to them in a text (although the text

> discusses this relation at some length). Furthermore, most students do not acquire this learning skill merely as a result of ordinary instruction in a physics course (Reif, Larkin and Bracket, 1976).

Similarly, deficiencies in processing skills have been found by Abercrombie (1960) in medical studies, by Richards (1929) in English literature, and by Perry (1977) in basic reading skills. Thus right at the start of the overall process students are failing to get at the real meaning of the information in the way that it is presented to them.

Evaluating the process of learning requires investigation and sampling *during* the process in order to isolate these learning skill deficiencies. Conventional tests and attitude questionnaires have been used to identify problems in processing, but more limited and direct questioning is needed to identify specific problems. Of particular value in identifying processing problems are interview or 'teach back' techniques (Laurillard, 1979, Pask, 1976, Marton and Saljo, 1976). Since answers to assignment questions tend to be vague rather than right or wrong, Lewis (1974) suggests that students should be asked to explain their answers.

How then are improvements to be made when processing deficiencies are revealed? The first point is that traditionally, and particularly in higher education such aspects are ignored or it is assumed that learning skills will be acquired by exposure to teaching. The experience of Reif *et al.*, (1976) that student do *not* acquire effective learning skills without explicit teaching, is more likely to be the case. The cognitive approach focuses attention on changing the learner. This does not, of course, rule out changing and improving instructional materials, but it recognises that developing processing skills is a long-term educational goal. Particularly in higher education, materials causing problems are often the very subject matter of learning. Practical considerations may preclude revision of teaching materials. This concentration on the learner contrasts with the 'test measurement' approach which assumes a direct link between teaching and learning, and so looks to change the teaching. In complete contrast, the illuminative and so looks to change the teaching. In complete contrast, the illuminative approach is largely unconcerned with either improving the learner's skills or revising instructional materials.

In looking at how students' processing skills can be improved, two issues need to be faced: the general or specific dichotomy, and the question of individual differences. It would be easy, but mistaken, to assume that what is needed are general learning skills, but as Gibbs (1977) has shown, such 'cook book' approaches rarely succeed because they do not relate directly to students' actual learning experiences and difficulties. Developing processing skills needs to be integrated into the mainstream learning experience both because an improvement in general skills such as reading needs to start with the student, and because some skills are specific to particular subject areas, such as the physics learning skill mentioned earlier. reif *et al.* (1976) identified the skills required and integrated their treatment into a 'Keller Plan' physics course. Abercrombie (1960) and gibbs (1977) both made extensive use of small group discussions (integrated into regular teaching programmes) which focused on particular learning problems. Sticht (1978) demonstrated the integration of literacy and learning skill training with basic army training, relating 'reading to do' to 'reading to learn'.

Cognitive psychology holds that each individual's cognitive structure and processing skills are unique and there is considerable evidence to show that individuals have different 'cognitive styles' or patterns of learning skills. This is a vast area, but the main issues are whether such differences are relatively fixed traits, i.e. 'serialist' or 'holist' learning patterns (Pask, 1976), and whether they are qualitative differences, i.e. 'deep' or 'surface' processors (Marton and Saljo, 1976). Laurillard (1979), however, found that students changed their styles of learning in terms of both Pask's and Marton's approaches, according to their perceptions of the demands of a particular learning task. This highlights the need to take processing skills seriously, at the very least alerting students that this is an important issue.

Processing and structuring are essentially a single process, and separating them, though convenient, is artificial. In looking at students' cognitive structures we are asking firstly whether they know enough to understand the new information; at one level it is as simple as asking if the language is understood. In terms of the information processing approach the following questions need to be posed: Is the student's cognitive structure extensive enough to receive new concepts? During instruction, does cognitive structure develop sufficient complexity to represent the subject matter? Is the structure sufficiently well organised to allow for easy retrieval? Each person's cognitive structure is unique, but there must be sufficient resemblance to the knowledge structure as a public entity to allow for communication with other individuals.

How to test for cognitive structure is a problem. A considerable amount of work has been carried out using word-association tests (see, for example, Shavelson, 1974). Stewart (1979) has highlighted the shortcomings of this approach and in a subsequent article (Stewart, (1980) reports the use of a 'concept-map line labelling task' and a very similar 'tree construction line labelling task'. Basically, students are required to arrange concept labels in a pattern and describe the relationships between the different concepts. This is using the information processing approach very much as a model or an analogy since such a basic representation cannot be said to have more than a basic connection with the complexities of cognitive structure in the brain, but it does reveal understanding and misunderstanding of subject matter. Where it is supported by interviews and analysis of normal testing procedures, a detailed picture of students' cognitive structures can be built up. Structure, like processing, is unlikely to be entirely absent, but it can lack the connections which make application possible.

Where there is evidence that students' cognitive structure is inadequate, two courses of action can be followed. The structure of the teaching material can be examined and where necessary made more explicit. There is evident that improving the structure of teaching improves student learning (Anderson and Lee, 1975, Trindade, 1972). This may not be as easy as it sounds because academic subjects tend to be studied, researched and taught as narrow, fragmented, specialisms with little or no attempt to relate to other academic areas. There is, however, a world of difference between improving the structure of a lecture or a chapter, and work carried out by cognitive psychologists under laboratory conditions. A more fruitful approach is that of encouraging students to take an active attitude to learning, to seek out and develop links between concepts. 'The ability to think creatively will presumably depend on the extent to which the memory has developed a multiplicity of unusual, but valid, interconnections' (Entwistle and Hounsell, 1975). How material is stored will, to a large extent, determine the ease or difficult with which it can be retrieved.

Most teachers will have had the experience of receiving a piece of work from a student, an essay or an attempt to solve a problem, which shows an almost total lack of understanding of the subject matter. Yet a couple of simple questions put to the student may reveal that he or she has the knowledge and skills but has failed to use them. In terms of the model, the student failed to retrieve information even though it was in his/her cognitive structure, and it is from this position that the question of retrieval will be considered. As with processing, the general/specific issue has to be faced. A considerable number of articles on how humans solve problems have been written by cognitive psychologists, notably

Newell and Simon (1972), and a number of studies have investigated the effectiveness of free-standing problem-solving courses (e.g. Whimbey, 1977). In spite of the benefit claimed for such general problem-solving approaches, it seems probable that development of problem-solving abilities needs to be embedded in the subject matter of the course. For example, given the specification of the skills of a physicist, social scientist, or historian, as part of the goals of a course, and the identification of that part of those skills which students will be expected to practise, it is important for this to be explicitly explained and opportunities for practice given. Reif *et al.*, (1976) shows that necessary cognitive skills are not acquired merely by exposure but that 'general cognitive skills necessary for effective performance in a science *can* be taught and should be considered a proper subject for explicit instruction'.

Course assignments, by themselves, rarely provide sufficient detail to establish the extent to which students have mastered the retrieval or problem-solving skills. There remains the risk of the student being right for the wrong reason. In a quest for a test of the quality of learning, Lewis (1973) proposes a three stage assignment in which the student is required to solve a problem, explain the solution and justify his explanation. Requiring students to explain how they solved a problem by presenting them with a structured test will reveal whether their solution has been arrived at in a valid way. There is a circular element in this, since problem-solving has to begin with processing information about the nature of the problem!

By focusing on internal processes which underlie learning skills, the cognitive or information approach emphasises an area which, traditionally, is ignored by academics. Hence the first result of such an evaluation is to turn the light on dark corners of the educational process. Although there are undoubtedly specific skills to be learned, the raising of awareness of the importance of the issue is the vital first step for both teachers and students. Mistaken perception of the demands of a learning task rather than skill deficiency may be the cause of learning problems (Laurillard, 1979), and while such misconceptions may result from outside influences, e.g. personal problems or exam pressures (Miller and Parlett, 1974), they may equally well result from simple lack of awareness of the demands of the subject matter. This is what Broudy (1977) calls 'knowing *with*' (to go with 'knowing *how*' and 'knowing *that*'), and links with the need to book skills and knowledge with the ability to select and apply them correctly for a particular situation (Greeno, 1976). To return to the model in Figure 5.1, this involves the development of the control processes, and the improvement of the ability to learn.

5.2 Evaluating the Process of Evaluation

Introduction—Changing Views of Evaluation

A decade ago, educational technology was generally seen as a systematic, prescriptive and objectives-based way of designing, carrying out and evaluating the total process of learning and teaching (e.g. Tickton, 1970). The methods of evaluation were thought to be similarly systematic, unproblematic and straightforward. Thus, for Popham and Baker (1970), evaluation consisted of just five basic operations: establishing specific goals; developing a measuring device; pre-assessing students; implementing an instructional plan; and measuring and interpreting evidence of student achievement. Their approach represented the general view, for it favoured the method of evaluation, now called 'congruent evaluation' (Stufflebeam *et al.*, 1971), which is concerned with measuring the degree to which the stated educational objectives for a course are congruent with what is achieved. Growing awareness of the limitations of that method—and of the prescriptive stance—is indicated by the many other models of evaluation and types of evaluator which have been identified and adopted since then; in 1972, Eraut was able to write of 11 such, while by 1978, Hawkridge had been able to raise this total to 30!

This diversity led to some uncertainty and 'role-reappraisal' by educational technologists, as evidenced by a description of evaluation as the '...unifying activity in which all those calling themselves educational technologists can join together. There is something for everyone [from]...participant observations of human interactions [to]...the empathetic "students'-friend" [who] can vet the course materials in advance....' (Rowntree, 1976).

Of course, one could modify the old prescriptive stance to make it more informed by evaluation, but this is not what was advocated. What was advocated was its rejection in favour of evaluation—which unfortunately does not guarantee that students' learning will improve.

The Students' Friend

As with any professional role, both the purely evaluative and purely prescriptive role, to be filled successfully, require access to reliable tools and procedures. But how reliable is the educational technologist's professional 'box of tricks' (Lewis, 1980)?

1. Are opinions presented as facts?
2. Do arguments loop and change?
3. Are there digressions or irrelevancies?
4. Are assertions grounded in theories?
5. Are ideas fully developed or related?
6. Is the material consistent?
7. Is the material presented systematically?

This list contains some rather arbitrary self-evaluation criteria which I tried to keep in mind when writing the present paper; different criteria might emerge for readers with a different reading purpose. It is not clear to me whether a single such check-list would be used by a 'students'-friend' in trying to anticipate readers' difficulties, or whether the 'students'-friend' would have several models of readers, and so several sets of criteria to apply. The former seems more probable to judge from one study where a group of 'experts' (actually teachers and student teachers) were asked to yet course material. Yet in this study, not only did they sometimes fail to identify problems experienced by students, but they also often detected supposed problems which created no difficult (Frase *et al.*, 1974).

The Professional Evaluator

Whatever type of evaluator we try to be, and no matter how good our procedures, certain questions seem to recur. For example, in negotiating with teachers, should we present them with evaluation *options,* and, if so, how should those options be presented? Again, once an option has been selected, how should subsequent evaluation reports be presented? These questions hide other problems, of which four will be considered now.

1. Choosing an appropriate sample size.
2. Resolving apparent contradictions in evaluation findings.
3. Recognising and allowing for mismatches in conceptions of education.
4. Reconciling ease of evaluation with ease of implementation of findings.

Professional evaluators should be able to cope with such problems with assurance, yet, as reported elsewhere (Smith, 1980), there is still no consensus in the literature on the question of sample size: most advice assumes that you need statistically significant evaluation data, and justifications have been given for sample sizes from as low as 10 to as high as 3,000, each of which meets some form of that statistical criterion! (Incidentally, if your intended sample size seems too small or not fully representative, Smith's own advice is to ignore the statistics and '....ask authors whether they will accept conclusions based upon the [group]....that you would like to use'.)

The literature is similarly vague on the second problem: how to deal with apparently inconsistent evaluation data, which may have been collected in different ways. The evaluator's report has to synthesise these findings in a systematic way (see the first list, point 7), a problem that is still unresolved in the possibly simpler context of synthesising research findings from different investigators (Pillemer and Light, 1980).

Whose Perspective?

The remaining two problems illustrate another point, to which I shall return: that the evaluator may not share the teacher's perspective, so mismatches may occur. The first possible mismatch I shall consider concerns one's conception of education. Even if a 'students' friend' can identify difficulties in advance, this may not be seen as any reason for action: although conventional wisdom might indicate that problems, once revealed, should be eliminated before students encounter them; others contend that—in higher education at least—some should left. The argument runs that 'real', rather than 'perfunctory' learning involves surmounting difficulties, becoming a critic, etc.; also, it is said that a learner's initial confusion is not necessarily a bad thing (Northedge, 1976). Clearly, if an author holds such a view, and the evaluator does not know this, but goes off to collect 'objective' immediate-performance-based evaluation data, some disappointment will ensue. That would be an extreme example, with at least one obvious cause, of evaluation data not being fully accepted by an author or lecturer. I must emphasise here that I am not advocating an unquestioning acceptance by an evaluator of a teacher's expressed aims, even though this may represent a change in role. The difficulty is that, particularly with courses which are experiential rather than didactic, the evaluator may be under pressure to adopt informal methods (Duchastel, 1976).

Yet those methods do not by themselves, assure use of evaluation findings. As Heilman (1980) has observed, people who do not like evaluation results often want to reject them, and the use of soft and informal methods can provide grounds for doing so. As he notes, if goals and perceptions shift, then 'Even the most sincere [teacher]....can find, in the end, that the "evaluation" answered the wrong question or missed the main point. When that happens, the active-reactive-adaptive evaluator is deprived of the principal rationale he or she had....[the teacher's approval]'.

Because of this difficulty, there has been a tendency at the Open University for large-scale evaluations to be of another type: *empirical developmental testing* (Henderson and Nathenson, 1976). In the past, that testing has been in the form of 'piloting' mimeographed drafts of our teaching material, before it is printed. In some ways, it is reminiscent of the older 'congruence' evaluation, since the variables which contribute to collecting useful and implemented feedback are seen as being: the relationship between performance data and other types of student feedback; the use of feedback in making revisions: the selection and motivation of testers; the development of data-collection systems; and the implementation of revisions. It has therefore been criticised as being '...based on the teacher's or evaluator's terms and taking '...no account of what is to count as an educational experience or achievement in the learner's terms. This evaluation contains the implicit assumption of producing one ideal teaching treatment, which does not recognise the wide range of students' abilities and learning styles' (Morgan *et al.*, 1980). While there is something in that criticism, piloting material in this way may well satisfy the demands of treatment-minded teachers.

The last of the four problems arises not from any disparity in views of what is *desirable* but from what is *practicable.* Recently, as Kirkup (1981) points out, some of the techniques of developmental testing have been transferred to a post-presentation evaluation of our New Technology Foundation Course. In that evaluation, the students' learning materials were in their final polished form; the idea was to use the first full cohort of students to identify weaknesses in the published course, with a view to revising it after two years. Unfortunately, while that methodology seemed, in the eyes of the evaluators, to provide data which was both useful and timely, it was not always the source of revisions. With hindsight, part of this can be attributed to the difficulty of maintaining teachers' commitment to evaluation and revision, over a time period at least one year longer than in the more usual piloting schemes. Perhaps as important is the great difference, not always recognised, between evaluating drafts and evaluating the final product.

For example, as Forman (1980) notes: when evaluating television programmes, for example, there can be 14 different evaluation stages for the television component alone. Evaluating the final stage—the polished programme—may be pointless if remake facilities are limited. As often demonstrated, more cost effective is the evaluation of the final script or the rough cut: for authors and producers may then be better placed to accept as implementable the findings from a 'treatment' (or 'statement of intention') evaluation, as used for the Foundation Course's programmes.

Mismatches

To summarise my argument so far, I have indicated a number of potential mismatches between evaluators' and teachers' conceptions of, respectively, education (e.g. Northedge, 1976); evaluation in education (e.g. Morgan *et al.*, 1980); evaluation expertise (Lewis, 1980); and evaluators' findings and the options available for change (Kirkup, 1981).

I shall consider one more: conceptions of evaluation in general. According to Clift and Imrie (1980), many teachers in higher educations still conceive of evaluation in terms of the congruence model, which apparently suggests to a teacher '....an exercise in which their performance will be rated along some continuum of effectiveness [and]....this current perception of evaluation [may be].....a major cause of resistance to and, in some cases, rejection of evaluation programmes by university teachers.' They therefore suggest a less-threatening 'intentional evaluation' scheme, which presents evaluation differently: '....as a learning situation in which staff and students learn how to handle and improve the contingencies of a course'. Put simply, this means involving staff and students more, so that implementation of evaluation findings is more likely. The actual mechanisms they suggest are, in my view, somewhat manipulative, but their scheme is interesting for another reason: while their data collection methods are not unusual, their description of the process of evaluation is cast in cognitive terms. By analogy with three stages of learning (apprehending, acquisition and remembering), they argue that evaluation can be viewed as apprehending, acquisition and application. They did not take that statement very far, but it has important consequences. In particular, as I shall demonstrate shortly, existing evaluation procedures might be modified to take into greater account the many ways in which individuals and groups—including evaluators—acquire and process information and make decisions.

Information Processing

Cognitive psychology tells us that each party involved in an evaluation project—the student, the teacher and the evaluator—is prone to errors of various kinds. This will be obvious to anyone who has asked students to comment on their learning both while they study and after they have studied some material; the concurrent and retrospective data may differ, partly because forgetting can be both general and selective, but also because students may not process consistently the teaching material and questions about that material. Memory distortion and selective perception are not the only factors to influence retrospective self-reports; the basis for the students' views of themselves and their performance may be changed by the material or by being asked questions about it, leading to the phenomenon of the 'response-shift' (Howard *et al.*, 1979). Similarly, the actual form of the questions may be a critical factor; rating scales which are labelled (e.g. excellent to poor) or numbered (e.g. 1 to 5) may be given different interpretations by different students (Frisbie and Brandenburg, 1979). Self-report measures can be made more reliable by relating them to a more meaningful yardstick (e.g. 'Look back to the rating you gave the last section: how does the present section compare?"), or by measuring students' intentions as an indirect measure of their feelings about the material—a 'behaviouroid measure' (Aronson and Carlsmith, 1968).

Many other familiar illustrations could be given of how the evaluation tools we use may determine the answers we obtain: I turn now to the question of how we deal with those answers. There is extensive evidence of the existence of a large number of factors which cause us to make consistent errors when we evaluate something, or when our evaluation of that something is itself evaluated by an author or group of authors. For example, we should all be aware that the sequence in which information (e.g. the text of an evaluation report; an audio-tape) is processed (e.g. studied; listened to) can influence the interpretation placed on it. Some of the influences will arise from the motives and fears of the recipient of the information, while others will be more obviously 'cognitive'. Further details can be found in books by Hogarth (1980); Nosbet and Ross (1980); and Mabry and Barnes (1980); and in papers by Shavelson *et al.* (1977); and Mitroff and Bonoma (1978). The latter proffer one possible alternative to 'the usual approach [to evaluation which involves the author] combining...his own biases with the [unknown] biases of the researcher and making a decision....both...must move backward from the data to confront both their own preferred background assumptions, [and]...competing but plausible set of counter assumptions. Second, they must [move] forward from the data to construct a set of policy options consistent with their preferred assumptions and with the competing assumptions'. Of course, that alternative takes the data as given. Some means must also be found of communicating to an author what assumptions have been made in obtaining the data.

In so doing, educational technologists should bear in mind how easy it is for evaluators or teacher to experience; misperceptions of randomness; unrealised overdependence on data from small samples; the related 'availability' bias; 'anchoring' bias; 'hindsight' bias; and the desire for redundant information (Lefrere *et al.*, 1980). Each can result in disproportionate (high or low) use of particular types of data, and inconsistent gathering of information; knowledge of how they arise might allow the criteria for reaching particular evaluation judgements to be made more explicit and less intuitive.

This brings me back to evaluators' views of education and the learner, and so to my final remarks. Easley (1977), in a paper on various possible perspectives on teaching and learning, writes of the need '.... to alert researchers and practitioners of various persuasions to the social and cognitive phenomena in which they play a part'. This I have tried to do here, although I have not tried to identify in any detailed way, better ways of communicating with authors. Those interested in that may find the way ahead is indicated by writers such as Moxley (1979), who advises that much current educational research is made unnecessarily complex and inaccessible because we cannot see the wood for the trees (and nor either can our clients and colleagues, the authors). He uses a three-way classification (subjective', 'individual' and 'aggregate') of the information we collect, a classification which seems capable of describing all the commonly-used evaluation models (as well as suggesting some new combinations). Translating such ideas into briefing documents for authors and evaluators might prove very useful, but I leave that to others. However, I must point out that this can lead to a change in role. I therefore close by noting the opinion of Robert Stake (quoted in Perloff, 1979). He sees a need for the professional evaluator to strive to separate his function as a data gatherer from his sentiments and values about someone else's material. Educational technologists may view evaluation differently, perhaps as just part of an educational technology service, where it is quite legitimate to attempt to improve the skills of all concerned. But in Stake's opinion: 'It is unethical to help improve the decision-making function, especially to make it more explicit and less intuitive if accomplished under the guise of an evaluation service'.

5.3 Conducting Programme Evaluations: Some Considerations

Introduction

Programme evaluation within an educational or occupational training context can be described as a systematic activity involving the analysis or documentation of programme-related components and process, the measurement of variables associated with programme interests, and the elaboration of recommendations based upon a consideration of the information. This definition incorporates Smith's (1975) suggestion that programme evaluation is more than assessment. Hawkins' (1980) emphasis on programme elements during evaluation, and the systematic nature of activities during a programme evaluation as emphasised by Hyman and Wright (1967) and Stake (1967). A means of translating these concepts into actual activities has been previously described by Moors (1979).

Many who are professionally involved in the planning and delivery of education programmes recognise the value of programme evaluation. The activity provides opportunities for feedback, accountability, and cost-benefit information, to name a few. In spite of these perceived outcomes, the actual mechanics of meaningful involving those who participate in the education activity (especially instructors) throughout a comprehensive programme evaluation sequence represents an obstacle. Educators tend to be well-versed in assessment techniques associated with their *primary* programme emphasis. For example, instructors tend to be able to assess curriculum, or administrators frequently audit their areas of programme responsibility. This in no way insures that professional educators can effectively participate in activities associated with the evaluation of a total programme especially in those activities which relate to components and processes beyond their sphere of primary programme involvement. As educators, we tend to lack the skills associated with evaluating aspects of the system peripherally related to our primary responsibilities.

The problem is similar to the earlier dilemmas experienced by many education boards who attempted to centralise curriculum development activities. In such circumstances, those who spent extensive periods of time out of a learner environment progressively lost the ability to produce viable products for use by classroom instructors. One effective approach to solving this was to have those instructors, who were to use the product, actively participate in its development. Instructors frequently require, and are afforded, the opportunity to upgrade their curriculum development skills in order to engage in such activities. This is a normal professional responsibility, and it is now a well recognised premise of many education systems.

This same need or requirement is applicable to the development and use of skills associated with programme evaluation activities. Developing these skills among the personnel of an education system can be viewed as an innovation. To be successful in the development of these skills throughout an education system, phases associated with the continuation and diffusion of the innovation can be described. Continuation refers to the ongoing nature of activities designed to develop the skills once such programmes are initiated. Diffusion refers to the use of information associated with the innovation by other educational systems or activities.

Reilly and Starr (1980) identify factors which positively influence the continuation and diffusion of an educational innovation. The two most important factors include the support and co-operation of (i) administrative staff and (ii) instructional staff. This paper describes an approach intended to develop, among instructors and others who are involved in the educational effort, the skills associated with participating in programme evaluation activities. It is assumed that the availability of such skills will assist in the development of support for the programme evaluation process among instructors and administrators, thereby facilitating the continuation and diffusion of the innovation. It is also assumed that the support necessary for the implementation of recommendations contained in any programme evaluation report would be increased because of instructor participation in the evaluation process. While this may be true for all programme sponsors, the influences of the effort on the instructors is of prime importance.

Who should Be Involved?

In order to infuse and maximise the participation of instructors and other programme personnel in the complete programme evaluation process, two interacting activities occur. First of all, the activities associated with the evaluation of a particular programme, including the development of a detailed plan, are directed by an evaluation committee. Each committee is structured to reflect the sponsors or stakeholders associated with the particular programme or educational activity being evaluated. For most occupational training programmes in

Nova Scotia, the committee structure begins with a representative of the funding source (Canada Employment and Immigration Commission—Regional Office) and a representative of the Nova Scotia Department of Education. Other sponsors (agencies who exercise influence over programme related activities) are invited to join the committee. While the standards or guidelines of committee membership continue to evolve, the usual procedure is to invite at least one instructor from the programme to assume committee membership.

One programme evaluation which is at present under way reflects this trend. For the evaluation of the Medical Laboratory Technology Training Programme in Nova Scotia, the following groups or agencies have been asked to name representatives to the committee:

- The Provincial Department of Education.
- The Nova Scotia Institute of Technology (where the first year of the programme is given).
- Each of the five provincial hospitals in which the second year of the programme is given.
- The Provincial Department of Health.
- The Provincial and National professional accreditation associations.

In this instance, instructors will participate on the committee as representatives of the programme delivery units. Administration involvement will occur through the Provincial Departments of Education and Health.

The second activity which insures involvement and support from critical levels is the operation of a workshop designed to develop the plan for the programme evaluation sequence. This workshop lasts over three days. The following is an example of the workshop objectives.

Programme Evaluation Workshop (Cape Breton Regional Vocational School)

Objective

To increase the skills of a selected group of Cape Breton Regional Vocational School staff members in the activities associated with planning a programme evaluation.

Each participant will, within two months of the completion of the workshop, provide a plan that identifies the sequence of activities anticipated during an evaluation or training programme in which they professionally participate.

This plan will be rated as acceptable by the workshop participant (author), the workshop leader and the Principal of the Cape Breton Regional Vocational School.

A more specific objective associated with the development of the evaluation plan during the workshop is as follows:

> Each participant will review the Moors (1979) programme evaluation model/narrative. Each participant will then suggest at least two activities for all of the model sub-systems as applied to the evaluation of their own educational or training programme.

Therefore, two products of the workshop activity can be described. The first is an increase in the level of information that workshop participants have associated with programme evaluation concepts. The second product is a detailed evaluation plan that provides the basis of all further activities associated with the planned programme evaluation. By 'front ending' each programme evaluation sequence with this workshop activity the persons who are to be involved in, and will be affected by, the evaluation sequence engage in a critical step towards eliciting their continued assistance, co-operation and support during the programme evaluation.

In summary, an important consideration in the activities associated with programme evaluation is the involvement and support of administrators and instructors. This relates to both the continuation and diffusion of programme evaluation activities, especially when the concept is at an innovative stage within an education system. Three important ways to facilitate this involvement include:

1. insuring that both groups are included on the programme evaluation committee;
2. providing persons with the opportunity to develop skills associated with conducting and participating in programme evaluation;
3. involving these persons in the development of the programme evaluation plan.

Determining Evaluative Questions

Evaluation sequences can run astray or remain incomplete because the evaluative questions and interests remain undefined. It is reasonable to expect that the areas of evaluative questioning will reflect the programme-related responsibilities of the various sponsors. It is also reasonable to expect that further areas of interest will evolve as the various components and processes of the programme become clarified during the initial stage of the evaluation sequence. An appropriate strategy for determining evaluative questions is to store evaluative interests or areas of questioning until the descriptive information relating to the programme has been documented. Following this, each of the stored evaluative interests are retrieved and related to the defined programme objectives. This permits each evaluative interest to be refined into a specific evaluative question and stated in terms of the programme perspective. The next step is to describe the research requirements of each question and the programme implications of the possible answers to the questions. This elaboration gives decision-makers the opportunity to put in order of priority the evaluative questions—to determine if the question and the associated research are worth the investment of the research. Decisions to pursue the necessary research are then taken in light of the time and resources available and the meaningfulness or importance of the resulting information.

This approach was used during the evaluation of an academic upgrading programme for unemployed adults in Nova Scotia and permitted the general type of question 'Are the mathematics learning activity packages (LAPs) effective?' to be refined to 'Are the mathematics LAPs effective (i) as resource materials in a self-directed learning situation, and (ii) as resource materials to instructors?' The question associated with effectiveness in self-directed learning situations could be answered by examining the number of self-test tries by a student to criterion performance for each LAP. The effectiveness of the materials to instructors could be measured by constructing an instrument for an instructor rating of the various LAP sections. Elaborating on the self-directed learning questions, the evaluation committee suggested a 70 per cent successful performance level of student 'first tries' on the self-tests would mean that no changes in the LAPs for self-instructional use would be recommended. A lower success score would indicate the need for revisions. Because the programme operators intended that the instructional situation would rely heavily on self-directed learning, this evaluative question was given a high priority by the evaluation committee and subsequently pursued.

In summary, identifying evaluative questions is an important activity within any programme evaluation sequence. One useful approach is to refine general statements of interest areas to specific evaluative questions. Research and programme implications associated with the question should be clearly identified. This allows for meaningful decisions relative to which evaluative questions should be addressed.

Instruments

The selection of instruments for evaluation purposes depends on the specific evaluative questions defined for further research. The traditional instrument categories have been outlined by Denton (1973) and are well known. These include: attitude/interest tests; criterion referenced tests; questionnaires or interviews; direct observation; and unobtrusive tests ('inference twice removed'). To these should be added the further categories of 'illuminative' instruments and check-lists. Illuminative evaluation instruments, as described by Morgan, Gibbs and Taylor (1980), have evolved because of the interest in qualitative evaluation techniques. Check-lists have become popular because of the necessity for job performance measures and include not only basic check-lists but also performance tests and observation scales. This necessity relates specifically to occupational and industry based training programmes and has been emphasised by Forman (1980). These two types of instrumentation are relevant to the present discussion because of the information they provide to instructional staff, both during and following the programme evaluation process. In short, they provide one basis for the diffusion of an innovation.

Check-lists which are developed for programme evaluation purposes can be effectively used in subsequent instructional situations. This is especially true of instances in which an industry supervisor works with the instructor to develop the instrument.

A type of qualitative instrument has been developed and employed within Nova Scotia programmes to determine the degree to which LAPs represent an effective instructor-used teaching resource. In order to develop the instrument, a group of instructors identified the most and least preferred characteristics of instructional materials associated with the various sections of LAP (objectives, prescriptive materials, self-tests, etc.). Through a conciliation rating procedure each of these characteristics was assigned a value and a weighting factor in relation to each of the other identified characteristics. This provided a basis for a five-point rating scale associated with each of the four most important characteristics during the assessment of the LAPs by other instructors. The instrument then not only provided data for evaluation purposes. Because it reflected qualitative factors (characteristics used in instruction), it was also an effective aid in determining areas for curriculum refinements and provided guidelines for future resource development. Thus programme evaluation activities should, where possible, select and develop instruments which can assist programme-related activities beyond the evaluation sequence.

Handling the Results

In the final analysis, programme evaluation should provide feedback information associated with future programme direction and activities. While support and commitment for the evaluation process can be generated by treating programme evaluation as an innovation, the activities an organisation initiates, based upon the recommendations of the evaluation report (i.e. the overall product of the evaluation process), truly determine the difference between attempts to examine quality control and efforts to maximise quality assurance. The difference in these two concepts in an education system has been identified by English (1980), who suggests that quality control is internal to the organisation while quality assurance is external. Within the present context, the evaluation process represents an attempt to identify information associated with quality control. Activities based upon the resulting recommendations fall within the domain of quality assurance.

By involving all sponsors throughout the complete programme evaluation sequence, the basis of the recommendations should be understood by the agency or stakeholder to which they relate. These recommendations should be circulated, in draft form, to the sponsor agencies through their representative on the evaluative committee. Within each sponsor organisation, the discussion, refinement, and conformation of the relevant recommendations can be 'brokered' by their committee representative. This person has the advantage of being able to elaborate upon the information placing it within its proper perspective. Following this, a final or 'confirmation' meeting of the evaluation committee permits a formal opportunity to refine and accept the evaluation report. A procedure which incorporates these, or similar, activities simply views the recommendations of an evaluation report as information to be diffused, again requiring the support and commitment of programme sponsors.

Conclusion

In conclusion, the nature of the evaluation process, to be meaningful, must establish a basis for programme sponsor support and co-operation. This suggests that activities should not be pursued which established an adverse relationship among the participants. Rather, planned activities which are designed to involve and develop the skills of various groups associated with the programme evaluation are necessary.

5.4 Evaluation Through the Aperture: An Analysis of Mediated Observational Techniques

Measurement and/or Observation

In many minds, measurement and evaluation have become synonymous (Gardner, 1977). This may be partly due to the application of scientific research models to educational evaluation. A basic assumption is that the phenomena in question possess significant measurable attributes and that instruments can be designed which can sensitively detect those attributes. Indeed, many of the failures of the measurement approach, according to Gardner (1977) can be attributed to violations of this underlying premise.

Measurement lends itself well to evaluation-by-objective

models (Tyler, 1942; Bloom *et al.*, 1970; Popham, 1969) since evidence of summative output based on specific behavioural events are identified in advance and serve as the evaluative criteria. Eisner (1972) and others (e.g. Stake, 1975) have argued that evaluation-by-objectives and associated measurement practices tend to obfuscate potentially critical differences which may manifest themselves only during the process of learning. Also, Stake (1975) points out that certain content areas, such as the arts, are not conducive to quantification and therefore should be evaluated by employment of less restrictive models such as programme portrayal. Observational methodologies and other qualitative evidence are suggested as alternatives or supplements to objective data under such conditions.

Unquestionably, the appropriateness of any measurement and/or observational methodologies is dependent upon situational and philosophic issues, which must be resolved prior to evaluation.

Human Observers of Human Behaviour

The prominent role of observation in inquiry has been touted in both literature and science. Sherlock Holmes was portrayed as possessing 'extraordinary powers of observation' upon which rested his 'science of deduction and analysis.' The contributions of Piaget (1926) and Gesell (1934) were founded upon observational methodologies which led, in both cases, to striking changes in our views of child development. Similarly, the sciences of ethnography and anthropology have relied heavily upon evidence collected through observation.

Human observers are, to a large extent, low fidelity recording instruments. They suffer from fatigue, expectation bias and a host of associated problems (Campbell, 1959), some of which can be corrected and some of which cannot. Even when they are highly trained, observer variability over time (Webb, campbell, Schwartz and Sechrest, 1966) represents a major threat which is difficult to foresee. Observers may become less observant as boredom sets in, or conversely, more attentive as the task becomes better learned or provides the opportunity for participation. An extreme case of observer participation is reported by Lang and Lang (1960). During a sociological study of a Billy Graham Crusade in New York, two scientific observers became so moved by the experience that they made the 'Decision for Christ' and left their observational vantage points to walk down the aisle. While such blatant observer participation bias may not jeopardise the course of normal educational evaluation, educational technologists should be aware of the extent to which variability may influence evaluative outcomes.

When one of the more descriptive evaluative models is employed, such as the naturalistic approach(es) suggested by Guba (1978), programme portrayal (Stake, 1975), or the case study approach (Stake, 1978), data coded into nominal categories may not be appropriate or desirable. Under these conditions, observers may be asked to write anecdotal notes or in some other way provide descriptive feedback concerning the phenomenon being studied. Mediated observational procedures may be most productively employed in such circumstances. The remainder of this paper is devoted to a brief review and description of mediated observation, its potential role within various evaluative frameworks and its methodological limitations.

Mediated Observation

It is not surprising that scientific disciplines which regularly employ observational methodologies have adopted mediated techniques (i.e. mechanical recording devices) to extend inquiry as well as to reduce human observational error. Collier (1967) reports that ethnographers were among the first to enthusiastically accept photographic data as the clearest evidence of a culture. Felix-Louis Renault produced ethnographic film as early as 1895 (Hockings, 1975), and

Heider's (1976) comprehensive book entitled *Ethnographic Film* touches everything from the history of photographic applications in ethnography to the use of such media in teaching. Collier (1967) and Hockings (1975) also report applications of photography to anthropological research, but both note that media are used by researchers in this field more to augment traditional naturalistic inquiry than as a primary data source.

For example, mediated observation has also played a major role in a number of other contexts. Video-taping has been used extensively with pre-service teachers (Ellett and Smith, 1975; Winn, 1974) and with in-service teachers (Fuller and Manning, 1973), as well as in a host of similar arenas (such as training and therapy). The primary focus in these applications, however, is on judging or modifying individual behaviour within a given context. Since the person being observed is typically involved in review, threats to interpretation are reduced, although, as Fuller and Manning (1973) point out, under certain conditions self-confrontation via video-tape may cause more harm than good.

As a research or evaluative tool, visual media (film or video-tape) clearly can provide an advantage over human observers in certain circumstances. Mediated observational records can overcome the problems of fatigue or observer participation mentioned earlier. Once produced, these records are relatively permanent, lending themselves well to repeated viewing, editing and reproduction. Mediated records also allow flexibility in analysis and interpretation. Images can be used as descriptive evidence or can be converted into categorical data depending upon the needs of the project and the model which is being used. Finally, technological advances like stop action and slow motion can make possible the description and analysis of complex interactions which might otherwise go unobserved. In short, mediated observation can aid the evaluator or educational technologist in a variety of ways given that its limitations are understood and taken into account.

Potential Roles of Media in Evaluation

There are a number of possible roles which media could serve in evaluation. These include (i) recording, (ii) evoking evaluative responses, and (iii) reporting.

Recording Role

As previously mentioned, the evaluation literature is replete with evaluation models which place a high premium on observational methodologies. Guba's (1978) naturalistic inquiry approach and Stake's (1978) case study model are prominent examples which borrow heavily from the anthropological-observational research methodology. Mediated observation seems a logical extension of these approaches. For instance, where the evaluator's emphasis is on programme documentation or portrayal (i.e. Stake, 1975), 'portrait photography' would seem to be directly applicable. In any evaluative model employing observational methodology, Collier's book (1967) *Visual Anthropology* could serve as an excellent field manual.

Mediated recording would seem to have a use within the framework of other models as well. Evaluators (Worthen and Sanders, 1973) argue for the use of multiple dependent measures; at the very least mediated observation offers a novel and potentially valuable data source. For example, media could assist the goal-free evaluator (Scriven, 1967) in gathering evidence concerning the multiple effects of the phenomenon under study. Wide angle and zoom lens techniques would seem to be particularly amenable to the evaluator seeking a broad view of programme impacts. Media might also be employed in connection with the judicial model (Wolf, 1975) where both sides collect evidence to document and dramatise their cases, or with the more objective models (i.e. Tyler, 1942) in an effort to record outcomes related to specific stated objectives. Or, media might be used only during certain phases of an evaluation—such as the input and process phases of Stufflebeam's (1971) CIPP model. Regardless of the evaluation model, media applications to evaluation represent a unique data source of vast potential for recording programme events and other outcomes.

Evocative Role

Once recorded, visual media can be used to generate a secondary data source. Seeing a photograph or video segment can serve to facilitate recall by clients and programme staff regarding the nature of events, personal reactions to those events and perceptions of the programme's effectiveness. This is not unlike the way in which photographs were used by psychologists as early as 1909 (DeBrigard, 1975), and to a great extent by anthropologists and ethnographers (Kreb, 1975). Researchers in teacher education have also used video records for the same purpose. Typically, representative samplings of teacher behaviour are recorded, but rather than using them to evaluate individual behaviour, the teachers themselves or panels of judges are asked to respond to the segments with descriptive and analytical comments. Thus, a new data set is created which can be analysed separately from the original visual images.

In a goal-free evaluation (Scriven, 1967) of a student orientation programme (Petersen, Brown and Sanstead, 1979) an attempt was made to assess the impact of evocative media upon the reactions of participants and staff. The sample was randomly divided into two groups and each was asked to respond to a questionnaire concerning the programme and its effectiveness. One group viewed programme-related slides as they responded while the other group did not. When questionnaire results were analysed across groups, no significant differences were observed. In this particular study, the questionnaire took on the structuring role for the respondents while the slides acted as supplements. However, the photograph could easily have served the same structuring role in which case different results might have been obtained.

Reporting

Slide-tape presentations or edited video productions will probably never replace the traditional evaluation report. Yet, in cases of programme portrayal, the use of such media seems both appropriate and desirable. Recently, a study (Petersen, Brown and Sanstead, 1979) was conducted to determine if such applications can have bearing on evaluative decision-making. A judicial model (Wolf, 1975) formed the framework for the evaluation of a large university residence hall. Two teams of evaluators were employed: an advocate and an adversary, both of which took photographs to represent the environment and operating milieu of the hall. One team used an evocative approach to solicit comments of the residents while the other team supplied their own interpretations. Results from independent jury deliberations (i.e. administrators assigned to independent juries), one with media and one without, indicated that the use of photographs significantly affected the evaluative outcomes. The two juries reached different decisions as to the need for renovations and organisational changes in the residence hall.

Stake (1975) strongly urges the use of multiple channels for communicating evaluative results, especially when clients or decision makers are removed from the physical setting under consideration. Media represent one means of providing concrete referents to supplement more abstract data. Though there is potential danger of media reporting becoming a multi-media extravaganza—a show with no substance—the other extreme to be avoided is the evaluator who, although he employs visual media in a recording capacity, makes no use of the medium in reporting. Even when recorded observational data are reduced to nominal categories, the actual visual images may serve as a potent methodological justification during the reporting stage.

Methodological Issues and Concerns

There are a number of issues regarding the use of media in evaluation. These include (i) bias, (ii) obtrusiveness, and (iii) ethics.

Bias

Subjectivity and bias are inherent risks in any observational methodology. In an earlier section, several forms of human observer bias (i.e. expectation, fatigue, participation) were pointed out and, to a certain extent, media applications can serve to reduce or eliminate these. However, mediated observation can introduce its own forms of bias. For instance, in representing one aspect of the visual field, others are necessarily excluded. Varying angles of view and aperture settings can give false impressions of size and depth, and still photographs are completely devoid of time referents. Close up views may ascribe significance to the trivial, and wide-angle views may diminish the important. While the significance of these, and other, limitations may be evident to those who regularly deal with media products, uninitiated respondents and consumers should be provided with the necessary qualifications in advance.

In addition to these technical limitations, bias may be introduced through human operators. Visual media possess the potential for both recording experience and artistic expression. Photographers are often referred to as 'picture-makers' rather than 'picture-takers' since they select a particular view from an infinity of possible views, so that the product reflects the photographer as well as the pictured object (Berger, 1977). Even under the best of circumstances, media can never provide a totally true representation of reality. However, care can be taken to avoid the propensity to record the attractive or the unusual to he exclusion of other possibilities within the visual field.

In order to counteract bias, anthropologists and

ethnographers have relied upon training in their disciplines to provide the necessary safeguards. Evaluation would do well to borrow some of their sampling procedures and techniques. The evaluator might also do well to borrow techniques to control observational bias from the psychologist. Base-lining, repeated measures, and time-sampling are examples of techniques which help reduce bias. Whatever approach is used, bias remains a problematic issue to be resolved whenever an observational procedure is employed.

Obtrusiveness

A second methodological problem inherent in the mediated approach is that of obtrusiveness. Both Heider (1976) and Hockings (1975) discuss the potential impact of the camera on human behaviour. Likewise, Webb *et al.* (1966) discuss the relative effects of obstrusive and non-obtrusive recording devices upon behaviour. There is little question that all observational methodologies inject an element of reactive bias into the observed setting. The Hawthorne effect is well-known and documented. However, through the use of specialised equipment (i.e. telephoto lenses) and appropriate attenuation and base-lining periods prior to recording, the effects of obtrusiveness can be minimised even when the most elaborate hardware set-ups are required.

Ethics

An issue which has received relatively less attention is that of ethics. Recording the actions of others, whether through photographic or electronic means, requires participation in another person's 'mortality, vulnerability and mutability' (Sontag, 1977). In an age concerned with confidentiality and rights to privacy, there are questions of who owns the images which have been recorded, and probably more importantly, how should they be used in the course of evaluation and how should they be treated afterwards. The issue of confidentiality comes to the forefront when media are used in evaluative reporting, since it is at this point that private information is made public. Aside from the legal ramifications, it is the responsibility of those concerned to obtain consent from the people being observed and to insure that the rights of individuals have been observed and protected.

Conclusion

The purpose of this paper was not to create yet another evaluation model, but rather to explore the potential utility of applying an existing tool to enhance and enrich the evaluation process. As with any tool, there are strengths and limitations. Mediated observation has a limited capacity to document certain cognitive events which are indicators of learning. However, in terms of observable events, media can play a direct role in recording and reporting, a secondary role in supplementing and checking other data sources, and even can be used to evoke responses for an auxiliary data set.

In illustrating potential applications of mediated techniques, at least three major issues were identified: bias, obtrusiveness, and ethics. While not unique to mediated observation, the nature of the data suggests special consideration, especially if the data are used in public reports. These issues cannot be resolved through rhetoric, but must be actively engaged through experimentation and field trials.

This paper began by suggesting that the educational technologist should become aware of and familiar with a variety of evaluation models and techniques. To a large extent, educational technologists are in a unique position to explore the utility of mediated observation, even to a greater extent than evaluators in other educational realms. Heider (1976) suggests that the best ethnographic films come from ethnographers who are photographers. Undoubtedly, the best use and applications of media to evaluation will come from educational technologists who are also evaluators.

5.5 Validation Processes for Instructional Systems

Introduction

In industrialised countries traditional instructional systems seem unable to reflect the dynamics of the society's development.

Problems which require new approaches and new tools for instruction and education are:

- the rising demand for education at all levels;
- the changing demands of the labour market;
- the development and dissemination of new technologies, methodologies and related methodologies pertaining to storage, elaboration and transmission of information;
- the rapid growth of scientific knowledge and an acceleration of the dynamics of the social need to which instructional systems are related.

To face these problems new, instructional systems have been developed to complement the traditional ones. Examples are the Open University in the UK, DIFF in West Germany, and the CAL systems developed for universities and schools. Even though these systems are quite different in their shape and content, they share several important features:

(a) they tend to rely heavily on modern communication means (TV, computer, teletext, viewdata, video-disc, etc.);

(b) they are reproducible in that they may be repeated in different places at the same time;

(c) they are used by many students;

(d) time and costs for developing the instructional material are very high.

Related to these features, new problems arise. Because these systems have a large audience, poor teaching will affect many students and will be difficult to rectify. Furthermore, production costs are justifiable only if the development systems are more effective than the traditional ones. Thus, a 'reliable' control of their quality is required. On the other hand, information about the quality of the instructional process, which emerges naturally in a face-to-face situation, is not available.

Thus, as far as non-traditional instructional systems are concerned, we need more information for controlling their quality, but we are deprived of the normal information we would get in a traditional teaching situation. As a result, new methods, techniques and tools based on the reproducibility feature are required in order to evaluate them.

Up to now, many different approaches to 'evaluation' have been put forth. It emerges from an analysis of these that there is much disagreement about:

- techniques (what to do in order to evaluate an instructional system and how to use the gathered data);
- functions (why a system must be evaluated and by whom);
- object (what must be evaluated in a system).

In addition, the term 'evaluation' is often used ambiguously for either quality control or student assessment. In order to overcome this confused situation, we think that it is necessary to begin with a clear definition of the nature of the problem and then to derive possible solutions.

The Nature of the Problem

In order to eliminate ambiguities, we will use the word 'validation' instead of 'evaluation'. Here, 'validation of an instructional system' is defined as a set of procedures aimed at:

(a) ensuring a compliance with specified functions;
(b) detecting the causes of deviation from the state behaviour;
(c) identifying the activities for correcting errors and weaknesses;
(d) ensuring the compliance with needs;
(e) detecting the causes of deviation from the needs;
(f) identifying suitable modification to the system.

Moreover, since the quality of the system changes with time, an activity is required to maintain it. This activity is called maintenance.

Let us examine the consequences of these definitions, starting from a model of the instructional processes. Figure 5.1 shows an instructional system in operation. During an instructional process an interaction takes place between the system and a learning population that is a part of the environment of the system. The results of this interaction are a change in the knowledge state of that population (and, consequently, a change in the environment) and the gathering of data about the instructional process.

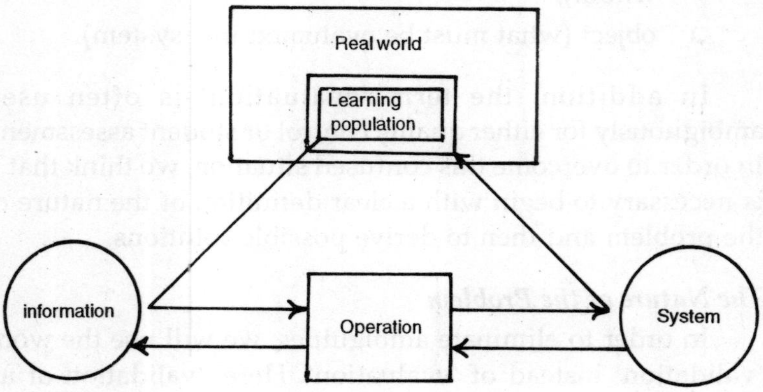

Figure 5.2. Schematic Representation of an Instructional System in Operation

Following the definition given previously, the first function of validation is to see if the system performs the functions for which it was built. This implies that the functions of the system must be clearly and unambiguously defined before producing the system. In addition, the gathered information has to be comparable against these functions, to detect if functions are correctly accomplished, and, if deviations from the stated behaviour are detected, then suitable corrected actions must take place. This implies that the system must be produced in such a way as to be easily changeable.

Many evaluation techniques follow this scheme. In these techniques the functions are roughly identified with the instructional objectives, and information is obtained regarding the students' behaviour. Unfortunately, however, most of them fall to identify the causes of discrepancies and, what is worse, they do not indicate what must be done in order to correct the system.

Another function of validation (as defined) is to establish whether the stated functions of the system fulfil the requirements defined by means of the needs analysis.

At this stage the functions are compared with the requirements, discrepancies are detected, and functions are consequently modified. Of course, this step must precede the production of the system.

However, the quality of an instructional system does not remain the same during time, but changes continuously because—as was shown in the Introduction—the environment to which it is related changes with time. This activity of continuous change, intrinsic to the nature of the instructional system, is called maintenance.

Thus the system must be maintained and modified during its life in order to keep its quality stable. This process continues until the production of a new system becomes more profitable than the maintenance of the old one.

According to our model, validation and maintenance are strictly linked to the developed process of an instructional system and they can be accomplished only if the system is developed taking them into account from the very beginning.

Instructional System Life Cycle, Validation and Maintenance

In this section we will describe our approach to validation and maintenance. In particular, we will discuss the following items:

(a) production phases of the system;
(b) validation processes related to them which take place when the system does not yet exist (these processes are called 'verification');
(c) valiation processes aimed at testing the system quality (they are called 'quality control' and take place during and after system implementation).

Production Phases

Figure 5.2 shows the input and output of the production process of an instructional system. The inputs are the needs related to the environment. The output is the system, called 'gross system' because it has not been tested yet. As shown in Figure 5.3, this activity can be broken down into four main sub-activities or phases, namely; requirements definition; specification; design; implementation.

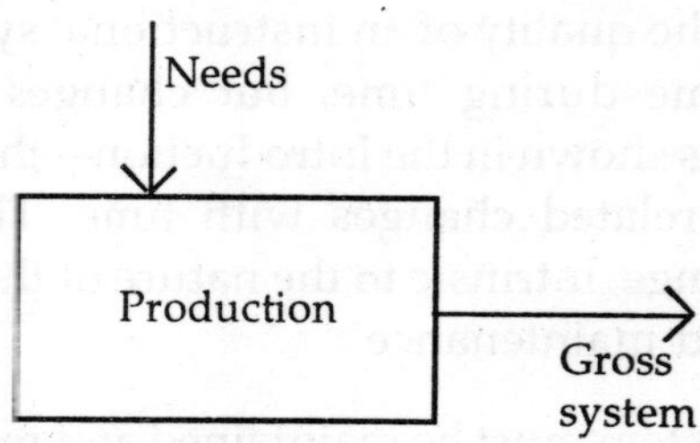

Figure 5.3. Inputs and Outputs of the Production Process of an Instructional System

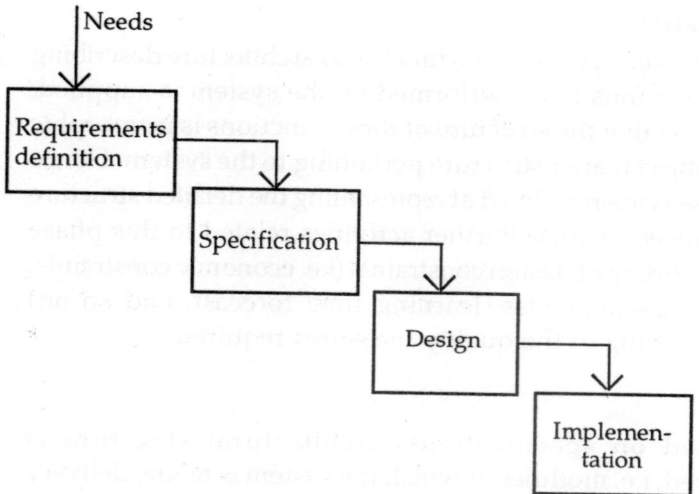

Figure 5.4. Phases Associated with the Production Process

In our approach, the outputs of the first three phases have the following three main functions:

1. To set requirements for the next phase.
2. To document the production activities of each phase.
3. To supply the basis for determining whether or not each phase fulfils the requirements set by the previous one.

Let us now briefly describe each phase.

Requirements Definition

This phase endeavours to clarify:

(a) the needs for which the instructional system must be developed;
(b) the general features of the system that meet these needs, i.e. aims and content;
(c) available resources.

Specification

In this stage, the system functional architecture describing all the functions to be performed by the system is supplied. We assume that the structure of these functions is isomorphic to the subject matter structure pertaining to the system. Hence this phase is mainly aimed at representing the detailed structure of the subject matter. Further activities related to this phase are the defining of design constraints (i.e. economic constraints, students' prerequisites, learning time forecast, and so on) and the stating of the quality measures required.

Design

Based on specifications, architectural structure is developed, i.e. modules of which the system is made, delivery strategy, testing procedures, etc. In this phase, the detailed design of modules is also developed describing the means for presenting information, problem-solving activities; and containing AV scripts, self-instructional material. CAI dialogues, and so on. Finally, quality control procedures are defined.

Implementation

The design is physically carried out. Modules, assessment tests, delivery strategy and the user's manual are produced.

Verification

Verification is strictly linked to the production process. In fact, it is an interactive process aimed at determining whether or not each phase of the production process fulfils all requirements set by the previous phase.

Initially, the requirements stated in phase 1 are compared with the needs. If they match these needs, the 'requirement document' passes to phase 2; if they do not, the requirements are changed and verified again. This process continues until they match the needs. In the same way, the specifications are compared with requirements, the design is compared with the specifications, and the gross system with the design.

Thus, verification controls the development of the production activities. It is allowed to go on to the next step only if it has been verified that the actual phase fulfils the requirements set by the previous one. In this way, errors and weaknesses are detected very early, before the system exists, and they can easily be eliminated. Thus, verification prevents building a system which deviates from the stated requirements.

Quality Control

Quality control is a process of organised use of the system under controlled circumstances to test its quality. It takes place during and after the implementation phase. Like verification, this process is also related to each production phase.

After implementation, each module is tested to detect and correct errors and weaknesses. In the current evaluation practices of instructional systems, this process is called 'formative evaluation'.

As all tested modules become available they are assembled into a system in an integration process and a system test begins. At this stage the integration tests is aimed at determining if the interfaces among the modules are correctly stated and work properly.

In the next step the system functions are tested to verify whether or not they meet the functions given in the 'specification document'.

After this function test, the system is compared with the requirements and the needs to determine if it can cope with them. Finally, an operation test is performed to detect all operational problems.

Following this stage the system is ready to be released. It

is at this point, as far as quality control is concerned, that validation ends and maintenance begins.

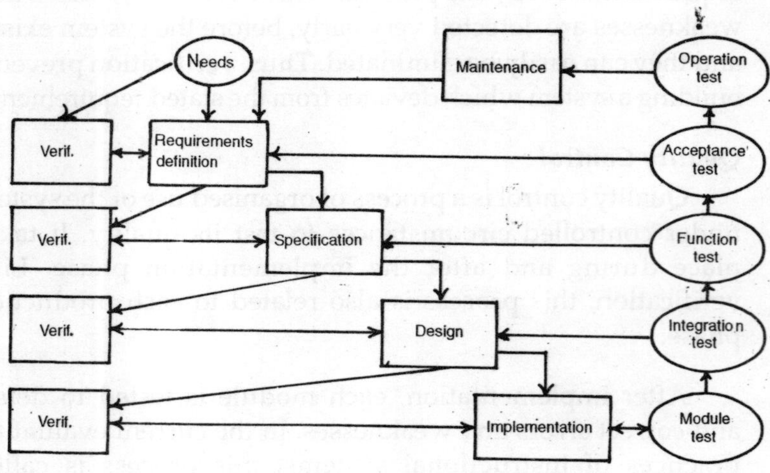

Figure 5.5. Relationship between Production, Validation and Maintenance

Maintenance

During the system operation, students learn the subject matter pertaining to the system by interacting with it. If during use, parts of the system are found to be wrong, inappropriate, or too restricted, or if the system does not cope with the needs any more because of the changing environment, the system must then be modified.

It must be emphasised again that change is intrinsic to the nature of an instructional system because the needs to which the system is related change with time.

Thus, it must be developed in such a way as to be as easy to modify as possible. In other words, the development process must embody the feature of the system's alterability. The development of a system according to a well-defined production process and the documentation of this activity make the system changeable. Each change is brought about following the production process from the beginning.

The model in Figure 5.4 shows the relationship between production, validation (verification and quality control), and maintenance.

As this model shows, all these phases are strictly linked to each other. Their union constitutes the life cycle of an instructional system.

Conclusions

In this paper we have described the nature of the problem which validation and maintenance must face. The main issue of the problem analysis is that validation and maintenance are intrinsic to the nature of the instruction systems and cannot be separated by the production process. We have discussed the relationships between verification, quality control, maintenance and the production process. Finally, we have summarised the model in a life cycle of an instructional system. In conclusion, we will make two brief remarks:

1. We have described only a general approach to validation and maintenance and not specific techniques. This reflects the fact that such techniques cannot be defined separately from the methodology, techniques, and tools related to each phase of the life cycle. Our present activity regards the definition of formal, comprehensive methodologies for carrying out each step of the stated life cycle and the associated validation processes.
2. The approach presented reflects the results of some research carried out in the software engineering field. Since a strong analogy exists between software and instructional systems regarding nature, problems and methodologies, it is possible and useful to transfer general approaches and, sometimes, specific

methodologies developed in software engineering to instructional systems. The approach to validation described in this paper is an instance of how this transfer can take place.

Finally, the ideas expressed in this paper may constitute a contribution to the definition of a possible common starting point for building general acceptable paradigms for developing and validating instructional systems.

6

THE INDUSTRIALISATION OF TEACHING

Introduction

Much of the early research work in distance education was accomplished by Otto Peters in the early 1960s. Peters worked at the German Institute for Distance Education (DIFF) at Tubingen in the Federal Republic of Germany, then at the Berlin Collage of Education before becoming in 1975 the foundation Vice-Chancellor (*Grundungsrektor*) of the Fernuniversitat in Hagen. In 1965 he published an authoritative analytical and comparative survey of distance institutions at further educational level throughout the world. This was followed in 1968 by a survey of distance teaching at higher education level.

Peters states that when his analytical and comparative analysis of distance teaching systems was complete, he proceeded to develop a theoretical structure for the field. He claims that the traditional categories of educational research proved inadequate for a didactical analysis of distance systems and he was forced to abandon them. Building up systems for teaching at a distance, he tells us, is structured so differently from conventional, oral education that the didactical analyst must look elsewhere for his models.

For Peters the most fruitful model was the similarities between the industrial production process and the teaching/

learning process in distance education. He analysed the industrial production process and found that not only did this provide a satisfactory basis for an analysis of distance teaching but that a fruitful explanatory and forecasting theory of teaching at a distance was possible when one considered it as the most industrialised form of teaching and learning.

Peters justified his search for a new theoretical basis for distance teaching on the grounds that it is a new form of industrialised and technological education. He states that from many points of view conventional, oral, group-based education is a pre-industrial form of education. In the universities of the Middle Ages, the ancient rhetorical form of education was replaced by the lecture, the seminar, and the lesson and these have remained permanent characteristics of traditional education ever since. The humanistic influence added the tutorial. These can all be regarded as pre-industrialised forms of education in which the individual lecturer remains in close contact with the whole teaching process just as an artisan does with his craft. Attempts to adapt the lecture, seminar, and tutorial to industrialised techniques by the use of educational technology will not prove successful because of the pre-industrial characteristics of the didactic structures in conventional universities.

Distance teaching, however, is recent. It could not have existed before the Industrial Era. It began, at most, 130 years ago, he says, writing in 1980. It was no historical accident that correspondence education and the industrialisation of society began about the same time because they are intrinsically linked. Distance education is impossible without a relatively fast and regular postal service and transport system: 'the first railway lines and the first correspondence schools were established around the same time.'

Traditional educational concepts are only of partial use in analysing and describing this industrialised form of education so new categories for analysis must be found and they can best be found from the sciences which analyse industrial processes.

All forms of human life have been heavily influenced by the industrial revolution. Only traditional forms of education in schools, colleges, and universities have remained outside it—except for the phenomenon of education at a distance.

Peters claims some basis for his comparative study from the fact that the production of learning materials for distance students is, in itself, an industrialised process and one that is, in its didactic procedures, quite different from book production.

Didactical Analysis

Peters' theoretical presentation of distance teaching commences with a didactical analysis. In this presentation distance teaching is analysed as a distinct field of educational endeavour and not as a teaching 'mode'. The analysis of the didactic structure of distance teaching (1967:3-17) follows exactly the structures proposed by Paul Heimann and Wolfgang Schultz, two German educational technologists who founded the Berlin School of Didactics—now also referred to as the Hamburg model, as Schultz became a professor at the University of Hamburg (Heidt 1978:48; Holmberg 1982:139).

Heimann and Schultz claim that all teaching-learning processes can be analysed in terms of six intrinsic structural elements: aims, content, methods, choice of medium, human pre-requisites, and socio-cultural pre-requisites. Peters analyses distance education, as Heimann and Schultz had analysed education in general, in terms of these six essential structures of the educational process and has little difficulty in demonstrating profound structural differences between distance education and conventional education for all six of the constituent characteristics (1967:4-16).

- *Aim:* The aim of distance teaching is determined by

structural considerations as in all forms of teaching. Specific structural differences in the cognitive, emotional, and practical domains are indicated for distance teaching.

- *Contents:* The teaching of knowledge, skills, and practical 'hand-on' learning are examined and the difficulties and/or possibility of teaching certain content at a distance is considered.
- *Methods:* The drastic reduction or complete suppression of interpersonal communication is treated and its substitution by written information carriers and motivators.
- *Choice of medium:* It is claimed that communication suffers an essential loss of substance in its transfer from human speech to the written word and the possible compensating role of other media is considered.
- *Human pre-requisites:* Employment conditions, age, diagnostic counselling for entry to courses are contrasted with the condition of conventional students.
- *Socio-cultural pre-requisites:* Ideological, political, academic status, and tradition aspects of distance education in different cultures (USA, USSR, South Africa, England, Sweden) are considered.

The conclusion for Peters is inescapable. Distance education and conventional education have been shown to be essentially diverse on each of the six constituent components of an educational process as defined by the most 'adequate theoretical basis for dealing with instructional media' (Heidt (1978:47) known to German educational theorists.

This analysis leads to a fundamental separation between direct and indirect teaching and the claim that educational theorists have focused on direct teaching, especially in its conventional, oral, group-based form to the virtual exclusion of that other component of the educational scene—indirect teaching—of which distance teaching is one of the elements.

He lists the other components of teaching which are not direct, but which are not, however, to be identified as distance education: education by letter; printed learning materials; audio-visual teaching; educational radio and television; programmed learning; computer-based instruction; independent study; private study; and learning from teaching materials.

Industrial Comparison

At this point in his treatment of the subject (1967, 1971, 1973, 1981) Peters presents a comparison of distance teaching and the industrial production of goods under the following headings: rationalisation; division of labour; mechanisation; assembly line; mass production; preparatory work; formalisation; standardisation, functional change; objectification; concentration; and centralisation.

- *Rationalisation* is seen as a characteristic of distance teaching when the knowledge and skills of a teacher are transmitted to a theoretically unlimited number of students by the detached objectivity of a distance education course of constant quality.
- *Division of labour* is the main pre-requisite for the advantages of distance teaching to become effective and is thus a constituent element of it. If the number of students enrolled in a distance course is high, regular assessment of performance is not carried out by those academics who developed the course and other elements of the teaching/learning process are assigned to others.
- *Mechanisation.* Conventional education proceeds at a pre-industrial level with the teacher using the tools of the trade (pictures, objects, books) without these changing the structure of teaching; in distance teaching mechanisation eventually changes the nature of the

teaching process.

- *Assembly line.* In distance teaching the staff remain at their posts but the teaching (manuscript for example) is passed from one area of responsibility to another and specific changes are made at each stage.
- *Mass production.* Traditional forms of teaching envisage small groups and can only be applied to mass education artificially (e.g. a loudspeaker from one lecture hall to an adjoining one). Distance teaching copes confidently with mass production which is essential to it.
- *Planning and preparation.* As in industry, distance teaching is characterised by extensive planning by senior specialist staff in special departments and prior financial investment. Success is linked to the preparatory phase in a way that is different from conventional teaching.
- *Standardisation.* A greater degree of standardisation is required than in conventional teaching and the educational advantages of the interesting deviation at a particular time with a particular group of students is not possible: the objective requirements of the total course profile dominate the particular interests of the teacher.
- *Functional change and objectification* are further essential elements of the most industrialised form of education, especially when the functional role of teacher is split at least three ways: provider of knowledge (distance unit author), evaluator of knowledge and progress (course maker or tutor), and counsellor (subject programme adviser).
- *Monopolisation.* Concentration and centralisation are characteristics of the management of distance systems and of industrial enterprise; distance teaching institutions have a tendency to monpolisation within a state or national educational provision.

Educational Technology

The completion of this comparative study of distance education and the industrial production of goods led Peters to an analysis of distance teaching in the light of the then current ideas (mid-1960s) about educational technology. He follows distance education through five groupings of educational technologists which he takes over from the German didactician Flechsig:

1. simulation models,
2. planning models (*Zweckrationalitat*),
3. materials development strategies,
4. systems approach,
5. curriculum development.

Peters studies the affinities between distance education and educational technology, especially programmed learning. He shares with Flechsig and the educational technologists of the period the belief that planning and technology will achieve educational success. It was felt that the application of technical categories to educational processes would achieve beneficial results and that systematic planning and rationalisation of educational means to reach defined goals (*Zweckrationalitat*) could achieve both educational and economic efficiency.

Conclusions

The final dimension of Peter's analysis of distance education is what he calls the historical, sociological and anthropological perspective. Humanistic attacks on the industrialisation of society and its contribution to mass culture lead Peters to expect criticism from humanists of his theory of distance education as the most industrialised form of education.

Tracing the historical evolution of educational structures back to early Indo-European origins, Peters finds them characterised by six elements:

- ❑ elitism
- ❑ sacral aspects
- ❑ hierarchical aspects
- ❑ family-small group structures
- ❑ personal communication
- ❑ time-place-person ties.

Distance education is the final phase of the evolution of education away from these sociological structures. It presents a new, strange, and foreign educational pattern that also has six characteristics, being

- ❑ egalitarian
- ❑ profane
- ❑ democratic
- ❑ aimed at a mass audience
- ❑ technological-based
- ❑ free from the dimensions of educational time, places and persons.

A sociological analysis based on the German philosophical *Gemeinschaft/Gesellschaft* positions taken from Weber, Tonnies, and Habermass shows that traditional, oral, group-based education follows the *'Gemeinschaft'* categorisation with distance education falling into the *'Gesellschaft'* grouping. In general terms *'Gemeinschaft'* structures are friendly and community-based; *Gesellschaft* implies a wider, society-based structure that may be unfriendly. The communication processes within these two sociological groupings show that the intersubjectivity and reciprocity of interpersonal communication in conventional education is radically to be contrasted with the 'context-free', mechanical communication of education at a distance. The possibility of alienation is not overlooked.

Peters sees as practical consequences of his theory that there is something unnatural about education at a distance. The process of communication is broken up and artificial substitutes for it are provided. The whole communication process is changed and this changes the teaching acts and the learning acts which take place in the education system.

Peters feels that it is a slow process for a teacher to adapt to a distance education system because there will always be clashes between traditional teaching and the carefully structured procedures of a distance teaching university, in which the unity of the teaching/learning process is split into many units performed by different persons and elements of the education system. The process of adaptation however can be furthered by reflection on the characteristics of distance education.

The student in an industrialised education system finds that instruction is available in such ways that he can choose his own way. Instruction is not linked to fixed times, to fixed places, to fixed persons. This throws new responsibilities on the learner that are not characteristic of pre-industrialised education systems.

Peters has no desire to criticise conventional education. His view, however, is that industrialised society of today has developed so many needs for education that it is absurd to imagine that conventional systems can satisfy them. New techniques are needed and these must be industrial.

He recognises that traditionalists will say: What happens to the highly valued traditions of face-to-face education? What happens to the spirit of the learning community? These are all, he admits, of value but you cannot have 40,000-50,000 students in a system like an open university and try to provide face-to-face tuition with finite means.

Almost alone among distance educators writing about distance education, Peters finds much to query in the industrialisation of education. He finds distance education unnatural; it breaks up the process of communication; artificial mechanical substitutes for interpersonal communication are provided; this changes the teaching behaviours and the learning behaviours; there is a definite propensity to alienation. If you are going to teach in the most industrialised form of education, he tells us, you have to be ready to live with the problems that the industrialisation of education brings.

Evaluation

Reactions and objections to Peters' thesis have been many and there are those who deplore the introduction of industrial concepts into an educational field. Four of these reactions are considered here: Christof Ehmann, Karl-Heinz Rebel, Manfred Hamann, and integrationist responses.

Christof Ehmann

Ehmann (1981:231) criticises Peters' position because of its dependence on faith in the value of planning in education and faith in technical progress. He claims that these faiths, strong in the 1960s, have been shown to be wrong in the 1980s and that 'the application of technical categories to social processes is just as questionable as the use of biological analogies'. Planning euphoria, programmed learning, faith in the calculability of processes—all central features of Peters' industrialised models—have all been dissipated before the 1980s started.

Ehmann's evaluation of Peter's contribution is negative. He feels that as an academic position it is largely dated because of its reliance on theories of planning and technical progress, that its influence on Peters' own institution—the Fernuniversitat—has been nil, as has been its influence on the world of commercial correspondence schools.

Karl-Heinz Rebel

Rebel complains (1983:200) that 'the basis of Otto Peters' assumption—the six interdependent elements that constitute each teaching-learning process (the so-called Berlin Didactic School of Paul Heimann and Wolfgang Schulz)—could never be expressed in such a way that research data capable of falsifying this theory could be collected'.

Manfred Hamann

Hamann (1978) argues that all forms of *Zweckrationalitat* whether they be called media didactics, learning psychology, systems theory, or information theory, have been without success: there have been occasional glimpses of didactic possibilities but no progress towards increased cost-efficiency in education. He accuses Peters of simply applying the structures of Heimann-Schultz to distance education and nothing more. This reproach is justifiable for only the didactical analysis part of Peters' presentation. The theory of industrialisation is certainly original and owes nothing to Heimann-Schultz either in its presentation or in its origin.

Integrationist Criticisms

There are critics of Peters' position who claim that he exaggerates the difference between conventional education and distance education. Many professors at the Fernuniversitat would argue that learning at university level consists of extensive readings plus occasional meetings with one's professor and distance education is composed of extensive reading plus occasional meetings with a tutor.

The long tradition of German university teaching is based on learning from textual materials so that Peters' position tends to over-emphasise the difference in the communication process in distance education. Australian systems, in which numbers of students are taught on-campus and off-campus by the same lecturer, reflect a similar position. In the external studies division of the University of queensland, for instance, each lecturer has responsibility for a defined group of students. For these students the lecturer devises the course, develops the learning materials, sees them through the production process, checks the proofs, marks the assignments for the students when enrolled, provides correspondence and telephone tuition as required, may visit the students either at study centres or in their homes, and conducts the examinations.

Where, representatives of this system ask, is the division of labour, the industrialisation, the mass production in this system? Where is the great role differentiation between the lecturer in a conventional and a distance system?

Peters has not replied to these critics. His most recent contribution to distance education theory (1981:47-63) merely restates his position. It implies that if he were to restate his theory today for the mid-1980s he would change only the references to economic theory and industrial analysis but would maintain the didactical structure of his position. He claims that by substituting more modern economic and industrial references he could produce a theory of the industrialisation of education even more convincing than what he has achieved so far.

It is disappointing to find that the 1981 presentation repeats word-for-word the formulation of the theoretical position as it was in 1967. The positions of scholars like Ehmann, Rebel, and Hamann have not been answered.

Peter's strength is his knowledge of distance systems as they were throughout the world in the period 1960-65 and the fact that his theoretical positions are clearly grounded in the data he accumulated at that time. The theory also has a certain heuristic value, in that it offers some explanation of the nature of educational institutions in which the warehouse and the production process dominate and in which there are few educational installations and that such systems have a propensity to alienation and monpolisation.

Peters' long period as foundation Vice-Chancellor of the Fernuniversitat has come to an end since the publication of the first edition of this book. His present research is on the relationship of study to work in contemporary society (Peters 1984).

7

INTERACTION AND COMMUNICATION

Introduction

This chapter presents writers who have emphasised interaction and communication as central to any concept of distance education. In very general terms Moore, Wedemeyer, and Delling tended to concentrate on the autonomy and independence of the student as the basis for their views, while Peters' focus is the functions of the institution developing learning materials. The authors in this chapter take as their starting point the role of the institution in providing a satisfactory learning experience for students, once the materials have been developed and dispatched.

Five authors have been selected, Baath, Holmberg, Daniel, Sewart, and K.C. Smith. Baath is particularly associated with an emphasis on two-way communication and Holmberg with a theory of guided didactic conversation. Daniel, Sewart, and Smith are, or have been, managers of distance systems. Their writings are developed from the day-to-day pressure of managing distance systems. Their inclusion is justified by the wide-ranging and influential character of their contributions.

Two-Way Communication

John A. Baath (pronounced 'boat') is Swedish and worked for many years for Hermods at Malmo. His work benefits from a knowledge of the literature of distance education in the Scandinavian languages, English, German, and French. During the 1970s he was associated with the concept of two-way communication in correspondence education. He would not claim to be the originator of the concept but he made an important theoretical and empirical contribution to establishing this idea as a major defining feature of distance systems today.

TABLE 7.1

Baath's Analysis of Teaching Models

Model	Two-way communication
B.K. Skinner's behaviour control model	Checking students' achievements; individualising functions; assess students' starting level; consider specialabilities; previous reinforcement patterns
E.Z. Rothkopf's model for written instruction	Helping students get started
D.P. Ausubel's advance organisers model	Determine each students' previous knowledge and cognitive structure; promote positive transfer to subsequent parts of course
K. Egan's model for structural communication	Individually devised discussion comments and 'reverse' assignments
J. Bruner's discovery learning model	Provide individually adapted help; stimulate students' discovery of knowledge
C. Rogers' model for facilitation of learning	Check 'open' assignments for submission; dialogue with each individual student
R.M. Gagne's general teaching model	Activating motivation; stimulating recall; providing learner guidance; providing feedback.

Source: Adapted from Baath (1979).

One part of his research aimed to relate modern education research to distance education. He examined the applicability of the teaching models of Skinner, Rothkopf, Ausubel, Egan, Bruner, Rogers, and Gagne to correspondence education (which he regards as a subset of distance education) (1980:12). He was able to show the functions of two-way communication in correspondence education in the light of each of the teaching models (see Table 7.1).

His conclusions are that:

- models with stricter control of learning towards fixed goals tend to imply, in distance education, a greater emphasis on the teaching material than on the two-way communication between student and tutor/ institution; and
- models with less control of learning towards fixed goals tend to make simultaneous communication between student and tutor/institution more desirable; this communication taking the form of either face-to-face or telephone contacts (1979:21).

Holmberg (1981:27) summarises Baath's presentation of the relevance to distance education of the authorities cited in Table 7.1:

- All the models investigated are applicable to distance study.
- Some of them (Skinner, Gagne, Rothkopf, Ausubel, structural communication) seem particularly adaptable to distance study in its fairly strictly structured form.
- Bruner's more open model and even Rogers' model can be applied to distance study, though not without special measures, e.g. concerning simultaneous non-contiguous communication (telephone etc.).
- Demands on distance study systems which would inspire new developments can be inferred from the models studied.

In a second volume, *Postal Two-way Communication in Correspondence Education*, Baath (1980) adds empirical analysis of two-way communication to the theoretical analysis of his previous book. In particular he studied:

- the relationship of submission density (frequency of assignment submission during a course) to two-way communication;
- the replacement of tutor-marked assignments by self assessment questions; and
- the introduction of computer-marked assignments as a form of two-way communication.

Baath's theoretical and conceptual contributions stem from his experience in Sweden. He tells us how his own situation led to his involvement:

> When writing correspondence course materials I was struck by the idea that it was possible to provide some kind of two-way communication within the material, by means of exercises, questions or self-check tests with detailed model or specimen answers. Could such two-way communication, to any considerable extent, replace the postal two-way communication induced by assignments for submission?
>
> (Baath 1980:11-12)

This combination of personal experience and theoretical and empirical investigation led Baath to place two-way communication as central to the distance education process and the distance tutor as central to his concept.

Baath writes well of the importance of the tutor in a distance system. He indicates that there is evidence to show that distance learners need special help with the start of their studies and that they need help in particular to promote their study motivation (1982:22). He sees the role of the tutor going well beyond that of correcting errors and assessing students' progress:

> This is the role of the distant tutor: he can have important pedagogical functions, not only that of correcting errors and assessing students' papers. He may play a principal part in the linking of learning materials to learning—by trying to relate the learning material to each student's previous reinforcement patterns (Skinner), or to his mathemagenic activities (Rothkopf), or to his previous knowledge and cognitive structure (Ausubel), or to his previous comprehension of the basic concepts and principles of the curriculum (Bruner), or by concentrating on the task of establishing a good personal relationship with the learner (Rogers)—as I have tried to demonstrate.
>
> (Baath 1980:121)

Baath quotes with approval the 100-year-old statement on tutors in correspondence studies:

> The correspondence teacher must be painstaking, patient, sympathetic, and *alive;* whatever a dead teacher may accomplish in the classroom, he can do nothing by correspondence.
>
> (William Rainey Harper 1880)

A query about Baath's work is that he does not seem to attempt a full theoretical framework for two-way communication in correspondence education. He has greatly furthered our understanding of two-way communication but has not explained how it would fit in an overview of this field.

Guided Didactic Conversation

Borje Holmberg (pronounced Burr-ye Holm-bery) is also from Sweden and today is Professor of the Methodology of Distance Education at the Fernuniversitat in Hagen in the

Federal Republic of Germany. He has written profusely on distance education in Swedish, German, and English.

A number of characteristic traits link together the publications of Holmberg across nearly 30 years. Among these are a generous, humanistic philosophy that values highly student independence and autonomy, an early concentration on two-way communication in distance education, an emerging concept of distance education as guided didactic conversation, a critical approach to non-print media and the provision of face-to-face sessions as components of a system and a concentration on assignment marking and its importance.

Like the dedicated humanist he is, Holmberg bases his view of distance education on his conviction that the only important thing in education is learning by individual students. Administration, counselling, teaching, group work, enrolment, and evaluation are of importance only in so far as they support individual learning. He would like to see systems with completely free pacing, a free choice of examination periods, and plenty of two-way communication for tutorial and feedback purposes.

Distance education is considered to be particularly suitable for individual learning because it is usually based on personal work by individual students more or less independent from the direct guidance of tutors. the distance student is in a situation where the chances of individually selecting what educational offerings he/she is to partake of can be much greater than that of conventional students. The student studying at a distance can, and frequently does, ignore elements of the teaching package that has been prepared for the course being studied. TV programmes or comments on assignments or face-to-face sessions or visits to study centres may all be ignored.

Holmberg characterises study in a distance system as self-study but it is not, he insists, private reading, for the student is not alone. The student benefits from having a course developed for him and also from interaction with his tutors and other representatives of a supporting organisation. The relationship between the supporting organisation and the student is described as a guided didactic conversation. The general approach agrees closely with Wedemeyer's. Holmberg insists on allowing students a maximum freedom of choice in matters of both content and study procedures, individual pacing of the study, and far-reaching autonomy generally.

Two-way communication in writing and on the telephone between students and tutors has been one of his chief concerns. Students' assignments are regarded as facilitators of this communication rather than as instruments of assessment.

Distance education is seen as a guided didactic conversation that aims at learning and it is felt that the presence of the typical traits of successful conversation will facilitate learning. The continuous interaction between the student on the one hand and the tutors and counsellors and other representatives of the institution administering the study programme is seen as a kind of conversation.

There is a kind of two-way conversational traffic through the written and telephone interaction between student and institution. More dubiously Holmberg also argues for what he calls simulated conversation from the students' study of the learning materials that have been prepared in a didactic style.

Holmberg's view of distance education as guided didactic conversation might be presented schematically as in Fig. 7.1. There are traces of these ideas in Holmberg's early writings but in recent years he has developed them into the basis for a general theory of distance education.

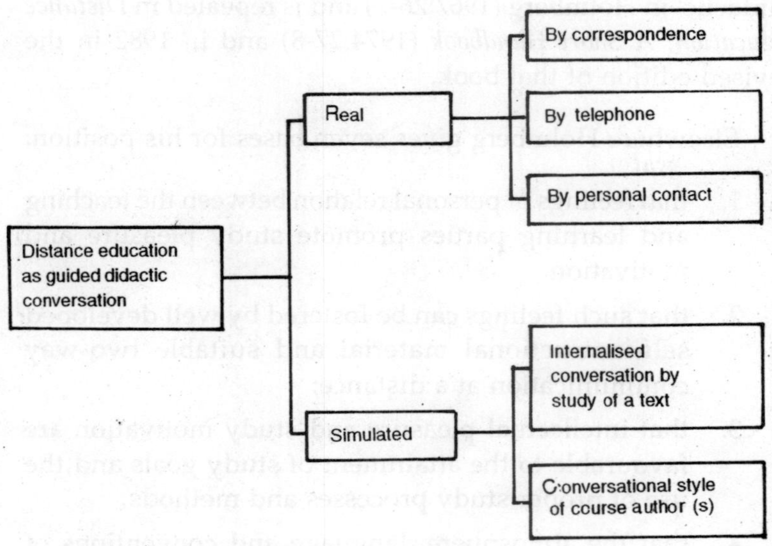

Figure 7.1. Guided Didactic Conversation (Holmberg)

In *On the Methods of Teaching by Correspondence* in 1960 he wrote:

> A considerable portion of all oral tuition can rightly be described as didactive conversation. In a great number of successful correspondence courses the atmosphere and style of such conversation is found. It is typical of the style of didactive conversation that advice is given on how to tackle problems, what to learn more or less carefully, how to connect items of knowledge discussed in different lessons and this also characterises many good correspondence courses. It seems to me that advice and suggestions should preferably be expressed in phrases of personal address, such as "When you have read these paragraphs, make sure that....".
>
> (Holmberg 1960:15-16)

The same paragraph appears with 'didactive' changed to 'didactic' in Holmberg (1967:26-7) and is repeated in *Distance Education: A Short Handbook* (1974:27-8) and in 1982 in the revised edition of that book.

Elsewhere Holmberg gives seven bases for his position:

1. that feelings of personal relation between the teaching and learning parties promote study pleasure and motivation.
2. that such feelings can be fostered by well developed self-instructional material and suitable two-way communication at a distance;
3. that intellectual pleasure and study motivation are favourable to the attainment of study goals and the use of proper study processes and methods;
4. that the atmosphere, language and conventions of friendly conversation favour feelings of personal relation according to postulate 1;
5. that messages given and received in conversational forms are comparatively easily understood and remembered;
6. that the conversation concept can be successfully translated for use by the media available to distance education;
7. that planning and guiding the work, whether provided by the teaching organisation or the student, are necessary for organised study, which is characterised by explicit or implicit goal concepts.

(Holmberg 1978:20, repeated 1983:115-16)

Distance learning materials developed in the light of Holmberg's theory of guided didactic conversation would present the following characteristics (1983:117):

- ❑ Easily accessible presentations of study matter: clear,

somewhat colloquial language, in writing that is easily readable; moderate density of information.

- Explicit advice and suggestions to the student as to what to do and what to avoid, what to pay particular attention to and consider, with reasons provided.
- Invitations to an exchange of views, to questions, to judgements of what is to be accepted and what is to be rejected.
- Attempts to involve the student emotionally so that he or she takes a personal interest in the subject and its problems.
- Personal style including the use of the personal and possessive pronouns.
- Demarcation of changes of themes through explicit statements, typographical means or, in recorded, spoken communications, through a change of speakers, e.g. male followed by female, or through pauses. (This is a characteristic of the guidance rather than of the conversation.)

If a course is prepared following these principles Holmberg (1977) forecasts that it will be attractive to students, will motivate students to study, and will facilitate learning. In two interesting experiments Holmberg re-wrote a Fernuniversitat post-graduate course on educational planning and basic Hermods course on English grammar in accordance with his theoretical position and replaced the rather analytical text-book-like approaches of the originals with a more conversational style designed to promote empathy with the student (Holmberg *et al.*, 1982).

By any estimation, Holmberg's contribution to the field of distance education is extensive (1979, 1980). His early pre-occupation with two-way communication in correspondence education provided an impetus for the research of Baath, Flinck and Wangdahl in the 1970s.

Although he is not the only scholar to recommend a conversational style for distance learning materials he has been the only one who has developed a coherent theory from his early statement that 'a correspondence course must by definition be something different from a textbook with questions. A correspondence course provides actual teaching by itself and is thus a substitute for both a textbook and the exposition of a teacher' (1960:8) and then submitted it to empirical testing. In general this position has been beneficial to practitioners in the field and has contributed to making distance learning materials now a recognizably different genre from textbooks.

Interaction and Independence

From 1973 to 1977 John Daniel was director of studies at the Tele-universite, Universite du Quebec, and then Vice-President, Learning Services at Athabasca University in Edmonton, Alberta, Canada. In 1980 he took up the post of Vice-Rector (Academic) of Concordia University, a conventional university in Montreal and moved to Laurentian University, a conventional university with a small distance department in the summer of 1984.

Daniel has thus had experience of academic management in both French and English distance systems and his thinking about distance education is frequently from a management perspective.

He sees the emergence of distance education systems as coming from three sources: a long tradition of independent study; modern developments in the technology of education; and new theoretical interest in open learning. The fusion of these elements has produced new educational enterprises which teach at a distance and fulfil important economic and political needs of societies.

When Holmberg and Baath write extensively of two-way communication in education at a distance they envisage constantly a situation in which the major part of the communication will be by postal correspondence.

Daniel (writing from the start from a university perspective) sees distance systems as comprising activities in which the student works alone and activities which bring him into contact with other people. The first grouping of activities he labels 'independent activities' and the latter 'interactive'. He provides a listing of possible activities in the two groups as in Table 7.2. A major function of distance systems is to achieve the difficult synthesis between interaction and independence—getting the mixture right. All learning in a distance system is achieved by a balance between the learning activities the student carries out independently and those which involve interaction with other people. The balance between the two is the crucial issue facing distance study systems.

TABLE 7.2

Interaction and independence (Daniel)

Independent	Interactive
Reading a text	Discussion on telephone
Watching television at home	Marking and commenting on assignment
Conducting a home experiment	Group discussions
Writing an assignment	Residential summer schools

The balance chosen between the interactive and independent activities in a distance system has extensive repercussions on the administration and economics of the system. Independent activities, he tells us, have great possibilities of economies of scale since the marginal costs of printing extra copies of texts or broadcasting to more students are low. However, the cost of interactive activities tends to increase in direct proportion to the number of students (Daniel and Marquis 1979:32).

Increasing the proportion of interactive activities improves student performance but it does so at a price. The cost of interactive activities is broadly proportional to the number of students involved. There is little opportunity for the economies of scale which characterise independent activities, and which are responsible for the overall cost advantage of distance education.

Daniel states that distance systems should be dearer: things done at a distance usually are. He then parts company from much of the writing on the economics of distance education by stating that there are two economic structures for distance systems: one for the independent activities in which economies of scale are possible; and one for the interactive activities in which they may not be (Snowden and Daniel 1980).

He believes that courses should not be designed that are entirely independent. Socialisation and feedback are the main functions of the interactive activities and whereas the importance of socialisation in education is less vital for adults studying part-time than for children and those involved in compulsory and full-time education, the feedback role of interaction is of crucial importance. Students want to know how they are doing in relation both to their peers and to the criteria of mastery set by the course authors. Distance students are only weakly integrated into the social system of the teaching institution and feel low involvement with it. Therefore they are at risk and the importance of interactive activities is enhanced.

The thrust of Daniel's thinking on distance education comes through clearly in his attitude to pacing (Daniel and Shale 1979). He suggests that the more freedom a learner has the less likely he is to complete the course. He is of the opinion that distance systems can either give students the dignity of succeeding by pacing them or the freedom to proceed towards failure without pacing. Holmberg, on the other hand, claims that students should be free to pursue distance courses without the pressure of pacing.

Where Moore and Wedemeyer emphasise autonomy and independence of the learner studying at a distance, Daniel looks for a balance between interaction and independence in the structuring of the system and shows how this affects the pacing of students and the cost structures.

Continuity of Concern

David Sewart joined the Open University of the UK in 1973. After a period in the Manchester regional office he moved to the university's central site at Walton Hall near Milton Keynes where he had managerial responsibilities for the provision of support services to students. In 1980 he returned to Manchester as regional director and then returned again to Milton Keynes.

Sewart sometimes tries to trace distance education back as far as the epistles of St. Paul but sees a rapid development in the last two decades. This he attributes to the new communications techniques which have been perfected in the twentieth century, the increasing costs of conventional education, and the rapidly expanding range of knowledge.

His theoretical approach to teaching at a distance can be summed up as a continuity of concern for students learning at a distance (1978). Teaching, he tells us, is a complex matter. It is an amalgam of the provision of knowledge and information plus all the advisory and supportive processes with which this provision is normally surrounded in conventional education.

He is unhappy with the notion that the package of materials in a distance system can perform all the functions of the teacher in face-to-face education. He shows that, if it could, it would become an infinitely expensive package as it would have to reflect the complex interactive process of the teacher and each individual student.

In many of his writings he discusses the efforts of course developers in distance systems to produce the 'hypothetically perfect teaching package'. He finds this unrealisable and seeks to prove this with his view of the role of the intermediary in complex civilisations. He argues that just as in most complex bureaucracies an intermediary is necessary (a social worker, a hospital orderly) to bridge the gap between the individual and the institution, so in distance systems an intermediary is necessary between the individual student and the teaching package (Fig 7.2). The intermediary is employed by the institution but works for the individuals in the system and individualises their problems when confronted with the bureaucracy.

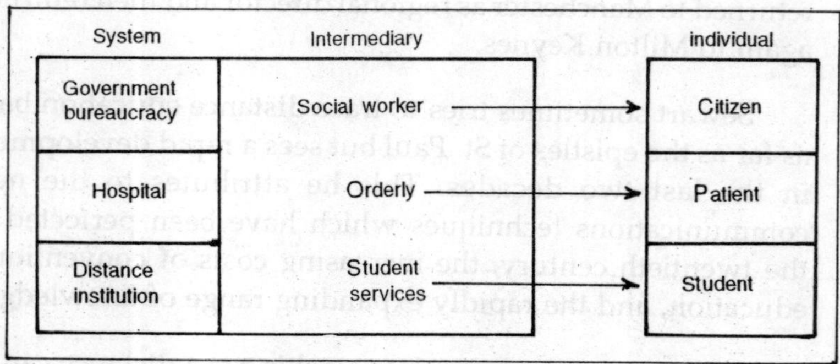

Figure 7.2. Role of the Intermediary (Sewart)

Sewart's clear emphasis on the needs of students learning at a distance, demands an interactive mode in distance systems which can hardly be supplied by the learning materials, however well they are developed. Failure to recognise this has, he considers, led to the almost universal lack of esteem for distance systems which he judges to have been the norm until quite recently. He considers that advice and support for students in a system of learning at a distance poses almost infinitely variable problems and this creates the need for an advisory and supportive role of a distance institution in addition to the provision of a teaching package.

Sewart writes of the differences between conventional and distance education and presents both the advantages and disadvantages of education at a distance. As advantages he lists:

- ❏ freedom from the 'strait-jacket of the lecture hall;'
- ❏ ability to study whenever and wherever desired;
- ❏ freedom inherent in the individuality of the distance students' situation;
- ❏ student not bound by the learning pattern of a learning group; and
- ❏ distance students' needs are not subservient to the needs of a learning group.

The debits are also well presented in Sewart's writings (1981):

- ❏ no measure of progress available;
- ❏ no framework of study for the distance student;
- ❏ no peer group clarification or pressure; and
- ❏ no benchmarks on progress or failure.

He considers the situation of the student learning at a distance to be quite different from that of conventional students because of the absence of swift feedback and because the learner's peer group does not act as a benchmark.

> Whereas the infant school class and the university lecture have easily discernible differences, they are generically similar in offering a group learning situation with a face-to-face teacher/student contact, and the subsequent possibility for instant feedback of an oral and visual nature. The group learning situation is itself supportive of the learning process,

> not only because of the potential interaction between students in relation to the academic content of the course—learning through discussion with one's peers—but also because the group learning offers a benchmark to the individual members of the group.
>
> (Sewart 1980:177)

Sewart concludes that the process of learning at a distance is generically different from the conventional mode. The swift feedback available from the face-to-face learning model is almost entirely absent (1980:177).

The differing study patterns of distance students, the need for intermediaries in complex processes, the absence of the learning group against which the distance learner can measure himself, and the infinite variety of individual problems all lead him to the conclusion that the introduction of the human element is the only way to adapt a distance system to individual needs. This provision should ideally be available whenever and as often as the student needs it and is part of the richness and variety of a system that can adapt to the needs of individualised, independent study. Unlike Peters, however, he clearly sees all education provision as a continuum with forms of distance education fusing into conventional provision.

Sewart's views provide an effective counterbalance to those who see distance education merely as a materials production process. He claims that it is the continuity of the institution's concern for the quality of support in a distance system that has been the Open University of the UK's success in soling the age-old problem of distance systems—the avoidance of avoidable drop-out.

Sewart represents his views in an article published in 1987. There is a continuum, he tells us, between a face-to-face dialogue between one teacher and one student and a 'pure' method of teaching at a distance. There is another continuum between teaching with the complete integration of preparation and presentation by one individual at one end, and the total separation of these functions at the other (1987:163). The problem is to locate on this continuum the position of the particular distance system that one is analysing or designing.

An Integrated Mode

When the University of New England, Armidale, New South Wales, Australia began teaching externally in 1955 it adopted a system of integrating external and internal teaching by the full-time faculty of the university. External enrolments were limited on the basis of a staff-student ratio similar to that already existing in the traditional lecture situation so that staff bore responsibility for teaching both student groups as part of their normal duties.

This system (which came to be known as the 'Australian integrated mode') has had two able proponents. Howard C. Sheath (1956-72) and Kevin C. Smith (1973-84). It would be too much to say that the writings of Sheath (1965, 1973) and Smith (1979) contain a theory of distance education; rather they present a series of heartfelt beliefs on how external studies should be administered.

Smith feels that institutions planning external studies must come to terms with an educational dilemma. The dilemma lies in the fact that external studies depend essentially on an independent learning situation and must be designed so that motivated mature-age students can plot their own path through a particular course with a minimum of outside assistance. On the other hand, systems which rely solely upon the stamina, perseverance, and intellectual capabilities of students to survive the rigors of external studies without assistance do not fulfil their academic responsibilities. The compromise is to provide a core of independent learning material but to add compulsory provision for staff/student contacts and regular student group activity.

In contrast to Peters' theory of industrialisation, Smith advocates dividing the work of the university faculty equally between on-campus and off-campus students. For the distance education students the lecturer performs all those functions, and more, that are performed for normal students: the design and presentation of courses, the marking of assignments, the conduct of residential and weekend schools, final assessment and examination of students. The external students enrol in the same courses, follow the same syllabus, are tutored by the same lecturers, sit for the same examinations, and are awarded the same degrees as the conventional ones.

Smith bases this structure on the following ideas (1979:31, 57):

- external teaching should not be done by part-time tutors but by the full-time university faculty;
- by being part of a normal university a distance system remains in the educational mainstream;
- a university has only a small pool of outstanding staff; external students should be in contact with them, not with what he calls 'part-time recruits';
- a university is a community of scholars and all distance students must become part of this community by attending compulsory residential schools;
- concentration on the 'learning package' can lead to a dehumanising of the learning process, as this is a social experience;
- distance education must not depend solely on correspondence methods. Some degree of interaction not only with materials but also with other students and the teachers is essential.

Smith also lists eight belief's about how a distance education system should be justified (1979:54):

1. *Legitimacy:* continuing education and external studies are legitimate functions of universities.
2. *Mainstream activity:* distance teaching should be undertaken by full-time academic staff as part of their normal teaching responsibilities so that it will receive the scholarship, resource allocation, and status it deserves.
3. *Commitment:* commitment is likely if the whole process remains the responsibility of the academic staff and is not divided; personal contact between academic staff and students is required; quotas are imposed to reduce external numbers to the same ratio as on-campus allocations.
4. *Parity:* parity of esteem for degrees can best be achieved if the same staff of the university teach and assess both categories of students.
5. *Interaction:* group discussions between staff and students and between students themselves are beneficial.
6. *Variety:* variety of teaching methods is recommended because of the diversity of students.
7. *Independence/pacing:* pacing of students is a characteristic of successful systems.
8. *Communication:* a distance system requires an adequate administration.

A critique of Smith's position is that he frequently puts forward the particular solutions of his own institution as normative for other institutions. The Australian integrated mode as it evolved at New England is certainly of interest as a model for a small system of less than 5,000 students, but even in other Australian universities which teach both at a distance and on-campus it has by no means been followed in all its details. Far from being in the mainstream of university studies as Smith (1979: 33) claims, the distance departments of many integrated systems appear to be well on the periphery with little influence on university budgets or planning (Rothe 1987)

There is the constant problem that when a lecturer's time is divided between the demands of conventional and distance education, both functions are done less than perfectly (Shott 1983).

If an institution is offering full degrees or diplomas in a non-traditional way it does not seem appropriate that such provision should be located amongst the continuing education and extra-mural departments which do not normally offer full university degrees (Townsend-Coles (1982:29-37), yet this is where one normally finds integrated distance departments.

Nevertheless, Smith's contribution is a refreshing one. It is of value to find a thoughtful basis for rejecting concepts of mass production, cost effectiveness, and industrialisation in distance education, especially when one finds emphasis placed on bringing the distance student into continuous contact with the best brains of the university and, secondly, the admission that the education of a distance student should be just as costly as a conventional one.

8

EVALUATION OF DISTANCE LEARNING SCHEMES AND MATERIALS

8.1 Designing Evaluation of Flexistudy

Flexistudy Schemes

These are operating in some 70 colleges and adult education institutes; they offer learning materials for home-based study together with counselling, tutorial support and access to facilities provided by colleges. Originating in the linked courses for correspondence students studying with the National Extension College (NEC), schemes are adapting to offer and to support other self-teaching schemes such as the NALGO in-service education programmes. By no means all Flexistudy students are preparing for public examinations even where following a GCE course; a number of the courses offered by NEC are for general interest, return to study, or for preparation for study with the Open University. Thus Flexistudy gives students a chance to discover whether they can cope with self-teaching.

Duration of study is negotiated with tutors, and students comprise largely those who could not (or would not) be drawn to day or evening classes currently offered by the institutions. Personal circumstances may mean that students spend periods 'sleeping' before resuming active study with tutorials and assignments!

Flexistudy can thus be seen to offer some qualities of 'openness' as a learning system giving discretion about course, subjects and study topics, offering choice of learning methods, command over pace and location of study, freedom to take or reject public assessment, and opportunity for students to avail themselves of counselling and guidance (Spencer, 1980). This face-to-face support is a special quality of Flexistudy.

There are inevitably variations between institutions in the quantity and extent of subject enrolments and of experience in administration of such schemes. In a study of 10 centres in 1980, we found most tutors looking after six to 20 enrolled students in their subject, most centres permitting continuous enrolment throughout the session and providing tutorials by telephone where appropriate. A few centres were able to offer practical workspace for science students. Where courses were offered by adult education centres--or adult studies departments—part-time teachers staffed the scheme; at City of Bath Technical College, the scheme was organised through the Learning by Appointment's Centre which already maintained a booking service for users of the Centre.

Evaluation

Evaluation studies could be made of any area of work in further education to appraise success in fulfilling declared intentions or effectiveness in using allocated resources; evidence from such studies would help in formulating college development plans. There would seem to be little justification for expecting greater accountability from innovative course teams than from those whose courses evolved earlier in the history of a college. Innovators themselves may, however, feel obliged to show how effectively they deploy scarce resources—and how worthwhile are the opportunities they create by the marginal shift of staff, space and facilities they occasioned.

Audiences for Evaluation

Evaluation techniques selected for the study of Flexistudy

will depend on the anticipated audiences described below, and the use likely to be made of the findings.

1. The providers of the correspondence course materials are a prime audience with an acknowledged role in improving learning materials and disseminating information through conferences and publications. Some of the knowledge and awareness might find its way back to students through the quarterly magazine from the National Extension College (*Home Study*), provided this were made available to individual Flexistudy students. A study by a local counsellor for NEC revealed problems facing many home-based students and devised some solutions (Lewis, 1980). A review of student reactions to self-teaching schemes served to point out widely reported problems of study skills that could be tackled in part by further attention in evaluation studies to the design of instructional text (Noble, 1980).

2. The course team might provide a second audience with a parallel interest in the quality of the learning materials as used by home-based students. They tend to develop instructional aids to augment, and, where necessary, compensate for, the published course materials. They are likely to have some interest in aids developed in other institutions offering the same courses, but they are hampered by the small proportion of their personal teaching likely to be allocated to any one Flexistudy course. Tutors are likely to be new to many of the processes of 1:1 and small group tutoring — and to allowing for the vulnerability of home-based students when sent marked assignments. Experience borrowed from the Open University such as MacKenzie (1976) many carry less conviction than the results of a sympathetic study of how recent students have been experiencing the courses. The course team have a third area of interest in how

similar courses are administered in other institutions, a need largely met to date through day conferences organized by the NEC, Garnett College and the development work done by the NEC/CET Development Officer (Sacks, 1980). The dissemination of findings has been assisted by the Council for Educational Technology (Spencer, 1980) but we may need to discover the most effective way of disseminating ideas to course tutors.

3. A third audience comprises the senior management of colleges to assist in their overall review of resource allocation. To this end, their interest would be financial and administrative with some account of the special opportunities provided. They can derive comparative data from the studies by Spencer (1980). It will be likely that at least one member of senior management in a college is actively sponsoring the innovation and this may determine the emphasis of any report considered; the college administrative officer and librarian would need to be included in any review. As flexible learning systems develop in conjunction with TEC, BEC, NALGO and other professional bodies, the public relations role of Flexistudy will attract the attention of senior management; local press and radio have provided publicity and might be interested in the human dimension of second chance course provision.

4. A further audience for these schemes is the potential adopter in other institutions. Their interest will be in updated overviews (Sacks, 1980; Spencer 1980) and in the special local circumstances that may vitally account for a Flexistudy scheme having taken root and survived in a college. An evaluation study that aims to provide evidence through case studies has to contend with the implications of not being able to preserve anonymity for colleges and course tutors. There are political implications in such portrayals

(MacDonald and Walker, 1977). A major difficulty in publishing any such account is the rate of change within pioneer institutions; any account needs frequent updating. (The 1978 Flexistudy Manual appeared in a second edition from the NEC in 1980). A few accounts of major reconsiderations in course design and in learning materials can be found in the literature but it is unlikely that much evaluative data will derive from institutions where courses are discontinued.

What would Constitute Evidence in Flexistudy Appraisal?

Direct comparisons with courses offered by conventional modes of study might not be valid; such full-and part-time courses are normally time-constrained with entry to a prescribed public examination. Flexistudy seeks to extend further education to those who find existing provision in some way inappropriate or inaccessible; in many schemes, a major flexibility is seen as the right to roll onto the course at whatever point in the year suits the student, together with the right to decide what, if any, public examination to attempt. It would be difficult to cite 'wastage' or 'discontinuance' figures, as students buy the course book and opt *into* any correspondence assignments and face-to-face tutorials. Some comparison of staffing costs per unit of coursework completed might be made with an evening class group using the same learning materials, but Flexistudy yields no neat cohorts of student admissions for such comparisons. Australian experience with wholly distant learners suggests that, for those who survive, results are quite comparable with full- and part-time campus-based learners (Goodman, 1973). Further international comparisons might be made with Denmark, where 'supervised correspondence study' or 'combined education' has been offered by official schemes of study in navigation, the management of small business, and marketing subjects in the post-secondary sector (Nedburgh, 1973). Between 1951 and 1972, Swedish government commissions have satisfied themselves on the effectiveness of linked courses in preparing students for university entrance (Holmberg, 1973). It would not be unreasonable to assume that Flexistudy would be at least as effective as more conventional course provision; evaluation could then be seen as just a normal part of course review leading to course developments.

Self-appraisal by course participants might be the best evidence for showing what staff and students value about Flexistudy schemes—and the locus and timing of any problem encountered. Ways of supporting students in the early phases of their home study would probably emerge as greatly valued and significant in preventing discontinuance—to judge from several reports (Goodman, 1973; Lewis, 1980). There have been sufficient day conferences of teachers with experience of Flexistudy to generate a provisional check-list of issues connected with tutoring and counselling. Experience derived from work with full-time students may not raise appropriate issues. If studies by course teams are made available to outside audiences, then some measure of situational analysis would need to accompany the accounts and profiles—something of the antecedents of the students, the subject commitment and concurrent experience of the staff, the pattern of course demands, facilities available, and something of the qualitative blend of these in the college in question.

Independent evaluation might be unduly intrusive in some very small-scale schemes but there are precedents for bringing responsive and sympathetic perceptions to bear on linked courses and self-teaching schemes (Stringer, 1979; Lopez and Elton, 1980; Lewis, 1980). There is evidence that independent evaluation of learning materials can be made an integral part of following a self-teaching course (Nathenson and Henderson, 1980).

Evidence about Flexistudy could be both quantitative and qualitative though comparative data would have to be interpreted in the light of many qualifications. Evidence intended for formative evaluation, to contribute to course development, would use case study methods, contextual accounts, and responsive or illuminative procedures (MacDonald and Walker, 1977). Even for accounts of administrative procedures, context helps to interpret preferred organisational styles (Spencer, 1980).

Collecting evidence for Flexistudy evaluation would draw on an established battery of techniques. Questionnaires and attitude inventories would establish participants' experience of the course and the intensity and saliency for them of issues presented. Interviews would permit a more responsive, exploratory and open account to be built up—telephone interviews were used by Stringer (1979) and would not be inappropriate in Flexistudy where telephone tutorials are offered by tutors in a number of colleges. Repertory grid techniques have been used in eliciting attitudes to reading (Thomas and Harri-Augstein, 1980), and could well be adapted to the detailed study of course components. These techniques would be equally appropriate for use with members of teaching staff, librarians, college administrators, editors and course-writers, and students. Feedback questions have been developed for use in developmental testing of learning materials and are peculiarly well-suited to Flexistudy schemes where tutors are regularly monitoring coursework. Nathenson and Henderson (1980) publish examples of questions for use with both book and non-book materials.

Context for Designing Evaluation of Flexistudy

College staff readily show interest in Flexistudy as is shown by attendances of 70 to 80 at information-giving conferences; there is intrinsic worth in a scheme that provides for an otherwise neglected public of mainly mature students returning to study—and that offers opportunity to continue course that have ceased to be viable in a particular academic year. (Few colleges keep records of courses that fail to enrol viable numbers). Most course tutors and Heads of Department are interested in administrative issues related to implementing the schemes within their institutions and to securing resources in negotiations with Local Education Authorities. Some of this information is now published (Barnet College of Further Education, 1980; Sacks, 1980; Spencer, 1980). Apart form departments of general and professional education, few will find learning materials in an appropriate correspondence format but the Polymaths course and the BBC Living Decisions course (Noble, 1980) both show how readily resource-based courses using publishing materials would adapt to the Flexistudy model.

If a college were to adopt flexible learning systems over a range of courses, studies would need to be made of the scaling-up issues in connection with the college office, tutorial accommodation and the library; at present, demands are marginal to the mainstream of college activities. It is likely that course developments in connection with Technician Education Council and Business Education Council courses and with the vocational preparation of the 16 to 19-year-olds have had much more significant impact on colleges than the introduction of Flexistudy. Perhaps only in the Library and Resources Committee of a college is the relative impact of course developments likely to be monitored.

A decision could be taken to defer *any* evaluation of Flexistudy if the process of evaluation we seen to focus undue attention on a small-scale innovation without providing the essential parallel data about existing courses to assist in appraising the allocation of resources within the college. It would still be relevant to design evaluation studies by or on behalf of the team to assist with monitoring Flexistudy in operation.

8.2 Designing Evaluation of Flexistudy

Organisers' Account

The workshop provided the opportunity for delegates to

reflect on the issues involved in any attempt to evaluate Flexistudy schemes. A summary of the intentions of one scheme was made available, stressing the wish to use a carefully structured published course, and to provide full access to staff and resources in the college.

Issues were explored in small groups, each of which looked at a different aspect of the learning system: students as sources for evaluation data; ways of exploring the 'learnability' of learning materials; performance measures; the tutoring role; and the qualities and procedures of administrative support systems.

Sources of Information

There had been some doubt in the discussion after the formal paper as to the validity of planning pre-focused evaluation studies, but workshop members agreed that objective data could usefully by collected from college enrolment and course progress records. The Flexistudy scheme was seen to provide evaluators with good contacts for studying those who discontinue or interrupt their studies. Assignments in the Flexistudy scheme are not intended to assess students so much as to assist their progress; so some though was given to how to appraise progress, given that heavy reliance is placed on learning materials which may not match the cognitive style of the students. Asking students to envisage hypothetical alternative materials was rejected but structured interviews were favoured to encourage students to make suggestions for changes.

Some sample questions were provided that might be used in any detailed study of the match between text, learning system and learner. Members considered that a sample of students should be studied to find *how* they blended and valued the tutorials, assignments and examinations.

It was suggested that course providers might expect to allow 14 per cent revenue to cover administration costs but that in the early stages, colleges would be looking to the goodwill value of open learning systems and justify the costs in these terms. If Flexistudy schemes came to provide for more than a marginal number of students, it was envisaged that there would be a threshold beyond which the process of scaling-up would become a significant issue in terms of space, staff and procedures.

Members considered how some evaluation might be implemented using no major outside funding but harnessing the skills of the small-scale research undertaken in departments of education and colleges of education (technical).

Appendix

Some sample questions that might be used in structured interviews with home-based students or that might be built into learning materials. (Derived from procedures described by Nathenson and Henderson, 1980).

Feedback questions in text

The self-assessment questions in this unit were:

very difficult..............................very easy

Please explain why you think the diagram on page 5 shows three heavy lines with arrows and two dotted lines...

Can you suggest why the author used 'evaluate' in paragraph 1, 'appraise' in paragraph 2... Can you offer other words that would have been possible?...

To explore the process of learning with text and tape

Did you listen to the audio-tape recording of the interview?

If not, do let us know why...

Would you have preferred a transcript to read?...

Would it have helped to hear the interview earlier in this section?...

What other questions do you think the interviewer should have asked?...

What was your reaction to the analysis of the interview given in the text?...

Will you attempt the assessment for this Unit?... Would you explain your reply?

To check out ways of studying where students may lack a facility for describing their own style

I read the text and readings before starting my essay...

I mapped out my essay before starting the text...

I answered the essay question without reading the text...

I could follow the text but found the readings difficult and did not try the essay...

I wrote the essay after having...

To monitor the workload

The hours I spent on the text for this Unit added up to:

<5.......................................>20

I really needed short tutorials by phone:

...not at all...once...twice....times

I had to do extra work in the college library for this Unit...

8.3 Evaluation of Distance Teaching: A Criterion Sampling Approach

The Emergency Science Programme

In 1976, the Science Unit of the Ministry of Education in Guyana was asked to set up a training programme to help overcome the drastic shortage of science teachers in the secondary and community high schools of Guyana. As a result, the Emergency Science Programme (ESP) was launched in 1977. This in-service science teacher education project uses a three-way distance approach; the students receive correspondence units, tapes and slides, and they attend weekly tutorial sessions and annual vacation workshops (Brophy and Dalgety, 1980). The correspondence units are prepared by local lectures, mostly from the University of Guyana, and the regional tutorial centres are staffed, on a part-time basis, by trained graduate science teachers. In the third long vacation the students are attached for a period of work study to a local industrial or medical laboratory.

Guyana is a relatively small country with a population of only 700,000, and although almost half of the science teachers are untrained there is a need for only a small number of trained science teachers. To date, approximately 60 teachers have been recruited to follow the ESP three year training programme. The first batch began in 1977, the second in 1978, and a third intake are currently being recruited. Twenty-nine of the 1977 intake have successfully completed training and have been awarded trained teachers' certificates which are equivalent to those awarded to students from the college of secondary education.

It is appropriate now to carry out an evaluation of the ESP programme, an evaluation which is summative in that it assesses the degree of success the programme has in training the first batch of students and formative in that it provides information on which to base improvements for future generations of students.

Many distance teaching programmes have been set up, yet we can offer little substantial evidence to show that they produce the intended results. From over 60 projects using distance teaching methods to train teachers (Brophy and Dudley, 1980) we have little more than 'circumstantial' and 'anecdotal' evidence with which we can assess them (Jenkins, 1980). A thorough evaluation of a project such as ESP would, therefore, be of benefit for those who are considering the setting up of new projects and for those who are considering modifying existing ones.

The Evaluation Strategy

The evaluation of ESP is being carried out using a number of different approaches including:

1. A comparison of the performance of ESP 'graduates' with that of college-trained science teachers 'graduating' the same year. Points for comparison are self-image, final teaching assessment grades, ratings by headteachers and teaching style as perceived by pupils.
2. A comparison of the economic cost of training ESP teachers with that of training college science teachers.
3. An evaluation of the on-the-job performance of a sample of ESP teachers using a criterion sampling technique.

One aspect of this evaluation, namely the criterion sampling technique, will receive particular attention in this paper.

Criterion Sampling

Two major characteristics of a criterion sampling approach (CSA) to evaluation can be deduced from its title. First, it is dependent upon criterion referenced measurement. Unlike traditional tests which use norm referencing, criterion tests assess a candidate's performance against a fixed standard and they do not judge it in relation to the performance of others. If a candidates achieves a score above the fixed, 'criterion' standard he 'passes'—irrespective of the supply and the demand for people with this 'pass' qualification. In these respects criterion reference testing involves 'quota free' selection (Hambleton and Noviack, 1973).

In traditional pencil and paper tests students gain marks by responding to stimuli which they are unlikely to encounter outside the examination hall. Pencil and paper tests require indirect, 'symbolic' responses from their candidates, responses which may have little to do with the individual's actual behaviour in the job situation. In a review of 50 years of research on general intelligence tests, Ghiselli (1966) found that the correlation between these tests and job proficiency was no more than +0.23. In a CSA evaluation, an individual is assessed by the score he achieves on a number of situational 'performance' tests, tests which reflect the real life situation.

A second traditional method of evaluation, with which most of us in teaching are familiar, depends upon the candidates being rated by his supervisor on his job performance. For example, student teachers are assessed or rated by their lectures on their ability to teach during teaching practice. This method has the advantage of allowing assessment to take place in the job situation but has the disadvantage that it is based on unstable—high interference—observation. Supervisors' ratings can be affected by many different uncontrolled factors. The second characteristic of the CSA approach is that it can control many of the variables encountered in the real-life situation by testing the candidate's performance on a sample of the tasks he would carry out in the everyday situation. CSA, therefore, attempts to standardise the test conditions while also approaching the authenticity of real life (Fredenkens, 1975). CSA has been described as an approach: 'in which the students' performance on standardised samples of tasks for which he has been trained is systematically observed, measured and evaluated'.

The CSA approach to evaluation is at present being investigated by the UNESCO Institute for Education, Hamburg, to see if it offers a suitable method for evaluating non-formal educational programmes. Distance teaching is one type of non-formal educational programme. At the request of the UNESCO Institute, a CSA evaluation was included with the other approaches being used in the evaluation of the Emergency Science Programme. This now forms one of four case studies which are to be used for the Institute's meta evaluation, i.e. the evaluation of CSA as an evaluation method.

The CSA Evaluation of ESP

In a CSA evaluation the first step is for the evaluator to identify the major goals of the project under review. For ESP this was relatively simple because the goals had been written into the original proposal for the programme as submitted to the Board of Examiners in Guyana. Its major goals can be summarised as aiming to:

> provide its students with enough theoretical and practical knowledge in science, education, earth science, English and mathematics to enable them to teach the West Indian Science Curriculum (WISC) and the community high school science programme, Secondary Departments Science Programme (SDSP).

So ESP was designed specifically to train people to teach WISC and SDSP.

The second step in the CSA approach is to determine the criteria to be used to evaluate whether or not this goal has been achieved. A CSA approach requires that we use measures of candidates' performance on a sample of the tasks for which they have been trained. The ESP evaluation required, therefore, that we determine what a teacher must be able to do to teach WISC and SDSP by answering the question: 'What are the criteria by which we judge successful science teaching in Guyana?' The answer was determined by means of a two-stage strategy. The first stage involved a thorough review of the literature to determine what competencies science teachers and science educators thought were important for science teaching. Nine such competencies were identified. A further study of the literature was then made to determine which skills were required for each competency. Eighty-eight such skills were identified. The second stage involved asking science educators in Guyana which of the nine competencies they considered to be most important for teaching science in Guyanese schools and which of the 88 skills were most important for each of the competencies they chose as being important. In this way we were able to identify both the skills and the competencies that Guyanese science educators feel to be among the most important for teaching science of Guyana.

Criterion sampling involves the sampling of the criterion behaviours for which the students have been trained. The UNESCO Institute for Education recommend that the evaluator draws up a Task by Skill matrix in which the rows represent the tasks and the columns the skills underlying the performance. This matrix can then provide the test plan from which the evaluator can draw a sample of the task skill combinations. Science teachers are required to perform an enormous range of tasks involving a great number of skills. A task by skill matrix for science teachers would contain a large number of task skill combinations, many of which would be of limited use in everyday teaching. The sampling method used for ESP, therefore, was a modification of that suggested by UNESCO. Instead of taking a random sample from the universal set of task skill combinations, it was decided to use a stratified sampling procedure. The three competencies which were rated by the Guyanese educators as being the most important were isolated. The skills rated by the educators as being most important for each of these three competencies were then listed and a random sample drawn of two skills from each of the three lists. In this way a random sample was obtained of the sills which Guyanese science educators feel are the most important for teaching science in Guyana. The six skills identified in this way were:

1. Observe safety precautions for any situation that is likely to arise in his or her teaching.
2. Use correctly all the different apparatus and materials

needed for the science curriculum being used by his or her classes.

3. Guide pupils to make conclusions from their observations.
4. Encourage pupils to record what they have observed.
5. Relate new experiences to pupils' previous experience.
6. Adapt a lesson plan to suit the specific local conditions of a school.

Both the WISC and the SDSP programmes have prepared detailed teachers' guides and an analysis of these was made to identify those tasks in which these six skills were necessary. Situational tests were then designed which would test the teacher's ability to perform these tasks. Where appropriate, random selections were made of the content to be tested. For example, one of the tasks a teacher would have to perform in order to use science equipment correctly (skill 2) would be to identify the equipment. A list of the equipment needed to teach WISC and SDSP was drawn up and a random selection made of 31 of the items, a 30 per cent sample. As part of the situational test for this skill, teachers were asked to identify this sample of WISC/SDSP equipment.

The situational tests were carried out in Guyana over a three-day period in January involving 16 of the 29 ESP teachers. Criterion performance levels for each skill were determined using 'inspection-based' and consensus judgements carried out by a panel of three representatives of the Guyanese science educators.

Results

Data from the CSA evaluation is still being analysed but some findings are already clear, for instance 11 of the 16 teachers tested had at least minimal competence in all the six skills tested, four were competent in five of the six, and one was competent in four.

TABLE 8.1A

Competence of ESP Teachers on Criterion Skills

Level of Competence	*Criterion Skill*					
	1	*2*	*3*	*4*	*5*	*6*
High competence	0	6	12	8	7	13
Minimal competence	13	10	4	8	7	2
Below minimal competence	3	0	0	0	2	1

TABLE 8.1B

Number of Criterion Skills in which ESP Teachers were Competent

	Number of Skills						
	6	*5*	*4*	*3*	*2*	*1*	*0*
High competence	0	1	6	3	3	2	1
Minimal competence	11	4	1	0	0	0	0
Below minimal competence	0	0	0	0	1	4	—

As mentioned earlier, the whole study has a dual purpose—one to evaluate ESP itself, the other to investigate how effective are the CSA tests at evaluating ESP. Correlations between CSA scores and final teaching assessments were low with the only correlation above +0.1 being that between teachers' assessment grade and score on skill 1—knowledge of safety precautions ($p = 0.37$). A stronger relationship might be expected between the CSA scores on the two skills related to subject knowledge and the teacher's performance on the final science examination. There was, in fact, a significant positive correlation between skill I scores and science examination scores ($r = 0.6$ $p < 0.01$). The correlation with skill 2—use of apparatus—was not significant at the five per cent level ($r = 0.26$). McClelland (1973), however, has argued that the criteria for establishing the validity of criterion referenced tests 'really ought to be not grades in schools, but "grades in life" in the broadest theoretical and practical sense'.

TABLE 8.2

CSA Scores of GCE and Non-GCE Teachers

Teaches GCE	*Skill 1*	*Skill 2*
+	73	78
+	70	96
+	64	85
+	64	84
+	63	87
+	63	83
+	61	95
+	58	88
+	56	85
+	55	79
–	51	66
–	49	75
–	43	80
–	43	61
–	43	43

Correlation between skill 1 score and GCE teaching
$r = 0.83$ ($p < .001$)

Correlation between skill 2 score and GCE teaching
$r = 0.58$ ($p < .05$)

Accordingly the question that arises is how 'grades in life' for Guyanese science teachers can be assessed. In Guyana, as in many developing countries, headteachers tend to give the higher ability classes to the teachers in which they have the most confidence—especially with regard to their academic and subject knowledge. In Guyanese schools, a good measure of the headteacher's confidence in a teacher's subject knowledge would be whether or not he timetables that teacher to take a GCE class. Notes made of interviews with 15 of the ESP teachers' headteachers showed that 10 of the 15 taught GCE science and five taught only junior forms. In a comparison of the CSA results of the 'GCE' teachers with those of the 'non-GCE' teachers on skills 1 and 2—those skills which related to subject knowledge—we find there is strong evidence to show that the scores of the teachers obtained via the CSA tests were consistent measures of their subject knowledge as perceived by their headteachers.

It might well appear that all we have to do to evaluate the teachers is to ask for the headteacher's opinion. However, our results show that while a headteacher's opinion correlates highly with a teacher's subject knowledge, it does not correlate at all highly with any of the other skills. So while headteachers may be choosing the most knowledgeable teacher they may not necessarily be choosing the best science teacher.

The evidence,, so far, confirms that CSA testing is both feasible and suitable for evaluating distance teaching. Situational tests can be constructed to sample job tasks that the 'graduates' of distance teaching programmes are required to perform, and such tests can be accurate measures of on-the-job performance. This is not to say, however, that the CSA approach is a panacea for all problem encountered in evaluating distance teaching. Indeed, the ESP evaluation has identified a number of difficulties still to be overcome.

Acknowledgment

The research reported here was supported by a grant from the Northern Ireland Department of Education.

8.4 Evaluating the Effectiveness of Distance Learning: A Case Study

Introduction

Unlike teachers in traditional universities, Open University (OU) teachers receive no direct feedback from students. In most institutions, a great deal of feedback in courses is said to emerge informally and automatically from close interaction between students and teachers. More formal methods of evaluation have therefore been given careful consideration at the OU. The University is engaged in a cycle of remaking courses and a variety of models of using feedback in the production of these courses have been tested (Nathenson *et al*, 1981).

This paper examines the evaluation history of the Science Foundation Course over 10 years. This demonstrates how feedback data can be used in the attempt to improve courses. Also, by considering the successes and failures of the remade version of the course, the contributions of the evaluation strategies to the improvements will be identified. The main conclusion is that, while the course team was able to respond collectively to large structural and content changes in the material, individual course team members did not respond appropriately in all cases to detailed feedback which dealt with individual components of the course.

A History of the Evaluation

The Course and its Production Process

The Science Foundation Course (S 100) was produced by a team consisting of 15 subject specialists, two editors, several BBC producers, and a member of the Institute of Educational Technology (IET). The course had four aims. These were:

1. To design an integrated multi-disciplinary course with contributions from the four disciplines (physics, biology and earth sciences) linked together in a way which would demonstrate both the unity and diversity of the sciences.
2. To offer a course which would be both satisfying and worthwhile for students whose only contact with science it would form.
3. To teach science in its social context to bring out clearly the relationship between science and society.
4. To provide an adequate experience for students not previously exposed to experimental work in the laboratory, the practice of which is both an accepted

part of the training of a scientist and a valuable learning experience in itself.

The course consisted of correspondence texts, assignment question papers, TV and radio programmes, a summer school, a home experiment kit and some mathematical texts.

Work began on the production of the course in 1969, and production and remake activities have continued until the present day. Figure 8.1 summarises the events which have filled these 12 years.

During the production phase of S 100, instructional material was drafted and redrafted several times. Each draft was scrutinised by course team members and feedback obtained through course team discussions. Some student reaction to materials was collected during this period but practical considerations made this an unsatisfactory experience of the course team as the tested materials were incomplete (Melton, 1977).

Feedback

Once the course had been presented to students in 1971, survey data could be collected. The first survey of S 100 was undertaken in 1971 by the University's survey research department. For each unit (a week's work) students were sent an identical questionnaire to find out how difficult, interesting or helpful they had found each component of the course and the amount of work each had taken both in number of hours and subjectively. Students were asked to indicate their reactions to the amount of work in each unit. They complained there was much too much work in unit 10. This general survey was useful in that it helped to identify major problem areas.

The course team decided on the basis of this information to spread the load in this unit over two weeks and make the study of à later unit, unit 13, optional,. The survey was repeated in 1972 and this showed that students felt less overloaded.

Where units had been identified as particularly difficult or overloaded, course team members wanted more information to help them rectify the problems. A more detailed survey undertaken in 1973 combined with reports from course tutors (part-time members of staff who give face-to-face tuition) provided this. The survey asked students for each unit to identify terms, concepts and principles they had found particularly difficult to understand. The identical questions were asked for each unit to provide a basis of comparison. Areas which authors should give most notice to in the redrafting of a unit could be identified by a rise in the percentage of students identifying them as particularly difficult ones.

However, text material is printed for four to six years and authors work on other courses, so the opportunity and manpower to make extensive changes to the course was not present at this stage.

Also, since 1971, student progress data has been collected by the survey research department. This consists of a detailed breakdown of the students studying the course in terms of age, sex, previous educational experience and occupation. This information has been updated over the years and can be used to draw conclusions about the relative success rates of groups within a year's cohort of students.

Decision to Remake

The original plan was to remake the course within a period of four years, but the demands made by the science courses students may subsequently study meant that consideration of what 'remaking' the course required was left until 1975. At a faculty meeting it was decided that the course content of S 100 was still appropriate, apart from the necessary updating. The majority view seemed to be that we should use what we had learned about S 100 to improve it

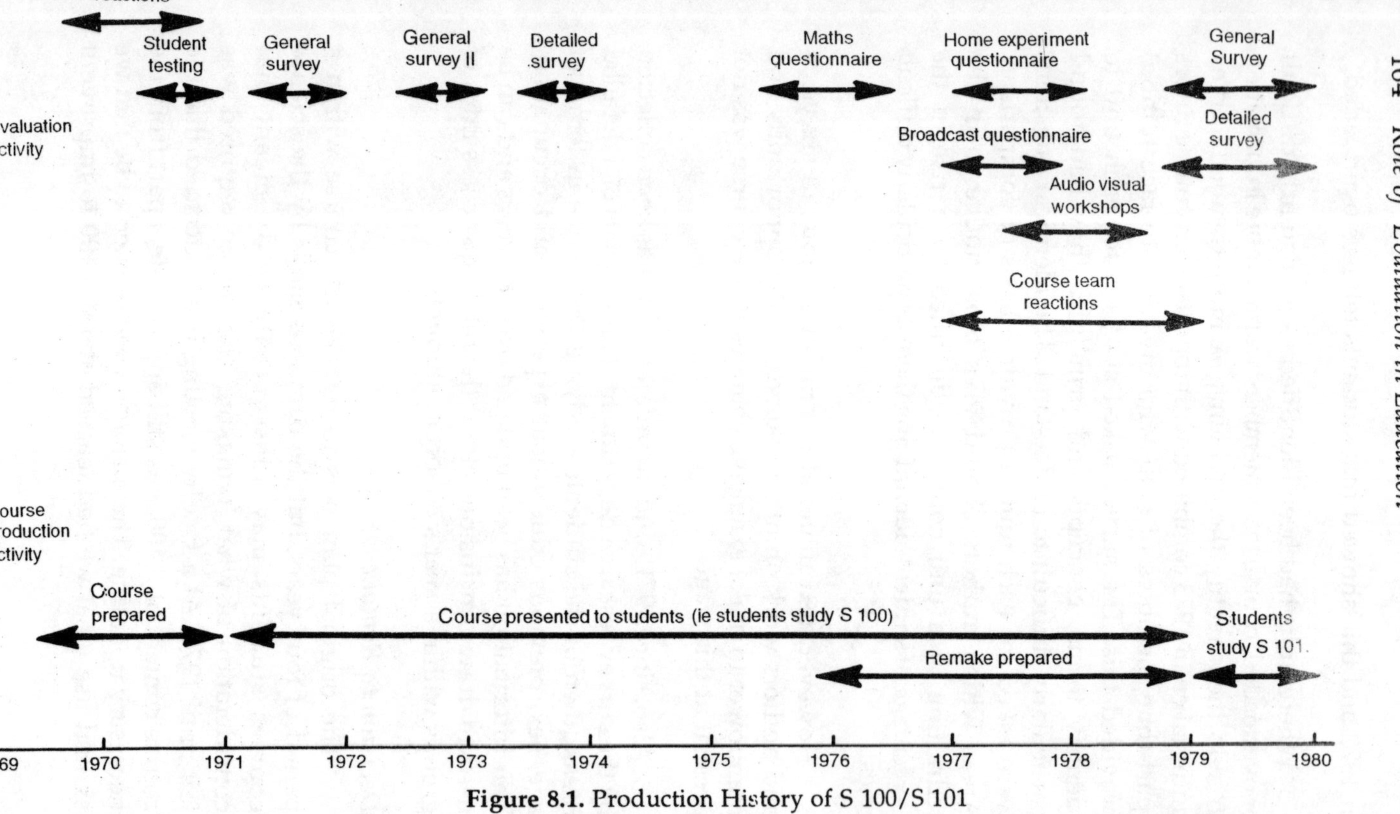

Figure 8.1. Production History of S 100/S 101

considerably as a course and make changes with that purpose only. We wanted to develop the new course S 101 so that its educational effectiveness should be greater than that achieved in S 100, and so that dropout and failure rates become no higher than their S 100 levels.

The existence of distinct trends in the characteristics of students enrolling for S 100 had implications for this aim. The percentage of students in professional occupations was increasing and also those in manual ones. The percentage of entrants with higher educational qualifications was decreasing and that of entrants with five O-levels or less was increasing. To maintain rates of success, especially for students with minimal educational experience, without sacrificing the standards necessary for proceeding with higher level courses, was thought to be essential. A major investment of effort in the S 101 operation could produce a much-improved foundation course and, more importantly, provide techniques and procedures to facilitate future remakes.

The Evaluation Project

A three-year evaluation project was set up in 1976. This was with the intention of concentrating attention on improving the course's educational efficiency. The aim was to devise a mechanism for ensuring that all the relevant information available was used effectively in the remake of the course. The remake team was enormous—it consisted of 45 members. Organisational structures were proposed to cope with this large number of people. This can be viewed in three ways (see Figure 8.2).

Later Evidence

When the remake course team assembled in late 1976, the evaluation group began to receive requests for information. Some of these could be met by considering the feedback already available. To assist in this process, two documents were prepared for each course team member:

1 A digest of general survey data (containing overall student reaction to the course).
2. A digest of information specific to the discipline group of which he or she was a member (containing an indication of particularly difficult sections in units, objectives students felt unable to achieve, together with tutor comment on the units).

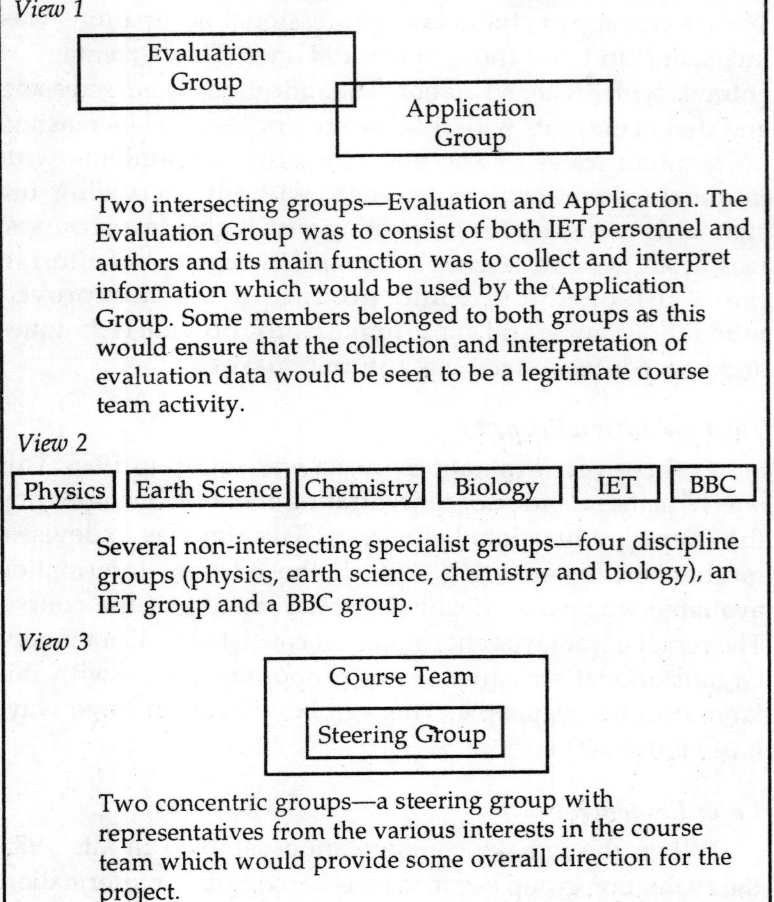

Figure 8.2. Course Team Structure

Members of the evaluation group discussed these reports with individual discipline groups to establish what other data should be collected. Several areas of interest emerged: three of these were as follows:

1. *Mathematics teaching in S 100.* A detailed questionnaire on the first five units of the course where most of the new mathematical ideas are introduced was prepared to investigate student use of the parallel mathematics text, together with a survey of other OU preparatory material.
2. *Home experiment strategies.* Information was collected in 1977 by questionnaire on reasons why students were not completing the home experiments. Statistics on the cost implications of different home kit strategies were collected and guidelines for experimental work were produced.
3. *Broadcasting.* A questionnaire was sent to students on the perceptions of the usefulness of certain features of S 100 TV and radio. Workshop sessions were held with the help of the audio-visual media research group of the University, examining examples of good and bad use of television from other courses. Guidelines for the use of these media were drawn up.

Final Structure of the Course

The final structure of the new course to emerge was as follows:

1. The number of units were reduced from 34 to 32.
2. There was a reordering of the topics covered aimed at making the more severe demands made by the course on the students appear somewhat later in the course than in S 100. The new introduction to the course conveys the relevance and utility of precise and quantitative analysis in science. The first three

units of S 101 attempt to introduce students to the general ideas of the 'scientific method'.

3. A preparatory package of four booklets dealing with arithmetic, algebra, graphs and geometry has been prepared. This package, available to all students in the six months preceding the course, provides students who are uncertain of their mathematical capabilities with the opportunity of practising them before the course itself starts. Each block of work is introduced by a 15-minute television programme. As we were uncertain of the level to aim at in these programmes, and since their prime function is to motivate students, a pilot of one of the TV programmes (on algebra) was made and shown to groups of S 101 applicants. Their comments were incorporated in the final version of the programme.
4. In S 101, as in S 100, students are involved in experimental work directly with a home experiment kit. The S 100 version of this kit was criticised by students for its inconvenience, bulkiness, and the packing system which was perceived as being designed with very little attention to the convenience of the user. The new kit is dispatched in two parts, one at the start of the course and one after final registration, and the design of each section of the kit is to maximise student use. The students also criticised the consistent under-estimation of the time taken to complete the experiment component of a week's work. In S 101, introduction of a unit on experimental chemistry, where practical work is the major component of the student's workload for the week, has meant an even closer scrutiny of the times estimated.
5. A number of audio-cassettes have been introduced to replace half of the radio programmes used in S 100.

Effectiveness of the Changes

An identical cocktail of general surveys, detailed surveys, reports from tutors and student progress data was employed to establish whether or not the changes made to the course were effective. The attempt to improve the pass rate while maintaining standards was successful.

Results from the first two years of S 101 show that the pass rate has increased slightly from 89 to 94 per cent. At the end of the year, students sat a computer-marked examination. Maintenance of standards was ensured by scrutiny of candidates' performance on selected market questions—ie questions which had been used in previous S 100 examinations and for which item analysis data was available. The first two years' results in the course suggest that we have been successful in maintaining, and slightly increasing, the pass rate of the least qualified students.

It is too early to assess whether S 101 provides a better foundation for higher level studies in science but a follow-up study on the first two years' cohort of students is in progress. The number of students successfully completing the course has not increased dramatically. Consideration of the drop-out rates for the last year of S 100 and the first year of S 101 show a remarkably similar pattern. Since the course team's revised introduction to the course was planned to be more gentle than the S 100 early units, this result is puzzling, especially since students agreed that the early units were comparatively easy. Other studies of drop-out rates at the OU (Burt, 1976) have suggested that initial high drop-out figures on foundation courses may be due to the student's unreal expectation of the demands an OU course will make on him or her.

Workload is an area in which the changes in the course have been less successful. There is little to choose between S 100 and S 101. However, S 101 students perceive the course as considerably more interesting then S 100 students.

The mathematics pre-course package and the integration of some basic mathematics leading in the early units of the course has produced students whose performance on simple mathematics tests improves during the course and whose confidence in mathematics has increased.

Home experiments are completed by many more students and their perceptions, both of the usefulness of the experiments they have done and the importance of experimental work to a scientist, have increased. On a more particular level the remade course appears more successful. Detailed surveys of S 101 units identify areas where the teaching of particular concept attracts more positive student reaction. The opinion of students on the teaching of elementary particle physics has increased markedly.

Not all sections of the course achieved this result and in particular the teaching of biochemistry and equilibrium in chemistry still causes students problems.

Conclusions

My experiences on the evaluation of S 101 lead me to the following conclusions. As the history of S 100 and S 101 shows, the effort expended in remaking the course did produce a somewhat 'better' course than the original—not enormously better, as the original course was itself a successful course. Large structural changes suggested by the evaluative data had been implemented with some success. However, at the level of individual units, the feedback was useful only in identifying areas where students had particular difficulty. Alerting the authors of the new versions of the units to these was helpful, but the detailed surveys show only limited success in the attempts of the authors to improve individual units. Progressive refinement in the course design process is required.

An example of this progressive refinement is provided

by the experimental chemistry unit. Owing to production difficulties with the home experiment kit, this unit was printed for one year only which allowed the author to act on the feedback collected in the first year of presentation to improve certain aspects of its teaching strategy with considerable success. This was no different from the techniques used in the unit S 100 remake process, but provided the author with the opportunity to polish the final version. Some of the remaining difficulties in the course might be removed in the same way.

But this process is dependent on the individual author's ability and willingness to respond appropriately to student feedback. He or she may be alerted to particular difficulties or confusions within the teaching text, but he or she must find his or her own solution to the problems the evaluator discovers. This process is time-consuming and, at best, the results are patchy.

On S 101, the course team was able to make large structural changes collectively with apparent success. This involved decisions about sections of work several units in length, to be studied by all students on the course. Difficulties arose where individuals had to make decisions about individual sections of work less than, or equal to, one unit. In these cases the evaluator's job becomes extremely difficult.

Effective evaluation is achieved not merely by the presentation of information in the most comprehensible and communicable form. It is vital when the decisions made are being implemented that the evaluator is available to discuss whether the action to be taken by the course team or individual author is an appropriate one in the light of the information being provided. Authors find it difficult to be objective about evaluative comment on their work. In S 101, the intersection of the evaluation and application groups was empty. No authors became involved in the collection of evaluative data. They had their own function to perform on the course team.

No evaluator prepared units. To ensure that attention is paid to feedback is a difficult and time-consuming job. For an author, responding to feedback which contains only information about which sections of his or her work failed and no suggestions for possible solutions is equally difficult.

Some questions remain to be answered by our future experiments in evaluation. The two most important ones are

(a) How can the author/evaluator relationship be improved?

(b) How can the process of evaluation improve an individual author's writing skills?

A possible solution could be for authors to adopt a purely evaluative function at intervals, on material which they have not produced, to increase their experience of assessing the effectiveness of teaching strategies. Coupled with this would be the insistence that evaluators be expected to generate not only negative criticism but to present clients with positive alternatives to the strategies they criticize.

8.5 Evaluating and Improving Learning Materials: A Case Study

Introduction

Clem Adelman has written that evaluators, in their desire to have their work well received by its audience, have concentrated too much on methodology and techniques and too little on preconditions and procedures (Adelman, 1980). 'Methodology and techniques', he argues, 'are premised on preconditions and procedures'. This paper examines the procedures by which formative evaluation data (Kandaswamy, 1980) on one Open University course have been dealt with in the process of revising the course materials. It argues that these procedures have had as great an effect upon the outcome of the evaluation as the choice of evaluation model and methods.

The study is of the evaluation of the Open University's new foundation course in technology: 'Living with Technology', which, in 1980, replaced 'The Man Made World', the original technology foundation course. A detailed description of the evaluation and some of its more interesting findings are being reported in a series of articles in the *British Journal of Educational Technology* (Nathenson *et al*, 1981). A detailed description of the course can be found in the *Open University Courses Handbook* (Open University, 1979).

Background to the Evaluation

When members of the Technology Faculty began discussing remaking the foundation course in their Faculty, it was generally accepted that the original course had been less successful than they wished, both in recruiting and teaching students. They therefore decided to begin again from scratch with a completely new course which would have different aims and philosophy. The team of academics (the Course Team) who began working on the course were enthusiastic and receptive to new ideas about teaching and presentation, as well as content. There was an atmosphere in which suggestions for evaluation were well received.

However, it is generally accepted within the Open University that evaluating course materials is 'a good thing', especially for long running courses with a large student intake. The foundation courses in the other four faculties had gone through extensive, although different, evaluations. That of the Science foundation course is described in another paper in this volume (Scanlon, 1981). It would have been difficult of the Course Team to have justified *not* engaging in some sort of evaluation. The decision was not really whether to evaluate, but what evaluation model to adopt, and the most important factor determining this was the close friendship between the Course Team Chairman and one of the educational technologists working on the course. These two travelled to work and back together every day and used that time to discuss which model would best satisfy the needs of the Course Team. The fact that the model adopted (a '2+6' model) was the most intensive evaluation the University has ever supported on one of its courses, was in great part owing to this friendship.

The 2+6 Evaluation Model

The 2+6 model is one of the many variants on developmental testing used within the Open University. This is a process in which learning materials (usually in draft form) are tried out on students, and is mainly concerned with examining learning rather than content issues (Henderson *et al*, 1980). In a 2 + 6 model, a course is evaluated during its first year of presentation, revised during its second year and the revised version is presented for the following six years. It is a rigorous model, since all materials are evaluated in their final form, rather than drafts, and larger and more reliable samples of staff and students can be used. It was these factors which appealed to the Course Team. However, there are two major drawbacks to this model. First, it is very expensive since revisions must be made to printed material, broadcasting and audio-vision after they have been produced in their final form. Second, it demands a commitment from academic staff to stay with a course past its exciting production period and into the second and third year of its presentation. Neither of these factor appeared important at the planning stage but they have since had a strong influence upon the revision part of the process.

Aims and Objectives of the Evaluation

The major aim of the evaluation was to provide the Course Team with information on which to base their decisions about revising material, and it had five objectives:

1. To identify the extent to which students were mastering the course objectives.
2. To provide quantitative feedback to the Course Team on various aspects of the course such as:

(a) the number of students dropping out of the course;
(b) the extent to which the materials matched the assumed entry level abilities of the students;
(c) student workload (e.g. how much time students were spending on each part of the course);
(d) students' perceptions of the relevance of broadcasting and cassette vision to the printed text.

3. To identify those parts of the course (both textual and audio-visual) which were conceptually difficult for students.
4. To try to determine the reasons *why* students were experiencing difficulties.
5. To try to elicit from students suggestions for improving the course materials.

Evaluation Procedures

The course is divided into seven 'blocks' of materials, each based around a technological issue. This structure provided a way of organising the evaluation data, and in 1980 data were collected for each 'block' from the following sources:

1. Item-analyses of students' assessment scores.
2. Computer-based survey data from all students.
3. In-depth feedback data from sample of students.
4. Open-ended feedback from all of the course tutors.

Short summary reports of the computer survey data, and the data from tutors, were distributed to the Course Team as they became available. However, the analysis of the in-depth student data, which was considered the most valuable and the basis for all revisions, took longer. The first evaluation report which integrated this data with data from the other sources was presented in November 1980. Reports on later blocks have been presented at intervals of four to six weeks.

During the course production stage the two educational technologists running the evaluation attended Course Team meetings and became involved with the production of the course. They also made attempts (mostly unsuccessful) to involve individual course authors more closely by asking them to identify any parts of their work they wanted given special attention. Their lack of success caused the evaluators to question the commitment of some Course Team members. The main commitment still came from the Course Team Chairman and the three course co-ordinators who, together, managed the development of the course. These co-ordinators became very involved with the evaluation and together with the educational technologists began to see themselves as a team. This team of five met regularly and produced joint authored reports and papers.

While the Evaluation Team was crystallising, the Course Team was disintegrating. This was not unusual since, in the Open University, both resources and job satisfaction tend to be concentrated on course production rather than evaluation or maintenance (the years during which the course is presented). During the years of presentation the course team is likely to consist of one or two academics and a co-ordinator. The production period for 'Living with Technology' had been long (four years) and many Course Team members were ready for something else. Some took study leave, including the Course Team Chairman; others began working on new courses; some pursued research interests; and some left the University for new jobs. Although there was a formal commitment from the technology faculty to the evaluation it was some months before there were enough willing academics to form a Revision Course Team. During this time the morale of the Evaluation Team fell very low since it was possible that without a Revision Team the evaluation would have to be abandoned.

The Revision Process

By September 1980, a Revision Course Team was formed. It was a mixture of some people who had been on the Production Course Team, and some new to the course, including a new Course Team Chairman. Each block had assigned to it one academic who was responsible for seeing that revisions were made to that block. Other people on the Team were evaluators, authors or monitors. The revision process could then begin.

However, from the beginning there have been pressures on the Revision Course Team both from within (because of conflict or confusion over the status of recommendations and data coming from the Evaluation Team), and from without (from the University committee structure). This external pressure was felt first through a demand, by the University, for an estimate of the percentage of revision that would be made to the course. The allocation of any resources at all for revision depended on the strength of the case presented. The Evaluation Team was therefore in the position of having, unwillingly, to produce such an estimate at a state when data were incomplete. Using a very crude measure of mastery of objectives a paper was produced which argued for revision of about one-third textual material and about one-quarter broadcasting, spread unevenly across all blocks. However, as expected, full-scale evaluation reports have contradicted this crude measure in many places, and the Evaluation Team have found themselves having to justify the contradictions. They have also had to argue against the Course Team using what was simply a committee document as a guide to revision.

Internal pressures have been reflected in both the procedure adopted for reaching a decision about revisions, and conflicts which arose within the procedure. Some structure had to be adopted so that the evaluation reports could be discussed and decisions reached, and although the Course Team is the official decisions-making body on course content and teaching techniques it can be too large to debate detail. Therefore, smaller sub-groups, known as Monitoring Groups, were set up for each block. These groups would discuss in detail the recommendations in the evaluation report, decide on revisions and report their decisions to the Course Team. With Course Team approval the authors would make such revisions, and revised material would be checked by the Monitoring Group and then sent to press. Members of the Monitoring Group would be authors engaged in revising material in that block, one evaluator, and certain Course Team members called 'monitors', whose task was simply to help make the decisions. Figure 8.3 shows diagrammatically the membership of the different groups for any one block.

Figure 8.4 indicates that the Monitoring Group now controlled the revision process and the Evaluation Team functioned simply to feed in data.

The first full-scale evaluation report was produced in November 1980, and since then two others have been produced and monitoring groups on two blocks have met to discuss them. However, it has become apparent that (from the evaluators' point of view at least) there have been deficiencies in this revision model. The primary one was that no one knew who had the final say in disagreements over revisions! It had been said at the Course Team that this lay with the major academic responsible for that block who should be free to act as he thought best; which would include ignoring parts of the evaluation report if he chose. Since only one evaluator has attended the Monitoring Group's meetings he has been in a powerless position if authors refused to accept the evaluation recommendations.

Reports from the Monitoring Group to the Course Team, which has met infrequently, have been very brief and for those unfamiliar with the full evaluation report very uninformative. Therefore it has been impossible for the Course Team to engage in any extensive discussion of the revisions from this document alone, and some members of the Course Team have said they do not wish to do so since their interests lie almost exclusively with their own materials.

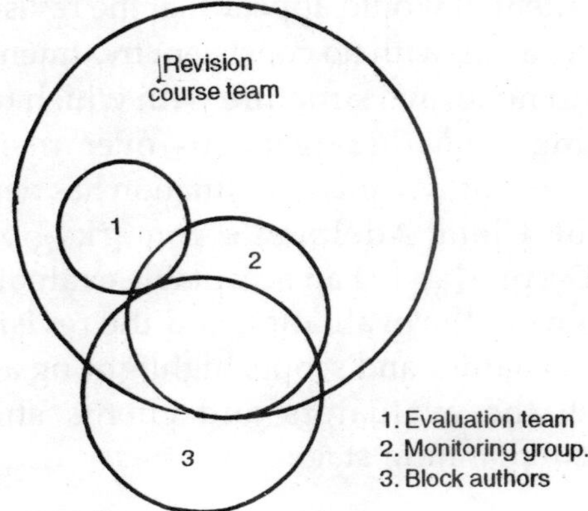

Figure 8.3. Membership of Groups for Any One Block

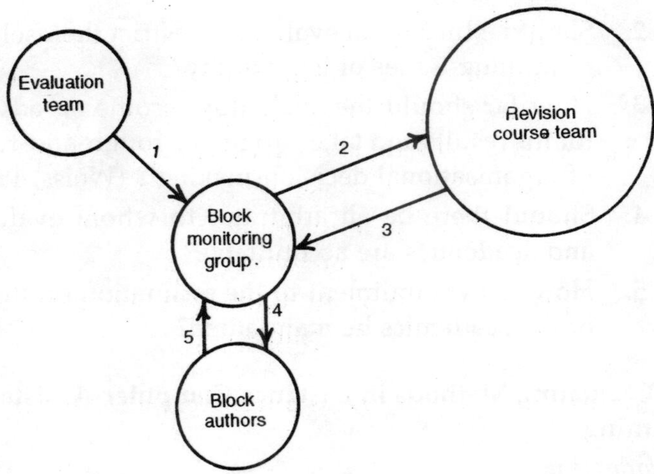

Figure 8.4. Sequence of Information between Groups for Decision-Making

Authors have accused the Evaluation Team of stepping outside their brief, i.e. that they have recommended changes in content which they are not considered competent to do. Strictly speaking this is true, but recommendations based on learnability may often suggest changes of emphasis to, or omission of, content. It would appear that the revision process has become piecemeal, with no consistent treatment of course-wide issues, and no formal structure with which to deal with problems arising from disagreements over revisions. The experience of procedures in this one situation has demonstrated the aptness of Clem Adelman's remark given in the Introduction. Despite having an acceptable evaluation model, the preconditions of the evaluation and the revision process have changed its nature and scope, highlighting a number of questions both the evaluators and clients should have addressed in the planning stage:

1. Can the organisation cope administratively with the evaluation model? (This is not a question of willingness.)
2. Should educational evaluators restrict themselves to examining issues of learnability?
3. How far should the evaluator become an advocate for his results and take part in the 'rough-and-tumble of organisational decision-making'? (Weiss, 1972)
4. Should there be an arbitrator to whom evaluators and academics are accountable?
5. How can commitment to the evaluation on the part of the academics be maintained?

8.6 Evaluating Methods in Distance Computer-Assisted Learning

Introduction

We would like to consider two questions in this paper:

1. How should Computer Assisted Learning (CAL) be evaluated?
2. What questions is the evaluation intended to answer?

To start with, let us take another two questions which evaluation studies often address. The first of these is: 'What is the cost of the system?', or 'How much?'. This is a reasonable question and a necessary one to ask, but it is difficult to provide a clear-cut answer and it is linked to the second question which is often asked of CAL, which is: 'Does it compare favourable with other teaching methods', or 'How effective?' The problem with this question is that this is not the right question to ask. It can be argued, in fact, that , if such a comparison can be made, then we are failing to realise the potential use of computers in education—as powerful tools for learning in ways which would not otherwise be possible. Even if, however, CAL is not introduced in such a way as to radically alter the curriculum, it rarely replaces a more traditional way of doing the same thing. The introduction of CAL is usually a new means to achieve new goals and is rarely an alternative to existing provision, and so the traditional 'comparative' statistical evaluation, where matched experimental and control groups are analysed, becomes meaningless. There is, however, more to the argument against this sort of approach than the impracticality of standard quantitative methodology, and this is the question of the philosophy and the assumptions underlying this sort of approach, which is largely derived from the behaviour sciences, especially behaviourism with its insistence on observable outcomes and the more reactionary strands of educational psychology which emphasise psychometric testing.

Evaluation Styles

The effect of this behaviourist tradition is for much of CAL to concentrate on *products* or *outcomes* rather than processes. This position has been attacked by protagonists of 'idiographic' evaluation such as Stephen Kemmis (Kemmis *et al*, 1979) who argues that construing learning in terms of attainment focuses attention on the content or subject matter, and the outcomes of the learning process, and away from that process itself—and from the students who are doing the learning. Thus evaluation studies concentrate on the extent to which the original objectives of the project have been met: these being, of course, the designer's objectives and not the student's for, to return to our original questions, to answer the question 'How effective?' we need to ask 'What were the objectives—and how far have they been met?'

Proponents of illuminative evaluation (e.g. Parlett and Hamilton, 1977) argue that the situation into which CAL projects (or others) are introduced is very complex and is one which is constantly changing: also that it may include perspectives which the project designer is unaware of.

To try to determine whether the project has achieved pre-determined outcomes, then, has certain pitfalls:

(a) there may be features salient to the success or acceptability of the project which are never discovered, because the information to look for has already been decided at the beginning of the project in a way which excludes 'unsought' information;

(b) the situation may change so that the original questions are no longer appropriate;

(c) if an 'experimental' model is adopted it is assumed that salient variables can be identified and controlled for, an assumption unlikely to be met in a real and complex situation.

We argue that the 'How effective?' question should be replaced by one in the form of: 'How is the project perceived from the client's point of view—and wheat are its salient and critical features which make its acceptability and success more or less likely?'

We can then consider the first question, 'How much?', because once we know the true salient features (rather than those the designers thought were important) we can ask

'How much are they worth?' There will be no unique answer to this form of the cost question—although we can get some estimates for what CAL costs per hour to produce. (It should be noted that similar estimates for face-to-face contact are hard to come by.)

Deciding whether the project is worthwhile is very difficult and involves weighing up the costs and benefits—where costs include time and effort as well as money and some of the benefits may not be tangible.

Evaluation should provide a basis for deciding what level of trade off is reasonable and acceptable. To do this effectively, it should not be the final stage of a project which will either give it the seal of approval or 'the boot'. Instead, we argue for a process of progressive refinement, where information from the evaluation can be fed back into the system. Evaluation thus becomes part of a monitoring and tuning process: by asking, ahead of time, 'How could the situation be otherwise if the feedback I propose to collect is positive or negative?', a basis is formed for acting on that information.

Figure 8.5 summarises two approaches to evaluation of CAL.

In the first 'static' model in Figure 8.5, outcomes of evaluation cannot affect the current system—although they may lead to decisions about maintaining it, dropping it or changing it. In the ideal version, 2, there is a feedback cycle based on built-in evaluation, which includes continuous tuning. To achieve this, the evaluation process should be built in to the system, which itself should itself be capable of being finely tuned. (A way of doing this is by the use of a production-rule system, O'Shea, 1979.) In the evaluation study we will discuss here, only a small part of the evaluation was built into the CAL system and the system itself is not easily modifiable; nevertheless, we believe that by adopting an eclectic approach we obtained information which we may otherwise have missed.

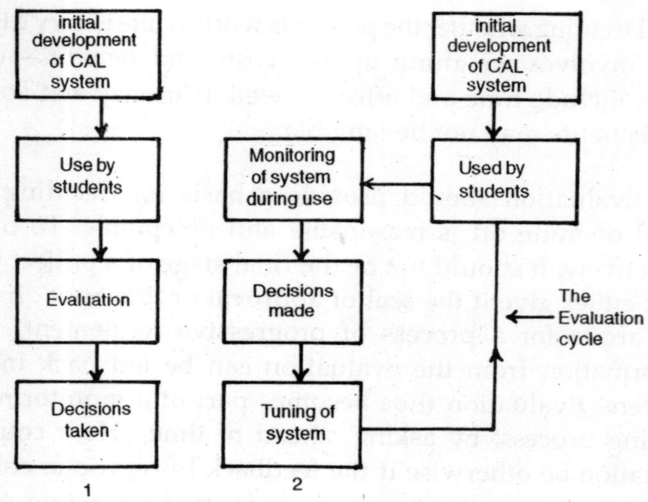

Figure 8.5. Two 'Models' of Evaluation of CAL

A Case Study

The CICERO computer-assisted tutorial system, which is used by people operating a range of courses at the Open University, has been described in detail elsewhere (Cooper and Lockwood, 1979) as have the various applications of CAL at the university (Bramer, 1980).

We intend to confine ourselves to discussing the evaluation of the use of CICERO on one particular course called Biological Bases of Behaviour. This study is part of a larger evaluation study of CAL in science and a full report of this particular study is available (Jones and O'Shea, 1981a).

CICERO tutorials can be used at any of the university's regional study centres which have terminals (currently 170) and are therefore theoretically available whenever the study centre is open, although students are advised to book in advance.

For each tutorial, a set of 'profile questions' relating to a specific block of the course is sent to students to answer at home: the answers to these diagnostic questions provide information about students' conceptual strengths and weaknesses related to specific objectives of the block and course. The completed answer form is taken to the study centre, the programme accessed and the answers typed in. Further questions may be asked to verify the diagnosis made and, according to the students' answers, advice and remedial help may be given. So, in an interactive form, the system offers the student a means of evaluating his or her understanding and further assistance if required. For the student unable to get to the terminal, a 'postal' version is available which provides diagnostic advice based on the profile questions, but cannot, of course, enter into further dialogue. To use this a student posts the answer form and receives a print-out within a few days.

We wanted to try to answer the question we posed earlier: 'How is the project perceived from the client's point of view—what are its salient and critical features affecting its acceptability?' and to consider what changes might be required (and how to implement them) in the light of the information we would collect.

Caste Study Methodology

We were broadly following the idiographic and illuminative approach discussed earlier, which does not prescribe a 'standard methodological package'. The evaluator must be eclectic and use whatever tools are at his or her disposal which may illuminate the situation.

Our methods included:

- An initial questionnaire sent to students, assessing intended use, expectations and attitudes.
- Questionnaires *built into* interactive tutorials and sent with the postal tutorials.
- Interviews with staff and students at a residential summer school.
- A final questionnaire sent to students following up earlier open-ended ones.

Case Study Results

Our main finding was a surprise: it seemed that the majority of factors influencing the decision to use or not to use the tutorials were not related to perceived educational benefits but turned out to be more affective in quality.

Students started off with realistic expectations of how they might benefit, and these included: diagnosing and correcting weak points, immediate feedback, remedial help, and a useful revision tool. Those who had used the system felt they had benefited in exactly these ways, yet use was low and the attrition rate high!

TABLE 8.3

Negative Factors in Using Computers

Factor	%
'Bad' computer experiences	23%*
Scared of using the terminal	12%*
Embarrassed at using in front of other students	13%

* Both these figures may under-represent the situation, as they only include those students who report 'strong agreement' with the statement.

Seeking out students who had not used the system, we interviewed 53 students at a residential summer school. These students reported a number of 'off-putting' experiences with computers and also revealed that many of them were scared of using a terminal and embarrassed at using it in front of other students. This was followed up in a final questionnaire. Table 8.3 give the percentage of respondents who reported strong agreement with the sentiments summarised in the table.

How Our Evaluation Study Affected Decision-Making

Although students were realistic in their expectation of how they might benefit from using CICERO, their views of the problems associated with its use were realistic too, and so take-up is low.

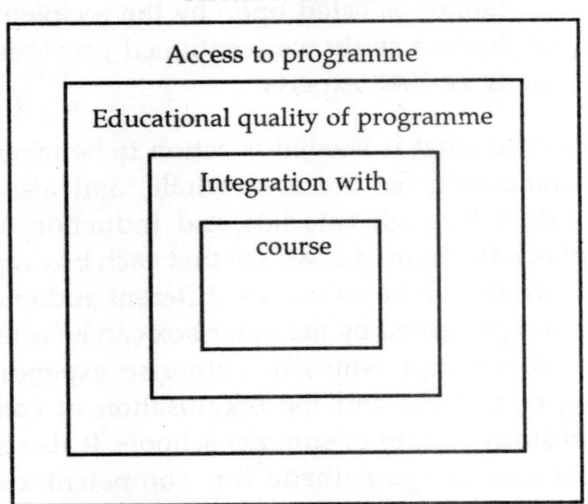

Figure 8.6. A View of CAL as the 'Chinese Box Puzzle'

The situation can be summarised as a number of barriers which students have to get through. From Figure 6 (taken from Jones and O'Shea, 1981b) we see that students must cope with access to terminals and to the programmes before the quality of the programme becomes a consideration. The point we want to make here is not that particular results of this study were surprising, but that some of these results would not have been obtained if a standard evaluation of educational cost-effectiveness had been carried out. For example, we discovered that some students were scared of terminals and embarrassed at using them in front of other students, by interviewing students who had not used the system. Students who did not admit to these feelings in open-ended questionnaires revealed this information in interviews. We were subsequently able to follow this up by telling students that we knew of instances of fear and embarrassment and asking them whether this applied to them.

This particular approach also reveals another aspect of our approach, which is that the discovery of widespread fear of computers cannot be acted upon by the recipients of the 'standard' evaluation study we mentioned previously, who would normally be CAL experts.

In this case what is needed is action to be taken by the Student Computing Service as a whole, and also by our regional tutors through tutorials and induction sessions. Referring back to Figure 8.6, we see that each box represents a problem which can be solved by different audiences. The information represented by the outer box can be acted on by university committees who can authorise expenditure on computing equipment and the organisation of computing facilities at study centres or summer schools. It also points to the importance of sympathetic but competent computer induction meetings—which lies in the hands of our regional staff.

'Access to programmes'—our next box—can be improved by such practices as always accessing the Help facility in programmes in the same way, and by giving users lists of options to choose from, to reduce their memory load. (The latter is usually referred to as providing Menu facilities—for obvious reasons.) These changes can be made by the Student Computing Service and some of these procedures are already, in fact, being implemented.

The inner box deals with the integration of the CAL material with the overall course and, in practise, the only group who can respond are the course team. In the past, the role of CAL in courses and in the university's organisational structure has been open to debate. Despite attempts to draw in the subject experts, both the production and maintenance of CAL lay with the CAL personnel in the Student Computing Service and this created certain problems. (This problem is not confined to CAL—Kirkup (1981) comments that the evaluation of courses is often perceived as being the sole business of the evaluator(s) as opposed to the course team.)

Finding the Audience

However, as information from our evaluation became available and was disseminated, potential clients from a particular faculty (Science) made themselves known to the evaluators. This led to the formation of a CAL in science evaluation group which includes members from the Science Faculty, the Institute of Educational Technology, and the Student Computing Service. The different mechanisms adopted by this group for reaching different clients include: internal technical reports; workshops; and reports to the Science Faculty board and to other boards and committees.

One result of our eclectic evaluation strategy is that it has helped to establish who the different audiences in the university are, and has also led to increased awareness of the role of and use of CAL in the university.

The main virtue of the evaluation process described here is that the various audiences addressed have a much greater potential for impact on the university's total CAL provision than individual CAL authors, who are only able to improve particular CAL programmes and are unable to affect other aspects of the total CAL context such as collective student attitudes and the mythology surrounding the use of computers and CAL.

9

SIMULATION AND GAMES

Introduction

Simulations and games, in many forms and for many subjects, are among the most recent innovations in instructional technique. Some are hardly "new media", however, because they are as simple and familiar as card or board games. Others involve technical equipment for use in transmitting facts and principles about their subjects of study. This chapter begins with a definition of simulation and considers ways in which simulations differ from conventional role-playing games. Then it reviews the purposes and forms of games and simulations, principally in the social sciences. Following this description of current uses, it summarises evidence appraising the impact of these new techniques as educational devices. Finally, it offers several recommendations for research and development.

What Are Simulation and Games?

A simulation is a miniature representation of a large-scale system or process (R. E. Dawson, 1963, pp. 1-3; Brody, 1963b, pp. 191-96). Laboratories provide arenas in which macro-processes are reduced in scale and complexity so that a teacher or student may manipulate the model of reality when he cannot manipulate reality itself. Biological, chemical, and physical laboratories are the original institutional forms for simulation. Test tunnels for small-scale models of planes, weapons, and other machines are newer examples of simulation. Training installations on miliary and naval bases include simulated use of weapons in confined spaces, but with the appearances and context of the real situations to which they correspond.

Simulations are also "dynamic" or "operating" models, as opposed to static or pictorial representations. Simulation and games usually imply use of replicas in phased sequences, and opportunities for change and development are present during all sequences.

This review of simulations is confined to social simulations—that is, representations of social processes as distinguished from physical or biological ones. A few of the social processes for which simulations and games have been devised are politics, economics, education, opinion formation, decision making, and administration.

Although we shall use the terms "simulation" and "games" interchangeably, some writers distinguish them according to the ratio of manual to computer activity. "Games" usually designates activities that are highly computerised. We shall not insist upon this distinction.

We should note that games and simulation do not necessarily bear any relationship to game theory. The theory of games consists of mathematical assumptions about behavior under specified circumstances of conflict. Games and simulation refer to social processes that are not necessarily subject to the kinds of theorising contained in game theory.

How Does Simulation Differ from Mock Congresses and Model United Nations?

Many high schools and colleges sponsor mock political conventions, mock congresses, moot courts, and model U.N.'s to impart information about important political activities. The American Legion annually holds week-long meetings of Boys' State and Girls' State throughout the United States, followed by Boys' Nation and Girls' Nation in Washington.

In all these activities students play out the central characteristics of different political institutions. Many of these activities can be conducted on a mass basis, with hundreds of people participating (some prominently, others peripherally), either during several days or weeks or in a shorter period of time.

The simulations we shall mention differ from these role-playing events precisely in the extent to which role-playing occurs in them. Although some games or simulations involve a relatively high degree of role-playing, they have even less of it than the mass mock conventions or congresses. Simulations tend to formalise and programme various aspects of the systems that they represent; that is to say, they permit less flexibility than do the free-wheeling mass conventions. Simulations concentrate more on the processes by which decisions are taken and devote less attention to the institutionalised and particular procedures of conventions or congresses. They require the participant to engage more in the dynamic interaction of the system and expect less of him in the way of second-guessing or of playing the role of a particular person or position.

Controversy abounds about the appropriateness of role-playing, but, in general, simulators distrust the student's or teacher's capacity to "dope out" the personality of a foreign leader, a state party chairman, or a similar figure (Greenlaw, Herron, and Rawdon, 1962, pp. 10-13). Instead, simulations emphasise the role as it interacts with other roles, and they require the participant to respond as he himself feels required to respond.

The de-emphasis of role-playing, the highlighting of process factors, and the formalising of programmes for the conduct of the simulation constitute the essential distinguishing characteristics of the new developments in simulation as compared with the more conventional mock programmes. These characteristics reflect the growth of knowledge in the study of decision and political processes, as opposed to the use of knowledge of formal procedures of particular institutions. In these respects, the simulation and games to be discussed here differ considerably from mock congresses and model United Nations.

Classification of Games and Simulation

Purposes

Although the original impetus for games came from professions interested largely in practical application of knowledge and therefore in developing games for instruction, many games and simulations are essentially research instruments. Indeed, with the exception of war and business games, most instructional simulations have grown out of games developed to investigate a particular system or process. Researchers usually have been ahead of teachers in developing these devices, and once the subject matter has been modeled in the form of a simulation, it has then been possible to teach the subject in a supposedly more challenging and more effective manner. Although this essay does not deal with simulations as research enterprises, it should be noted that in simulation activities a separate but equal policy segregating instruction and research may be unfortunate. Teachers will find it useful to be familiar with the latest models and simulations in their subjects in order to provide the best instruction possible for their students.

Instructional Uses of Games Include Both Teaching and Training

Teaching usually means the transmission of knowledge about subject matter through operational models. Training usually means the transmission of information or prerequisites for a particular role in professional or business life. In practice, simulation for teaching is likely to be found in the social sciences with a liberal arts or a general education orientation. Training activities are likely to be emphasised in professional and technical schools, where the objective is to prepare individuals for specialised tasks, such as business or educational administration.

The question is open whether simulations for teaching are appropriate for simulations for training. Indeed, with respect to the study of public affairs, one way wonder whether a simulation of a local government or of foreign policy making should be the same for supplementing a college course in political science and for an intensive short course for city managers or foreign service offers. Research has yet to discover whether training for policy making and training for citizenship are similar, or whether they differ sufficiently to require different educational programmes.

Games for War, Business, Politics, and Other Subjects

War games are the earliest known effort to train practitioners through the use of operating models of their field tasks. In the late nineteenth century the Prussian general staff developed war games, and military organisations in other countries have since adopted them on varying scales (Gorlitz, 1956; Greenlaw, Herron, and Rawdon, 1962, pp. 7-8, n. 15; Kahn, 1962, pp. 155-72).

Undoubtedly, the most influential and active diffusion of games has been in business education and training. There are probably as many business games as there are other forms of simulation put together. The one hundred business games developed since 1956 vary in their complexity and in the content that they teach. Games are available for training prospective businessmen in many aspects of commerce and administration, including marketing, production, inventorying, investment, personnel, and organisational decision making. Some business games are relatively simple operations that can be played largely with paper and pencil, in or out of the classroom, for short periods of time. Others are highly developed, large-scale, complex games that extend over a semester or a year and involve faculty members as well as students. The most sophisticated and best known of the complex games is the Carnegie Tech Management Game. It could hardly be said to be representative of business games, but it is doubtless the leading example at the present stage in the development of games (Dill, Jackson, and Sweeney, 1961, pp. 44-80).

The Carnegie Tech Management Game is the most complicated of the business simulations, and probably the most expensive. It consists of three teams of five to ten players, each team representing a detergent company. Teams make one hundred to three hundred decisions every "month" for future operations of their firms. Decisions cover raw material orders; additions to work force and overtime to expedite production, inventory, marketing, advertising, and consumer surveys. When the decisions have been made, they are entered in a computer that contains a model of the economy, industry, and company. The computer determines, according to this model, the outcomes of each company's decisions. Results are then reported, and team begin a new period of decision making.

The game requires analytic or intellectual tasks, represented in the decisions that must be made. Although the model for assessing the outcomes of the competing teams decisions is deterministic, its complexity precludes devising an optimal strategy. In addition to requiring performance of analytic tasks, the game allows within each team for roles that are differentiated enough to offer organisational tasks of some complexity. Interpersonal skills and relations, coordination, communication, and other organisational characteristics are important.

New business games frequently appear; often, they are reported in daily papers as well as in scholarly or technical journals. One implication of the increasing use and design of games is that, for one who knows the basic characteristics of his field, games are not necessarily difficult to design. In fact, it deserves to be stressed that teachers need not be frightened by games. Often the prospect of using computers, devising arithmetic formulas to state the parameters of a game, and other parts of the design seem forbidding and impossible to people whose experience has been primarily traditional classroom instruction. Nevertheless, games unquestionably vary in their simplicity, and the evidence from the business games indicates that one need not be inhibited from designing some games simply because one lacks highly complex equipment.

One of the subjects in which games have proliferated most quickly is politics. Most of the political games used for teaching or training were originally designed for research. The influence of the RAND Corporation in developing games for playing out potential political and diplomatic strategies was responsible for the first games for teaching (Goldhamer and Speier, 1959). These games were followed by innovations at Massachusetts Institute of Technology (Bloomfield and Padelford, 1959), San Francisco State College (McClelland, 1959), and the University of Wisconsin (Cohen, 1962). Such exercises ordinarily deal with particular political problems in international diplomacy. For example, scenarios re- or pre-create situations comparable to some past or prospective international situations. Various games have played out the East-West conflict over Berlin, a revolt in a Latin American country, and similar "real world" events. The RAND, M.I.T., and Wisconsin games adopt real-world names for their countries and sometimes assign decision makers to represent particular international figures. These games also have umpires or referees to rule on the appropriateness or realism of strategies that players propose. The M.I.T. game has been played with students at other New England institutions, providing a league for diplomacy to correspond to leagues for athletics. These games can be played at a single point in time, as during a weekend, or over extended periods in the manner of chess-by-mail. The most frequent practice, however, has been that of playing the games on a college campus on a Friday afternoon, Friday evening and Saturday morning, with time at the end of the game reserved for discussing its relation to the purposes of the course that it supplements.

A different simulation of international relations was designed by Guetzkow and his associates at Northwestern (Guetzkow, 1963). Unlike the RAND and M.I.T. games, the Northwestern Inter-Nation Simulation does not identify its nations with real-world nations. Rather than calling a country Great Britain or Poland, the Inter-Nation Simulation creates the fictitious names Algo, Ergo, Ingo, and so on. Further, titles for roles are decontaminated, and the aseptic title Central Decision Maker replaces that of prime minister or president; foreign ministers are referred to as External Decision Makers, and military officers are called Force Decision Makers. Real-world concepts such as GNP are replaced by Basic Capability, public opinion polls give way to an index of Validator Satisfaction, and concepts of democracy and government control are replaced by Decision Latitude.

The abstract character of the Inter-Nation Simulation is explained by its origins as a research instrument. Guetzkow and his colleagues proposed to simulate what they regarded as central features of inter-nation processes without regard to cultural and historical contexts. In other words, in their initial efforts they tried to control for certain features that vary greatly in the international environment and to concentrate on other basic characteristics of international systems. Without denying the importance of the cultural heritage and historical precedents of a nation, they attempted to hold such factors constant during their simulations.

Thus, when simulation was converted from research to instruction, it was already in a decontaminated form. The aseptic character of the Inter-Nation Simulation has several advantages over the rich, real-world quality of the RAND political exercises. For one thing, college students are simply not qualified to play Kosygin or Johnson. Although, when they are given such an assignment, they may read up on the person they are to play, still one runs the risk that they will "bootleg" as much inaccurate or irrelevant motivation as correct motivation into their performance of a world dignitary's role. Although playing an anonymous role may not encourage the student to extend his knowledge to the biographies of current leaders and their policies, it also may not lead him astray as he plays out the roles in the simulation. In fact, he will be challenged to play the role as he personally would play it, gaining some insight into his own performance and considering which model of diplomacy and negotiation he would like to adopt for himself.

Broadly speaking, all simulations are role playing to one degree or another. One may play the role of politician as opposed to some other role. He may represent a decision maker from a real-world country such as Brazil or a fictitious one such as Omne. He may represent a particular figure or position. All simulations involve some acting out of roles, but we shall reserve role playing to identify those games in which greatest emphasis is put upon close correspondence with the person who holds an identifiable office in a real-world state.

Compromises may be found between the extensive role playing of the RAND and M.I.T. diplomatic games and the Guetzkow nonrole-playing Inter-Nation Simulation. For example, Wood, also of M.I.T., has designed a local politics game in which the names of cities and participants do not correspond to the real world, but in which the parameters and variables are conventional and identifiable in the real world (Wood, n.d.). The vote in Wood's simulation corresponds to the vote in the precinct, whereas in Guetzknow's game, elections are represented by conceptual formula that has no operational counterpart in world politics.

In discussing business games, we said they are manageable enough so that independent investigators and teachers can design games for their own purposes. However time consuming the design of the first political games, they are simple enough to be picked up readily and used by people who did not design them. For example, Guetzknow's Inter-Nation Simulation has been used by several at his Northwestern colleagues, none of whom was intimately connected with the design of the game. Bretton and Jacobson, of the University of Michigan, adapted Inter-Nation Simulation to their large international relations class after one day's visit to Northwestern, and they in turn were able to conduct a day's run of simulation for a seminar in national security policy at the Ohio State University. Orbell and colleagues at the University of North Carolina organised an eight-hour run with the aid of published materials and without any outside assistance. Preparation, of course, requires careful study of documents as well as trial runs, but the fundamentals of a particular simulation can be grasped without much prior exposure to the technique. Unfortunately, at this writing an adequate "how to do it" manual is not yet available for interested persons, so that diffusion principally on word of mouth and personal visits.

Probably the most vigorous and technically advanced work in developing simulations for teaching is in progress at Johns Hopkins University, under the direction of Coleman. Coleman's first game, an election campaign game (Coleman and Waldorf, 1963), was designed for research and commercial uses, but it is now one of a series of teaching games that includes a career-choice game and a legislative game.

Coleman's model of high school behavior starts from the assumption that each boy and girl attempts to maximise his self-esteem (Coleman, 1962). Each student may be assumed to have his own level of self-esteem, and as he makes choices about time, friends, activities, and the like, he increases or decreases his estimate of self. In the game of high school, each player takes the role of a high school student. Parents and teachers are represented through the calculations prepared by those who designed the game. Players make both long-term and daily choices of activities, and a choice of persons' judgments to pay attention to. As these decisions are made over an extended period of time, the consequences gradually unfold. Results are reported to the players, and they may use the knowledge of previous outcomes in making future decisions.

The purpose of this game is well summarised by Coleman, and, indeed, it is the central purpose of most educational simulations: "It allows a boy or girl to act through situations *before* he faces them in real life, to see the *indirect and long-range consequences* of choices he may make, *before* it is too late, and he must face the consequences in real life" (Coleman, 1962, p. 4).

The International Business Machines Corporation several years ago began to consider the implications of new simulated learning environments for investment. Its interest was not in programmed learning through teaching machines but in computer and other technological developments that might simulate learning environments on an individually paced basis. In the summer of 1962, IBM awarded ten summer fellowships to outstanding teachers in the York-town Heights school system (more than one hundred applied) and organised a seminar in which each teacher began to design a simulation for this specialty. Subjects on which work was done included the development of Sumerian civilisation, qualitative analysis in the study of light in an elementary science course, principles of art discrimination, instrumental music, and French through a simulated United Nations environment. Progress in developing simulations for each of these courses has been uneven, but by the end of 1964 the Sumerian game was ready for experimental use and could be played from a typewriter terminal hooked to a 7090 computer. The qualitative analysis simulation was also made ready in late 1964, and its materials were tested at a California teachers college.

Impact

The popularity and increasing use of games and simulation are apparent from the record since 1956, when the first business game was designed. What is less evident is whether games serve the purposes attributed to them, whether they do so more or less effectively than alternative modes of instruction, and whether they have any unanticipated consequences. Questions of this sort call for "quasi-experimental" research that varies and controls for hypotentically important characteristics of games (D.T. Campbell, 1957; D.T. Campbell and Stanley, 1963). Designs for such research are often difficult to formulate and more difficult to execute in practice. Moreover, so many different games exist that it is impossible to evaluate and compare anything except the central features of a few simulations.

Should Games Be Evaluated?

In many quarters, even among professors of education, low priority is given to the systematic and controlled evaluation and comparison of teaching techniques and supplementary aids. For some the disinclination to study teaching methods is part of the popular anti-educationist syndrome. Barzun (1963), in justifiably praising William James's *Talks to Teachers,* goes so far as to assert that book "still contains nearly all that anyone need know of educational `method'." For others, the lack of enthusiasm for comparative studies of methods stems from the plethora of negative results and "no differences" found in early experiments. Indeed, experimental devices that occupy only a marginal part of a student's time may scarcely be expected to have much observable or unusual impact upon his learning.

Part of the reluctance also comes from physical and natural scientists who retreat from extending scientific methods to the study of human affairs, and from social scientists who hesitate to study their own teaching with the same rigor they apply to industry, government, and other objects of social investigation. Mayer (1963, p. 168) summarises the philosophy of the physicists, all distinguished researchers, who revolutionised the teaching of secondary and college physics.

At not time did the scientists place any great weight on "scientific measurements" of what they were accomplishing. They did work with the Educational Testing Service to design a test to assure that PSSC students would not be penalised in the bureaucratic world of admissions and to guarantee themselves against gross over-optimism about what they were accomplishing. But impressionistic, intuitional feedback from those who were teaching and learning the material weighed much more heavily than test results when the committee sat down to analyse how it was doing. The committee is still analysing and revising on the basis of judgment.

Impressions, intuition, and judgment are unquestionably sources for discovering ideas in education, as in physics; but as they would not be relied on for demonstrable verification of the movement of electrons, why should they be overweighted in verifying the advantages of one curriculum or teaching device over another?

This hesitation to evaluate is not confined to physical scientists; one finds it among hardheaded economists, operations researchers, and other social scientists who profess science. I recall observing this at the first teaching conference I attended several years ago. One of the large foundations had invested considerable money in encouraging business schools to design and use games in their curricula. Unfortunately, perhaps, no evaluation was built into the budget for this large programme in gaming, but the foundation did have the good judgment to call together some of the people who had used games to pool their personal experience. Because of my interest in political games and in their evaluation, I was invited as the one outsider. I am afraid I made myself more of an outsider by offering homilies about the importance of knowing what we are doing and asking what evidence is available for the claims for games, evidence of the quality we would expect in out own technical work, whether economics, business, or political science. The number of evaluations has not increased, apparently; yet such research on instruction seems to me the soundest way to understand what we are actually doing, to avoid fads, and to give students the fairest and best available mode of instruction that reliable knowledge affords.

Games at the Secondary and Elementary Levels

Simulation of the simple games variety promises to be particularly appropriate for elementary and early secondary education in civics. Pre-college instruction in government, citizenship, and public affairs is notoriously unsophisticated. The discrepancy between scholarly descriptions of political processes, on the one hand, and the public school teacher's description of the checks and balance system, on the other, is likely to be greater than that between reliable scientific knowledge of family matters, courtship, and marriage, and the increasingly frank treatment of these subjects in schools. Gradually, realistic discussions of rectitude have lost their taboos, but politics usually remains outside the domain of the schools.

While teachers and administrators gingerly ignore the topic, boys and girls nevertheless acquire perceptions of politics, and attitudes and values about government. Recent research on political socialisation documents that preadolescence is usually the critical period for the development of political interests and orientations (Easton and Hess, 1961, 1962; Greenstein, 1965; Hyman, 1959, chaps. 2-4; Wahlke *et al.*, 1962). If the finding is borne out in the next stages of research, we shall have cause to wonder whether student senate campaigns, college internships, and mock congresses can do more than confirm the already politically inclined in whatever values they have previously acquired.

If education in politics is to reach more than select group, it will have to begin earlier and/or take a form that will reach many more youngsters than can be affected by campaigns, internships, and mock conventions.

At Johns Hopkins, Coleman and Boocock have evaluated the use of their election simulation in four Baltimore high schools. In two schools the game was played during a two-week period, and in a pair of similar schools the game was not used at all. Student interest and performance at the four sites were compared.

Although there was little evidence that the presence or absence of the game affected students' learning of factual material, considerable data supported the impressions of teachers and investigators that students liked the game and that it increased their interest and involvement in course work. The researcher's explanation for the absence of a relationship between use of simulation and learning about social studies is that the game was not intimately related to course materials. Nevertheless, little doubt exists (as indicated both in questionnaires filled out by students themselves and by observations taken by the researches) that student motivations were affected by the game. Moreover, attitudes toward politics also seem to have been affected, with realistic and critical attitudes increasing among the students participating in the game (Boocock, 1963).

Secondary schools may well be the most appropriate settings for simulations about politics and public affairs. Assuming that adolescence is a critical stage in the acquisition of political orientations, this may be the point at which students ought to be challenged to think through critically their choices of party affiliation, values, and the like. To the extent that they motivate students and penetrate their developing but unconscious "set" toward politics, games may be effective instruments for acquiring self-insight.

A Comparison of Simulation and Case Studies in College

In 1959 Alger began using Inter-Nation Simulation in undergraduate international relations and international organisation classes at Northwestern. He solicited student comments and criticisms and reviewed various uses of other games and simulations as supplementary teaching devices. On the basis of this initial exploration, which extended over parts of nearly two years, it was possible to formulate a series of hypotheses about the effects of simulation in the classroom (Alger, 1963; Robinson, 1961). To strengthen the devil's advocacy, we considered a strong challenge to simulation—the much tried but never evaluated case-study method, for nearly a century a staple of the law schools, and more recently a popular adjunct to curricula in business and public administration, legislative politics, decision making, and other subjects. In planning a quasi experimental comparison of simulation and cases, we knew that our evaluation of one form of simulation, even if done in several courses with different teachers, could not necessarily represent all simulations. Accordingly, we were hopeful of studying hypothetical effects that had been commented upon by users of other games.

The six hypothetical effects that we investigated are among nine mentioned during the Tulane University Conference on Business Games (Dill, Jackson, and Sweeney, 1961) and eleven listed in a review by Cohen and Rhenman (1961). Five of our six alleged effects fall within the Tulane list and the Cohen and Rhenman list, while seven from the Tulane list and ten from the Cohen and Rhenman list can be translated to ours. This led us to think we were studying some central hypotheses and that our comparison of Inter-Nation Simulation and political case studies might be relevant to the evaluation of other games.

Below we will review six hypothetical effects of simulation and then report preliminary efforts to see whether they are in fact produced by simulation and differ in any way from those produced by the case method.

Interest The major claim for gaming or simulation is that the method heightens student interest, thus enhancing learning. Snow (1960, p. 23) recommends putting the student in the position of the original discoverer as a way of exciting him about science and enticing him to creative work. So far, most of the observations of motivation in simulations have been anecdotal, but the testimony of several directors of simulations is that motivation is strikingly increased by simulation. However, the reports are not uniform. At Carnegie Tech, where the business game extends throughout a semester and is the equivalent of one of five graduate courses, the game is disliked by some students. At the University of Wisconsin boredom and absenteeism were observed among students who occupied relatively unimportant roles in a political game (Cohen, 1962).

By interest we mean the student's involvement in the course. We assume that students who are highly interested will attend class more regularly, buy more reading materials and read more of them, participate in more peripheral activities such as lectures, and undertake more volunteer work than students who are not highly interested. When these assumptions about interest or involvement are clearly stated, a number of "nonreactive" instruments for measuring interest come to mind. Use of closed reserve materials in the library, attendance at nonrequired discussions or lectures, book purchases at local stores, student comparison of time spent on a course using simulation with courses not using it—all these are among possible devices for measuring interest. In addition, each course in likely to have a graduate teaching assistant who can act as informant, and teachers may find it useful to keep notes identifying the students who ask questions, stay after class, come to their offices, and exhibit other signs of interest.

Initially, we thought of interest only as an intervening variable, one of the mechanisms that produce learning of principles and facts. Even if we are not in the business of interesting students for interest's sake, it may be that different techniques differentially affect substantive interests, and therefore subsequent reading, and perhaps even career plans. This is what is meant when evaluators say that the effects may be long term. We tried in one experiment to follow up on two groups six weeks after their course ended and to give them tests for retention, as distinguished from tests of recall. However, the costs of seeking out the students, given all our other experimental commitments, led us to drop this important feature.

Feedback One of the most influential current theories of learning holds that reward for successful or approved action reinforces one in a way that encourages similar performance in subsequent situations. Simulation provides results of participants' decisions shortly after they are made, thus giving the student feedback, or evidence, of the quality of his decisions. This validating or nonvalidating mechanism is not ordinarily present in case studies, problem papers, class discussions, and other conventional learning methods, and it appears to have some of the effects of teaching machines.

Time is greatly compressed in games and simulation. Decisions are made hourly that represent real-world decisions of a month's or a year's duration. For example, in Inter-Nation Simulation budgets are prepared usually every sixty minutes, so that the fiscal year corresponds to an hour. Results are reported within a half-hour for use in making decisions in the next decision period. This feedback gives the student, or simulator, evidence of the appropriateness of his decisions. If the assumptions about "learning by doing," "learning through participation," and the like are right, students who experience simulation feedback ought to learn differently, at faster rates—and perhaps they ought to learn different things.

Explicitness Freudian psychology and psychoanalysis emphasise the value of rendering the implicit explicit. Individuals cope with their personal problems more adequately when they understand clearly the sources of the problems. Businessmen, teachers, and doctors supposedly improve their performances through others' reports on their work and through detailed discussions of their procedures, many not always noticed by themselves. Self-observation is a technique through which one may "escape *to* freedom" from practices one unconsciously pursues but would not consciously prefer (Lasswell, 1963, pp. 125-42, 224). Beginning scholars are advised to acquaint themselves with the choices available to them for approaching and treating their subjects: "the assumption is that these choices are likely to be wiser if they are made deliberately and self-consciously..." (Van Dyke, 1960, pp. vii-viii). In short, the hypothesis is that explicitness or awareness about one's position, role, problem, job, or situation improves one's performance.

Simulation and games allegedly make participants more explicit about what they are doing, seeing, or hearing. Students are then led to interpret their activities in terms of "principles" and "concepts" discussed in other course materials. Explicitness may be defined as the capacity to identify consciously elements of a problem in an analytic or technical sense. This skill is more than "knowing" the existence of an abstract quality or object, and more also than being able to define a term or a concept. It is not merely having a "feel" for a situation in the sense of experiencing insight through a sudden surprise or a "eureka" experience. It is the conscious recognition that a particular experience belongs to a certain class of phenomena; it is recognising the analogy between Event A and Class M. It is the skill to identify an object in a context and to be able to give it a technical label, which then throws the object open to interpretation in terms of the principles associated with the technical concept.

For example, Simon reports that "satisficing" is characteristic of alternative selection in problem solving and decision-making. to "satisfice" is to adopt the first solution or alternative that seems "good enough" to solve one's problem or decision; it is less "rational" than the optimal decision postulated by classical theories of economic and administrative decision making, but it is also more typical and more descriptive of human activity. Lectures or case materials may identify and stress this fact of decision making, and students may be able to define the term, match it with its definition in a list of definitions, or regurgitate it in an essay examination. Beyond this, however, one object of teaching is to help the student discover such behavior in its rich, manifold context.

The effects of simulation on students' interest, feedback, and explicitness may be regarded as intervening procedural mechanisms, which in turn have impact on the content of learning. The ultimate impact of simulation and other methods will be reflected in students' command of the principles of whatever subject they are studying and of the discrete factual information relevant to their inquiry.

Principles Learning of principles is general and structural; it is not confined to specialised content and issues. Such learning creates in the student's mind an abstract "model" of international politics, foreign policy processes, or whatever the field may be, without regard to specific policy issues such as aid to underdeveloped areas, the use of nuclear weapons, or the role of the Federal Communications Commission in regulating television.

Facts Factual learning refers to discrete bits of information, historical as well as contemporary. Lasswell (1960, p. 216) has remarked that in classroom simulation, "Motivations to study past events are kept high since the uses of history are demonstrated by the search for suggestive likenesses or differences."

Empathy Still another kind of learning concerns neither principles nor facts, but rather an appreciation of, or empathy for, the predicaments of the real-world decision makers. One form of empathy this experience usually results in is an increased capacity to take the participant's perspective in analysing or evaluating a decision or event. This is not to say that the student abandons a critic's viewpoint but only that he incorporates an additional datum, namely the participant's perspective, into his analysis.

Students who participated in the simulation called this effect to our attention. Frequently, they reported that, after representing a small country, they "understood" how small nations' representatives see the world, or that, after experiencing a communications breakdown in an overloaded information system, they could comprehend that organisational factors, not merely "original sin," can explain unwanted decisional outcomes.

Important as we think this effect, is, and confident as we are that some such mechanism is at work, our efforts to operationalise empathy repeatedly were unpromising. Finally, lest other aspects of the research be compromised, this variable was put aside.

Experimental Procedures

To evaluate claims for simulation, we chose three upper class courses at Northwestern in 1963-64. The first, "American foreign policy," had fifty-seven students; all attended two lectures weekly, thirty were in a three-hour simulation section, and twenty-seven were in a two-hour discussion of case studies. Subsequently, courses in international relations (forty-seven students) and administrative decision making (thirty students) were similarly subdivided.

The experimental procedure was the same throughout all courses. All students met together for two one-hour lectures each week; then one half attended a simulation section and the other half attended a case section. The simulation group met one afternoon weekly for three hours to participate in a simulated decision situation and to discuss the relevance of the simulation to the course; the case section met on another afternoon of approximately the same length of time to discuss cases and to relate them to other course materials. The assignments of students to sections were made during the first week of the courses on the basis of intelligence (as measured by scores on the Scholastic Aptitude Test), grade point average, and other personality characteristics on which data were collected at an early class meeting (i.e., motivations toward achievement, affiliation, power, and cognitive style).

Personal motivations toward or needs for achievement *(n ach)*, affiliation *(n aff)*, and power *(n power)* were measured by an adaptation of the Thematic Apperception Test developed by McClelland *et al.* (1953) and Atkinson (1958). Students were designated as high or low in need for achievement, high or low in need for affiliation, and high or low in need for power according to whether their scores fell above or below the class median.

Cognitive style refers to levels of abstractness concreteness in cognitive structure. Harvey, Hunt, and Schroder (1961) suggest that this level varies according to the "stimulus boundness of the individual." The more concrete the person's cognitive style, the more bound to the stimulus he is (i.e., the stimulus tends to dictate his response). The more abstract one's cognitive style (i.e., the less bound to the stimulus he is), the greater will be his ability to abstract relations from experience and organise them according to their interrelatedness. Cognitive style was measured by the Situational Interpretation Test, which ranks individuals by quartiles along a continuum from the most concrete to the most abstract. We will refer to the four groups as concrete, moderately concrete, moderately complex, and complex.

The personality variables listed above were selected for

several reasons. Fist, student motivations toward achievement and affiliation have been found to interact with teaching methods and practices in other educational experiments. If our research were to contribute to the continuing development of educational psychology, this decision seemed imperative. Second, these same motivations, together with motivations toward power, have a history of interest to political analysts, and as far as possible, we hoped to fit our teaching experiment to some of the continuing concerns of political theory. McClelland's (1961) study of the relation of *n ach, n aff,* and *n power* to economic growth is perhaps the most impressive demonstration of the relevance of these personality variables to politics. The theory and research inspired by Lasswell (1930, 1934, 1948; Rogow and Lasswell, 1963) on the relation of power and personality to politics constitutes another interest of political analysts, to which we hoped our work might not be unrelated. Third, Driver (1962) has studied the influence of variations in concreteness-abstractness of cognitive style on decision making in an earlier use of Inter-nation Simulation. If relations could be found between cognitive style and decision behaviour in simulation, it seemed reasonable to investigate hypothetical relations between cognitive style and learning in simulation.

Findings on Interest and Learning

We undertook to develop and use several measures of interest, assuming that interest is probably multidimensional and that findings supported by several measures deserve greater credibility than findings supported by single indicators. In all, we had ten measures of interest, including the students' reports of the amount of reading they did on the subject matter of the course, their comparison of their interest in the course with interest in others taken simultaneously, their perception of interest in political science, their preference for case or simulation, their attendance in class, their visits to the instructor's office, their use of special reading materials placed in the reserve room of the college library, their descriptive evaluation of the course at the end of term, and their rate of participation in lab section.

Data on these ten indicators of interest were available for twenty-three "subsets" among the participants in the three experimental courses. These subsets consist of all the students enrolled; all men; all women; men and women separately grouped according to high and low achievement, high and low affiliation, and high and low power; and men and women separately grouped in terms of their cognitive style.

When one lists the findings, as in Table 9.1, they seem to have no pattern. Certainly, neither simulation nor case is clearly more effective than the other in stimulating interest. And most certainly, the results do not fit the predictions, namely that simulation would be uniformly superior to case in exciting student interest and involvement. Nevertheless, an unexpected pattern emerges. Apparently, case is more successful than simulation in eliciting student interest as measured by students' *perceptions;* but measures of student *behaviour* indicate that simulation is more successful than case in affecting student interest and involvement.

Perceptions of Interest

Our way of eliciting perceptions of interest was to ask students a number of questions on a course evaluation questionnaire at the end of the term. This was administered at the last regular meeting of the course; the cover sheet instructed students to elect one of their number to collect the questionnaires and deliver them to the office of the secretary of the department of political science, where they would be held until the instructor filed his grades for the course. This procedure was adopted to assure students that their evaluations of the course would not influence their grades. As far as we could tell, students did not doubt the integrity of this procedure, and in each course they co-operated by responsibly handling the deliver of the questionnaires.

TABLE 9.1

Summary of Ten Interest Measures for Twenty-Three Groups

Groups	*Perceptual Measures*					*Behavioural Measures*				
	A[a]	B	C	D	E	F	G	H	I	J
All students	*b*				PC			PS		PS
All males					PC		PC	PS		PS
All females					PC			PS		PS
MEN										
High *n ach*					PC				PS	PS
Low *n ach*					PC		PC	PS	PC	PS
High *n aff*		PS			PC			PS	PS	PS
Low *n aff*					PC				PS	PS
High *n power*					PC			PS	PS	PS
Low *n power*					PC		PC	PS	PS	PS
Concrete cognitive style					PS	PC			PS	PS
Moderately concrete cognitive style					PS				PS	PS
Moderately complex cognitive style					PC					
Complex cognitive style					PC			PS	PS	PS
WOMEN										
High *n ach*					PC			PS	PC	PS
Low *n ach*					PC			PS	PC	PS
High *n aff*					PC				PS	PS
Low *n aff*					PC			PS	PC	PS
High *n power*			PS		FC	PS			PS	PS
Low *n power*					PC			PS	PS	PS
Concrete cognitive style					PC			PS		PS
Moderately concrete cognitive style			PC		PC		PC		PC	PS

	A	B	C	D	E	F	G	H	I	J
Moderately complex cognitive style					PC				PS	PS
Complex cognitive style			PS		PC					PS

[a] Columns correspond to the following variables:

A. Perception of amount of reading on subject (differences analysed by chi square test)
B. Perception of relative course interest (chi square test)
C. Perception of interest in course (chi square test)
D. Perception of interest in political science (chi square test)
E. Perception of interest in lab section (no test of significance)
F. Behavioural interest expressed by reading (t test)
G. Behavioural interest expressed by visiting professor (t test)
H. Behavioural interest expressed through attendance (t test)
I. Course evaluation essay (number of cases too small for test of significance on any groups except all students, all men, all women)
J. Behavioural interest expressed by rate of participation in lab section (t test)

[b] A blank line indicates no significant difference between case and simulation sections in amount of interest observed by indicators for this variable. PC (pro-case) indicates significantly more interest in case section, except in Column E, for which no test of significance was possible for small groups. PS (pro-simulation) indicates significantly more interest in simulation section. 0.05 level of probability was used to define significance.

As Table 9.1 (Columns A—E) indicates, four of the five perceptual measures of interest did not discriminate between simulation and case sections. We found virtually no differences between the two in students' perception of the amount of reading they did for the course, or in their interest in the course relative to other courses, or in their estimates of the degree to which interest in the subject had been stimulated by the course or how much their interest in political science had been stimulated by the course.

Perception of interest in lab section. The one discriminating perceptual measure of interest was a question asking the student to indicate, regardless of the lab section in which he participated, his preference between simulation and case. The course evaluation form asked:

Had you been able to choose the type of lab session to attend at the beginning of this quarter, which would you have preferred? Case Study Lab_____. Simulation Lab_____. Would your preference be different now? Yes_____. No_____.

We computed, for each group, the percentage who preferred case and the percentage who preferred simulation. The percentage who preferred the section other than the one to which they had been assigned was subtracted from the percentage who preferred the section in which they actually participated. This yielded a measure of perceived interest in or preference for one section over the other; those who voted for the section opposite theirs presumably showed less interest than those who voted of the section in which they had been members. The data for all students are displayed in Table 9.2. Only two groups, the men with greatest and with moderate cognitive concreteness, preferred simulation to case. The range of percentage differences in favour of the case was from 1 to 75 per cent. No test of significance was applied to these data, but the interpretation is clearly that students perceive case as preferable to simulation.

Behaviours of Interest

To the extent that students' perceptions of these two supplementary teaching methods vary, they favour the case. It is striking, however, that observation of actual course behaviour, i.e., participation, indicates just the reverse—that more interest is displayed by students in simulation than in case. Three of the five behavioural measures revealed important differences between the two sections.

Behavioural interest expressed through attendance. The instructors did not keep attendance records at lectures, but observers who were present at each section meeting noted who attended, who remained after the formal close of the section meeting, who was tardy, and who left before the official termination hour. Each individual was given an attendance score consisting of the number of times he attended his section, plus the times he remained afterward, minus the times he was tardy or left before termination.

TABLE 9.2

Section Preference (Number of Students)

Section	*Section Preference*			*Total*
	Case	*Simulation*	*No Response*	
Simulation	26	44	1	71
Case	46	15	2	63
Total	72	59	3	134

This objective measure of interest revealed that in twelve of the twenty-three subsets the simulation section displayed more interest than the case section. This was true for the aggregate of all students, for all men, for all women, and for men with low *n ach,* men with high *n aff,* men with high *n power,* men with low *n power,* men with the most complex cognitive style, women with high *n ach,* women with low *n aff,* women with low *n power,* and women with most concrete cognitive style. Table 9.3a, b, and c reports data for all students, all men, and all women.

Behavioural interest expressed through course evaluation essay. At the end of the course evaluation form, students were asked an open-ended question to which they could respond with any additional comments about the course and the section in which they participated. In contrast to the perception of interest questions, there was no element of forced choice about this item; indeed, students were invited rather than instructed to answer. Thus whether they commented, and the direction of their comment, is a manifestation more of behaviour than of perception. The question read:

> If you feel there are things about American Foreign Policy [or International Relations, or Administrative Process] which you had thought you'd like to get out of this course and didn't, would you please list them in the following space.
>
> The rest of this page is for any additional comments which you would care to make.

TABLE 9.3

Attendance Scores

Section	*Mean Attendance Score*
	A. All Students
Simulation	57.3
Case	48.7
Difference	8.6[a]
	B. Men
Simulation	58.6
Case	50.4
Difference	8.2[a]
	C. Women
Simulation	54.8
Case	45.4
Difference	9.4[a]

a Significant at 0.05 level as determined by t test.

These responses were analysed for the presence of positive comment, negative comment, or a mixture of the two. For sixteen of the subsets, students in simulation made more positive comments than students in case, but in four of the subsets the case section students offered more positive comments. The data for all subsets are not subject to tests of significance because of the reduced number for analysis, owing to the fact that students could abstain from commenting if they so desired. We have reported the direction of their comments, either positive or negative, although for the sixty-four students writing either strictly positive or strictly negative comments, the differences are not significant, as Table 9.4 shows.

TABLE 9.4

Comments (Positive or Negative), by Section

Section	*Comment*		*Total*
	Positive	*Negative*	
Simulation	15	20	35
Case	11	18	29
Total	26	38	64

Chi square = 0.167, not significant at 0.05 level.

Behavioural interest expressed by rate of participation in lab section. Rate of participation was computed by counting the number of communications of each student in the lab sections and dividing by the number of lab sections he attended. The number of participations per section attended was overwhelmingly greater for simulation than for case. In fact, the differences between the means for simulation and case for twenty-two of the twenty-three subsets were statistically significant; only men with moderately complex cognitive style did not have significantly higher rates of participation than the corresponding men in the case section.

In one sense, this finding is not surprising, because simulation sections include national conferences, bilateral and multilateral conferences, and other small group sessions in which the opportunities for student participation might be expected to be more numerous than in traditional discussion sections. It is not trivial, however, because the promotion of activity may be one of the key ways of motivating students.

Summary

The major conclusions from the behavioural measures of interest are (1) that they are more effective than the perceptual measures in discriminating between simulation and case sections; (2) that three of the measures—attendance, course evaluation essay, and rate of participation—indicate greater interest among simulation sections; and (3) that these behavioural measures differ from the one perceptual measure in the direction of student interest.

Learning Outcomes

The most fundamental reason for studying teaching methods is to determine what methods under what conditions favourably affect student learning. If different methods do not have different effects, one can leave to taste and cost the selection of one method rather than another. If, however, for some kinds of students, one method is more effective for learning than another, the presumption rests with that method, assuming that cost and other factors are equal.

We undertook to measure student performance for two kinds of learning: mastery of factual materials and understanding of principles. For each course, we administered equivalent tests for fact mastery and learning of principles at the beginning of the quarter and again at the end. The pretest-posttest design allowed us to analyse covariance to determine whether teaching method is related to changes in learning during the course rather than relying only in difference in performance on the final exams.

We predicted better performance on both fact mastery and learning of principles by simulation sections, and we expected that any exceptions to this generalisation would relate tc particular personality subsets. An analysis of co-variance, however, revealed no statistically significant differences between simulation and case for any of the twenty-three subsets with respect to fact mastery. The same was true of all sets on the objective part of the examination on principles. That is, no statistically significant difference in pre- and posttest performance was evidenced for any of the sets. Virtually the same finding held for performance on the essay part of the examination; only one set, men with low *n aff*, fared significantly better in simulation than in case on the essay on principles.

In short, simulation and case hardly differ in their relation to performance of these two learning outcomes, fact mastery and understanding of principles. If simulation and case differ at all, assuming internal validity of our procedures, the differences are complex and indirect. No simple and direct associations between method and learning were found. Let us now consider interest as an intervening variable which, when controlled for, might mediate the direct influence of simulation or case.

Interest and Learning Outcomes

To see whether interest intervenes between method and learning, we shall consider the four interest measures that discriminated between simulation and case (see Table 9.1, Columns E, H, I, and J). These are the perceptual measures of lab preference and the behavioural measures of attendance, course evaluation, and rate of participation.

Table 9.5 displays the mean improvement on the two learning variables for men and women according to whether they preferred their own section or the opposite one. In all but one set, those who preferred the other lab section scored better on fact mastery (i.e., showed more mean improvement between the pre- and postcourse scores) than did those who preferred their own lab. (The one exception was women in case section, and for this set, those women scored higher who preferred their own lab; however, the number of those who preferred simulation was quite small [three].) The differences in mean improvements were not great between those who disliked and those who liked their own labs, except for women in simulation. In that group, the eleven who preferred case had a mean of 18.9 compared to a mean of 4.8 for the thirteen who preferred to stay in simulation.

In addition to revealing a difference between students who preferred their own lab and those who preferred the other, Table 9.5 also indicates a difference between students preferring case and students preferring simulation regardless of the section they were actually in. Taking each of the four subsets (i.e., men in simulation, women in simulation, men in case, and women in case), we observe that in three of the four sets the mean pre- and posttest improvement was greater for students who preferred case.

TABLE 9.5

References and Mean Pre-Post Improvement

Preferences	*N*	*Mean Pre-Post Fact Mastery*	*Improvement Principles*
Men in case preferring case	30	9.6	8.3
Women in case preferring case	18	11.3	9.6
Men in simulation preferring simulation	31	11.0	11.4
Women in simulation preferring simulation	13	4.8	7.2
Men in case preferring simulation	12	9.7	14.6
Women in case preferring simulation	3	4.0	17.0
Men in simulation preferring case	16	13.6	7.1
Women in simulation preferring case	11	18.9	14.6

When we examine the relation of lab preference to learning of principles, we see the same kind of relation noted between lab preference and fact mastery. That is, except for one subset, men in simulation, those who preferred the other lab did better, i.e., showed more mean improvement between the pre- and postcourse examinations.

The relation between object of preference and learning of principles, however, is exactly opposite to that between object of preference and fact mastery. In three of four subsets, students who preferred simulation did better.

TABLE 9.6

Correlations, Between Attendance and Fact Mastery, and Fact Mastery and Learning of Principles

Attendance	*Fact Mastery*	*Principles*
Case men	– 0.3	+ 0.11
Case women	– .3	.04
Simulation men	– .03	.16
Simulation women	+ 0.1	+ 0.24

Now we take up the behavioural measure of interest as expressed by attendance and its relation to fact mastery and learning of principles. Table 9.6 reports the correlations between rate of attendance for men and women in case and simulation and fact mastery and learning of principles. Although none of the correlations is large, two points stand out. First, for three of the subsets the correlation between attendance and fact mastery is negative, but all the correlations between attendance and learning of principles are positive. Second, the high positive correlations between attendance and learning are for men in simulation and women in simulation.

We come now to the behavioural measure, course evaluation essay, and here we have findings reminiscent of those on the perceptual measure of lab preference, in which those who preferred the opposite lab did better than those who preferred their own. Table 3.7 displays mean improvement scores for both men and women by section, and according to whether they evaluated the course positively or negatively. In all subsets, negative evaluators have higher mean improvement on fact mastery than positive evaluators, although this is significant only for men in simulation. Likewise, in all subsets, negative evaluators show a higher mean improvement on principles than do positive evaluators, but none of these differences is significant.

TABLE 9.7

Evaluation and Mean Pre-Post Improvement

Evaluation	*N*	*Mean Pre-Post Fact Mastery*	*Improvement Principles*
Case men, positive evaluation	6	7.0	5.3
Case men, negative evaluation	9	10.0	9.9
Case women, positive evaluation	5	11.2	0.0
Case women, negative evaluation	9	15.8	14.1
Simulation men, positive evaluation	10	4.7[a]	6.9
Simulation men, negative evaluation	12	16.7[a]	13.9
Simulation women, positive evaluation	5	1.4	9.8
Simulation women, negative evaluation	8	4.13	13.5

[a] The differences between these means are significant at the 0.05 level as determined by t test.

Next, we consider rate of participation as an interest measure intervening between method and learning. Table 9.8 reports correlations between rate of participation for men and women in case and simulation and fact mastery and learning of principles. Notable in these data are the relatively low correlations, with only two of the eight higher than 0.3. Moreover, five of the eight are negative correlations, and men in simulation are the only subset with positive correlations between rate of participation and both fact mastery and learning of principles.

TABLE 9.8

Correlation Between Fact Mastery and Learning of Principles, and Rate of Participation

Participation	*Fact Mastery*	*Principles*
Case men	– 0.11	– 0.28
Case women	+ .05	– .02
Simulation men	+ .33	+ .23
Simulation women	+ 0.19	– 0.48

Summary

The relations between simulation and learning outcomes may be summarised in the following propositions: (1) No direct and unmediated relation exists between simulation and fact mastery or learning of principles. However, a number of indirect, rather complex relations were observed. (2) Those who preferred the other lab section did better on fact mastery and learning of principles, i.e., they showed more mean improvement between pre- and postcourse scores. (3) In general, those who preferred case, regardless of whether they were in case or simulation, did better on fact mastery. (4) However, those who preferred simulation, regardless of section, scored better on learning of principles. (5) Attendance and fact mastery were negatively correlated, but attendance and learning of principles correlated positively. (6) The high positive correlations between attendance and learning of principles correlated positively. (6) The high positive correlations between attendance and learning of principles were among students in simulation rather than case. (7)

Negative evaluators had higher mean improvement on fact mastery than positive evaluators, especially among men in simulation. (8) In general, participation and learning correlated negatively. (9) The strongest relation between participation and learning was among men in simulation.

Conclusions and Implications

The claims we made and the expectations we had for simulation were not borne out. It is not uniformly superior to case studies as a supplementary teaching activity, nor are the exceptions to this generalisation quite as we predicted. We expected more differences between personality subsets than were found. Nevertheless, the somewhat pessimistic conclusions from the data should not obscure one important finding, that behavioural measures of interest reveal simulation to be more involving and more interesting than case studies.

This observation is similar to findings from another recent experimental study of games. (It must be remembered that very few empirical evaluations of games and simulation have been undertaken, so it is a sparse literature to which our results are relevant.) As noted earlier, in four Baltimore high schools, Coleman and Boocock have studied the use of an election simulation (by computer) in two schools and its nonuse in two others. They find, and to a greater degree than we did, that the game excites interest and motivates students on virtually every measure of interest. Nothing comparable was found in the control schools without the game.

In spite of this claim for differences between simulation and case or other materials, the "so what?" question remains: What differences do these differences make for learning? We have pointed out in the section on learning outcomes some differences, but they are small. Yet these are differences obtained from small differences in treatment. Virtually everything in the courses was the same for both groups, except for their three-hour laboratory periods held on one afternoon each week. And the number of "treatments" with case and simulation were only eight or nine during an academic quarter.

Moreover, the subjects in this experiment were college students, many of them already interested enough in politics to be political science majors and/or to recruit themselves into these curses. It is important to bear this in mind in assessing the implications of the small differences obtained from this experiment. If there is anything we know from modern studies of political socialisation, it is that political interests and skills are often acquired early, i.e., by adolescence, and they are not altered much except by dramatic social events or traumatic personal deprivations. Thus any differences at all may be regarded as socially and theoretically significant.

Our, optimistic interpretation of pessimistic results, our positive reading of small differences, is reinforced by comparison of our findings with those of the San Francisco State College three-year programme to develop and evaluate new and different ways of teaching international relations. McClelland's (1962, pp. 269-70) summary of that experience indicates both the difficulty of making any noticeable impact on student learning and a likely explanation of that difficulty:

> The outcome that we have to report is that the course work did not affect the body of students in any significant way that the evaluations could take into account. That is, they did not, as a group, change their beliefs and attitudes perceptibly, they did not gain a greater mastery over the subject matter that was tested for, their understandings of various objects and conditions in the international environment remained very stable and unchanging, and they did not make measurable gains in critical abilities and techniques.

Some tentative conclusions and hypothesis requiring further investigation have been reported earlier on the reasons for the failure of students to change very much. The most important of these is that these students kept firmly in their possession a frame of reference which will accept only a limited amount of information and meaning about international relations and which, also, causes the rejection of those things which did not fit readily into that frame of reference.

The challenge to educators is to find ways to penetrate the firm "set" that college students bring to courses on politics and international relations. Student's perspectives and orientations toward public and world affairs are ordinarily developed by the time they reach college and are largely beyond amendment, except for some unlikely confrontation with an irreversible learning experience. It would be too much to claim, at this point, that simulation constitutes such an experience, but our data indicate small and important differences whereas other methods yield virtually no differences. We cannot yet boldly recommend revision of instructional policies, but we have grounds for confidently recommending further research and replication to help decide whether our vision of an effective technique is a reality or a mirage.

Training

One training use of simulation is in doctoral programmes in social sciences. Teachers and scholars in economics, psychology, sociology, and political science are likely to be required in the near future to master a considerable body of material on both computer and noncomputer simulation. Simulation is a new direction in experimental research techniques, and doctoral training in social science cannot avoid including it. Some dissertations will be researched with simulation. As a harbinger of this prospect, we may cite Brody's (1963a) exploration of the consequences of the sharing of nuclear weapons among several nations, and Driver's (1962) study of the effects of stress upon decision makers' perceptions of nations. Both these dissertations were based on data from the same run of Inter-Nation Simulation at Northwestern in the summer of 1960. Several other examples have been completed or are now in progress at various universities (C.F. Hermann, 1965; M. Hermann, 1965).

Costs

Innovations deserve to be considered partly in terms of the new costs they impose on the budget of an institution's instructional programme. There are "opportunity" or "behavioural" costs for the teachers, expenditures for forms, equipment, etc., and requirements of space.

Some games, like those of the paper-and-pencil variety or mere classroom role-playing exercises, are relatively inexpensive. For these games, the chief outlay is that of the teacher's time and imagination in writing a scenario of the kind Lieberman (1962) prepared to introduce her third-graders to the proposition that the United Nations is more than a building on a postcard. The design of any simulation involves this investment, and for the complex and long-running games it can be a heavy one. At Northwestern several years of graduate assistants' time, not to mention the sustained labours of a full professor, have gone into the development of Inter-Nation Simulation. At Carnegie Tech, four or five faculty members devoted several months to the initial work on a management game, and additional time has come from other colleagues who have served as auditors, as members of boards of directors, and in other supervisory roles during the conduct of games. Time given to designing and learning games is time denied to other activities of scholarship and teaching.

Costs for the actual conduct of a game may be illustrated again by the use of Inter-Nation Simulation at Northwestern. Alger (1963, p. 165) estimated that a single run of three hours added $65 to the budget for one of his courses; in an academic quarter of ten weeks, the additional cost was $650. This includes expenditures for student help, decision forms, message forms, secretarial time, typewriter rentals, calculator rentals, and so forth. It assumes, however, that some equipment is already available—for example, laboratory space, tables, chairs, in and out baskets, and clocks. Our use of simulation in teaching at Northwestern and at Ohio State has not required purchase of some of this "capital" equipment because it was already available for research. What it would cost to replace this equipment is hard to estimate. If laboratory space, or the equivalent, is not available, running the simulation is out of the question. At one institution, faculty offices have been cleared for a weekend's run, but this is surely unsatisfactory for a regular activity. Otherwise, the strain on inter-departmental comity can be an obstacle to further gaming.

Even the expenses for simulation for doctoral research run higher than usual. Two dissertations were recently written at Northwestern from eleven runs of ten hours' duration each. Counting the "overhead" charged by the university on research contracts and grants with government agencies, these two dissertations cost $15,000 each. Where is the university that will allocate that amount of its own money to graduate students' research?

Policy Recommendations

In conclusion, it is appropriate to suggest ways for consolidating, as well as initiating, simulation gains. A number of alternative policies are available to governmental and private institutions dedicated to sharing enlightenment and enhancing skills. Some of these relate to disseminating information about simulation and games more widely, and others bear on establishing a firmer base of knowledge of the use and consequences of simulation.

Training Manuals

Except possibly for business games, the use of simulation has been confined largely to educational elites, such as are found in the graduate schools and in government. At present, diffusion of information about and instructions for using games depends on word of mouth, personal visits, and the narrow circulation of incomplete dittoed or mimeographed material characteristic of innovations in research and educational institutions. Wider and better use depend on publication of workbooks or manuals with instructions sufficiently detailed and complete that teachers and students can put the model into operation without any further help. These manuals of procedures should contain copies off all forms to be used in any given game, such as the forms on which messages are recorded and published, the documents that represent the basic characteristics of the game, and all supplementary materials required for conducting a single exercise. Ideally, such manuals should also include options for the use of a particular game, so that simple but reliable modifications could be made in order to extend the use of the simulation to other related purposes.

There are now enough operational simulations in use by teachers at several institutions that a half dozen or so modest Office of Education contracts could result in as many manuals within a year or two. Thus it would not be difficult to extend and improve the dissemination of these new techniques.

Films

Similarly, mastery of such new techniques as simulation and games could more quickly be realised by an accompany half-hour film which would show the game or simulation in operation. This would stress the units, concepts, roles, and activities of the whole stimulation, as well as focus on particular points to be learned. Among the shots to be included in such a film would be a caselike following of a particular nation or firm throughout a whole period of the game, so that the primary activities of the simulation could be illustrated in depth as well as introduced in breadth.

In order to disseminate more general information about a number of games, an hour-long film covering several different kinds of simulations should be produced. This ought to be available to high schools, junior colleges, and universities in which teachers and administration contemplate adopting new media and techniques of instruction.

These visual media for introducing others to simulations and games are especially necessary in the judgment of many of the scholars who have invented these new techniques. They are frequently called upon to describe their games, and a well-packaged set of films would, in the aggregate, be a reasonably inexpensive means of communicating these new developments and would probably be an efficient way of doing so. In all cases, of course, the film should be made with the advice of those who have created the games, but the skills of those who are specialised in communicating by film and related visual modes would surely help in devising effective ways of presenting the new techniques to wider audiences.

Research Relevant to the Evaluation of the New Techniques

Strong judgements about the values of games and simulation for teaching and training should await the completion of research evaluating particular simulations both intrinsically and in relation to alternative forms of instruction. The number of projects critically evaluating simulations is still too small; only the efforts at Northwestern and Michigan are known to the author. Further studies can justifiably take any of several objectives, depending upon the researcher's interest in short-or long-term outcomes of the techniques, his interest in teaching undergraduate students or in training specialists for particular occupational roles, or his concern for assessing effects for aggregates of students or for individual types.

Many topics deserve a prominent place on the research agenda, but we should like to emphasise the critical importance of investigating the usefulness of games and simulation for different age groups. As has been said, research in political socialisation indicates that political attitudes, values, and orientations are acquired principally during adolescence or pre-adolescence. By the time most students have an opportunity to participate in the newer techniques of political and social science instruction, they probably have already, consciously or unconsciously, adopted their "set" toward politics and society. If one of the tasks of education is to help people to clarify their values and to find means to achieve their goals, the consequence of delaying political and social science work until late adolescence or early adulthood may be that a large segment of society is deprived of the opportunity to engage in systematic clarification of values about politics.

Therefore, those concerned about this social problem would welcome the development of instructional media and techniques that introduced people at early ages to the concepts and problems of political analysis. Because games and simulations are abstract, they can afford to save the student from many of the details and minutiae that he ordinarily discovers when confronted by the real world, but at the same time introduce him to what research has discovered to be the central and distinguishing characteristics of political behaviour. As the student grasps the essentials of one game, he can appropriately be introduced to more complex games, thus first seeing a tree and then encountering a forest, a but without losing his appreciation for the basic concept of tree.

10

EMOTIONS AND LEARNING

Defining Emotions

Literally speaking, pains is a physical experience and not an emotion as such. Emotions are complex and multifaceted processes, and I think it is a mistake to equate them with biological or physiological states. The point has been made by others, including Macquarrie (1973) and Evison and Horobin (1985). The concept of 'emotional pain,' however, suggests that some emotions are rather like experiencing physical pain, in that they are unpleasant experiences which 'hurt,' and which at the time we would rather be without. Some emotions are unpleasant without being painful, rather like physical discomfort, and again are feelings that we prefer to avoid.

Macquarrie (1973) warns against regarding emotions as phenomena separate and distinct from thought processes, and Evison and Horobin (1985) suggest that emotions inevitably have 'real time' meanings inseparable from and integral to them.

People probably differ in the way they label or pigeonhole their emotions. The labels I give mine may well differ from the ones you give yours. In recognition of this, I provide some examples below which simply serve to make the point suggested by Berne (1975) that people are likely to draw different meanings from similar predicaments and attach different painful or unpleasant emotions to them. The examples are not drawn from open and distance learning situations, because I want to set a more general context first.

Anguish seems to me to be associated with the discovery that we have been responsible for an accident, an unskilled or clumsy action, or a misjudgment that has had unfortunate consequences. During a group exercise I may make a mistake that only I notice, and feel private anguish because I have let my colleagues down.

Shame seems to be associated with the public exposure of such an error. I may admit may mistake, or it may come to light in a debrief after the exercise. In describing some past experience of mine, by way of contributing to a group discussion, I may suddenly realise, on being questioned by others, that the episode I have described illustrates quite clearly that I acted insensitively, carelessly, etc., and I now feel rather ashamed.

Anxiety and fear, for me, are similar kinds of emotion. In anxiety, I suspect than I am not equipped to deal constructively with something that is unknown or unpredictable, for which I have no ready programme or 'script' to guide my actions. This may happen to me during a somewhat unstructured personal development workshop. Middle managers would, I imagine, have similar feelings during workshops say on 'the skills of interpersonal influence,' or similar topics where they are expected to take part in a series of structured exercises. Fear, for me, involves focusing on challenges of a more specific nature, where there is reason to believe that I may not cope well with the situation in prospect. I may fear a visit from a particularly aggressive student whose work I have just failed, either because of an incident in my past when I was attacked or because the student has a reputation for making life difficult.

Suffering for me, is the growing awareness that one has been experiencing psychological damage, impairment, harm or stunting. On a life planning workshop, a participant may come to realise the extent to which he or she has relied overmuch on an over-protective mentor, has specialised too narrowly, or has failed to recognise opportunities in time, all of which may serve to arrest personal development and damage confidence. In addition, the participant may suffer during discussions because of a failure to articulate and explain ideas to the other participants, becoming ever more aware that there is something wrong with his or her skills of communication or self-management in a group context.

Whether a feeling is one of depression or a despair, is, for me, a matter of degree. In despair, I find myself to be a prisoner in an imperfect world, without a hope of realising my most cherished values, seeing no way forward and no way out. Depression is rather less shattering, felt perhaps by some change agents in organisations, whose best attempts to create a more humane, supportive and purposeful climate of human relations receive continual set-backs or are treated with apathy and cynicism.

For me, all such emotions are painful ones. Other emotions, such as the boredom I feel when unable to find a creative response to a familiar, uninspiring impasse, and the confusion and indignation I feel when people do not act as I expect them to and think they should, are, for me, merely uncomfortable and unpleasant, without being painful.

Because I rcognise that the ways I experience my emotions and associate them with particular meanings are special to me, the focus here is on rather a board range of them, and I will deal in general with the difficulties posed by painful and uncomfortable emotions in the open and distance learning context. Regrettably, space does not permit a critical consideration of the interrelationship between the learning process and emotions that are pleasurable or comfortable.

Emotions and Learning

The connection between a learner's emotional state and

the fruitfulness of an intended experience is not a straightforward one. This is the case even with boredom, which on the surface one might judge to be wholly dysfunctional to the learning process.

Boredom

Little has been said in support of boredom as something that may in some circumstances be helpful in a learning context. Colaizzi (1978a) states emphatically that one should not bother learning or pretending to learn anything which one finds boring. Colaizzi's view of learning is that it is a process in which learners build up personal meanings that are of central significance to their lives. Nevertheless, I believe that it is still possible to regard boredom as having a value, since the experience of it may guide someone away from learning in certain areas and thus help them to decide on others.

Marsh (1983) also presents a negative picture of boredom in relation to a learning situation. In her study of boredom on a training course, she reports learners' comments that compartments in the brain were closing off, there was no energy, they wanted things to be different, but did not wish to take responsibility to change what was happening or identify its causes. As she understood the phenomena, other feelings, such as the fear of taking risks, confusion about the role of the two tutors (who also were bored), frustration, and anxiety, appeared to contribute to and be part of an overwhelming and imprisoning atmosphere, which served to block off any learning. She speculates that had the boredom been painful, rather than dull and uncomfortable, it might possibly have had some exploitable value as a spur to action, but in the circumstances it was wholly dysfunctional in that people merely endured it.

The Value of Painful Feelings

Evison and Horobin (1985) hold that 'negative' feelings

those which are subjectively unpleasant such as being anxious, disgusted, cross or gloomy, and which are nasty and possibly painful, focus attention narrowly on the source of distress, impair problem-solving ability and block off all forms of learning except the process of conditioning.

Skemp (1971), discussing emotions in relation to the learning of mathematics, claims that feelings of dislike, bafflement, despair, anxiety or revulsion towards the subject are negative 'patterns' which prevent further learning. He singles out anxiety, in particular, as a major problem, even if it has its roots in early classroom experience and the learner is now an adult trying to learn independently through working with a text. Such feelings, he asserts, are the fault of teachers who have presented material as a set of meaningless rules and procedures insulting learners by requiring them to accommodate their schemata of thoughts to assimilate meaninglessness.

As with boredom, however, the idea that other 'negative' emotions are always dysfunctional to the learning process seems to be an over-simplistic conclusion.

Revans (1979) implies that emotional pain may be experienced on occasion by managers engaged in the process of 'action learning,' which he characterises as a process of development of the self by the self that can involve the manager spending 'more than an occasional afternoon in some Chamber of Horrors that he eventually recognises as himself. Revans (1984) argues that the process of developing questioning insight in this manner entails, among other things, 'quandary, query, and qualms,' and may involve times of violent opposition, vigorous contradictions and hostility towards fellow learners. Revans also, of course, emphasises the importance of supportive comradeship among learners. He does not imply that painful or uncomfortable feelings serve a particularly valuable role, but that they are part and parcel of the development process.

Boydell and Pedler (1979) concluded from data shared by participants on a workshop that most significant personal development involved a period of perturbation, crisis, shock or surprise, often accompanied by feelings of embarrassment or fear (although frequently the feelings were more pleasurable). They point out that perturbation does not necessarily lead to developmental outcomes, but that learning resources could concentrate on helping people to learn from it.

Macquarrie (1973) points out that some existential philosophers have regarded feelings such as anguish, anxiety, boredom and nausea as fulfilling an important function in illuminating the grimmer aspects of the human condition and raising questions concerning the meaning of one's life.

Casey (1985) implies that the process of significant new learning entails the turbulent upheaval of deeply-held beliefs, and is marked by feelings of incredulity and fear. He implies that such traumatic change is preferable to periods of stasis where managers may operate in comfort but are imprisoned by unquestioned ways of seeing the world.

Colaizzi (19786), in trying to illuminate what is involved when significant learning comes from reading a book of one's choice, suggests that the contents point back towards the reader and provide self-illumination that is as likely to be threatening and painful as it is to be consoling. Efforts to uncover personal meaning in this manner are likely to involve effort and struggle even though they will be carried out enthusiastically.

Summary

In drawing together the implications from these various perspectives, I shall distinguish between the processes of learning and of development as Davies and Easterby-Smith do (1984). I regard 'learning' to be a matter of taking on board lessons in the form of knowledge and of tricks of the trade. 'Development,' on the other hand, I characterise as the unfolding of individual potential and the building up of mature personal qualities, including an increased competence in the learning process.

Five points emerge from a consideration of the different perspectives so far discussed. First, where the intention is to provide learners with the opportunity for development, it is very likely that they will experience a measure of emotional pain or discomfort resulting from both the new insight they may gain into themselves and the very process of moving from the known and familiar into the unknown. To seek to prevent such pain in such circumstances is tantamount to attempting to block personal development, as the risk of some pain appears to be inherent in learning of this nature, rather like the growing pains some children experience.

Second, where the intention is to provide learners with the chance of developing their understanding of a body of intellectual knowledge or ability to use a set of practical techniques, such as in the field of numeracy, learners may experience painful or uncomfortable feelings arising from memories of insensitive ways in which they have been taught in the past or from the way they are currently being taught. Pain stemming from such sources is dysfunctional and educators are justifiably concerned with ways of preventing it.

Third, whatever it is that the person is learning, some emotional pain or discomfort may arise from the social context within which learning is taking place. Some learners may find their relationships with others to be uncomfortably close. Some may perceive other to be coldly indifferent towards them and feel lonely and anxious as a result. Whilst such discomfort or pain may be a stimulant for personal growth and development, it may also serve to divert attention away from any particular body of knowledge or techniques that the person may be attempting to learn.

Fourth, even if the learners' intention is a narrow one of acquiring an understanding of some body of knowledge or techniques, they may in the process also derive some personal development from becoming more aware of their personal strengths and weaknesses as learners. Although such awareness is valuable, it may be difficult, uncomfortable, or painful to come to terms with.

Fifth, no one advocates the provocation or stimulation of emotional pain or discomfort as a means of promoting learning or personal development. When the intention is to help someone to learn a body of 'content,' most concern centres around ways of preventing such feelings, and the extent to which it is feasible to do so. When the intention is to encourage and support the process of personal development, the wider concern is expressed about how to deal with unpleasant feelings.

Strategies for Dealing with Emotions

I have discussed the interrelationship between pain or discomfort and learning or development, as a preamble to a discussion of strategies for dealing with painful or uncomfortable emotions in open and distance learning. The context of 'distance' is one where a programme has been designed to be followed in geographical separation from those with the professional role of supporting or facilitating the learning. Normally, this is also an 'open' context, in the sense that constraints on access to the programme are fewer when attendance requirements are minimal. Ideally, part of this context will include an 'open' philosophy of education which encourages learners to establish their own purposes of learning, and decide on the means through which these purposes are pursued.

I will consider four main strategies for addressing emotional pain or discomfort: prevention, masking, soothing, and working with and through feelings. For each strategy, I will give examples of its actual or potential use, discuss the limitations on its application, and make a subjective assessment of how it may be used to best effect.

Prevention

Those adopting a strategy of 'prevention' will attempt to anticipate what is likely to give rise to pain or discomfort, and try to steer well clear of this in their designs.

Examples

One source of painful emotion that designers of open and distance learning programmes may anticipate is the association in learners' minds between the experience of using the materials and the experience of study in a school classroom, or of doing 'homework.' It is often said that school experience has been for many people emotionally painful. Consequently, attempts may be made to create texts that are as unlike the standard school textbooks as possible. Materials may instead be glossy, contain cartoons, have a journalistic and documentary rather than a didactic style of presentation, and may attempt to tell a story rather than signal the need to engage in rote learning. There may be wide spaces in the margin to write, in, but not, importantly, instructions to fill in blank spaces between words. There may be a low word density but not big writing. Any exercises included would not have 'right' answers to look up in the back, any work submitted would not be graded, and any progress report from a tutor that resembled a school report would be avoided.

Designers of interactive video programmes may attempt to prevent the phenomenon of 'getting stuck,' with its attendant feelings of self-doubt, frustration and anger, by means of programmes that do not consist of taking learners through a series of loops and gates, but encourage the learners to browse at will through different parts of the programme, cheat as much as they like, and skip bits that are boring.

Similar steps may be taken to prevent impasses with text-based material. It should be possible to design texts that cover quite complex ideas but are conducive to browsing, with a certain degree of skippable redundancy of explanation built into them. A note in an accompanying study guide might advise learners to keep on reading in the event of an apparent impasse, or to skip to the next section if they feel they are going over old ground.

Designers ought to be aware of racism, sexism, and other cultural assumptions within their materials which may cause offence, and which may discount and marginalise groups of the population. Piloting programmes with members of a wide range of minority groups should help to prevent such phenomena, including that of 'tokenism.'

The learner's frustration at wishing to argue a particular point about the materials, but having no means of doing so is preventable by designers inviting and responding to personal correspondence.

Limitations

The limitations on the extent to which emotional pain or discomfort can be prevented stem form the impossibility of predicting and controlling human experience or actions, or of catering for the diversity of ideas and social values. This is illustrated in the following examples.

A designer cannot know precisely what will spark off painful associations with the past for any particular learner. Piloting materials with large numbers of learners may reveal some general trends in adverse reaction, and the materials may be modified accordingly, but to be sensitive to every possible reaction is probably not feasible. Indeed, modifications intended to prevent pain for some types of learner may aggravate the pain of others.

A 'user friendly' computer programme may be designed to prevent learners form making harsh self-assessments, by using kind and soft language to deal with inaccurate responses or illogical decisions. Yet learners reach their own self-assessments in their own ways. My experience of using interactive video as a learner suggests that, however kind and supportive the language on the VDU, if I get the sense that I have been making slow progress I leave the terminal in a rather depressed and subdued mood.

Boot and Reynolds (1984a) have clearly demonstrated that, regardless of the intentions of the designer, exercises intended for personal development give rise to meanings among learners that cannot be predicted and can be emotionally painful and uncomfortable. Engaging with factual or expository material can have similar effects, especially if learners choose to consider questions such as 'What are the implications of understanding this for the work that I do?,' and 'What does this tell me about the organisational world in which I have to live?' Painful conclusions may be reached about the career one has chosen. For example, learners may conclude from working with a package on secretarial procedures that the work of a secretary is characterised by high levels of subservience. A programme on personal practice may portray this, in the eyes of the learners, as unpalatably manipulative. Facing up to such meanings in relation to the work one has based one's career on is likely to set in motion a painful process of self-examination.

Evaluating the Case

Least promising approaches to preventing emotional pain or discomfort involve attempts to predict and control the learner's experience. For example, some designs include branching programmes of such sophistication that every 'reasonable' sequence of learner responses is assumed to be catered for and any potential moments of pain assumed to have been removed. More promising approaches attempt to empower learners to control their own experience. These regard prevention as the prerogative of the learner rather than as a strategy designed in by someone else on the assumption that they can manipulate the learner's experience towards painlessness. A strategy of prevention alone is clearly inadequate to tackle the challenge of painful and uncomfortable emotions in learning, especially where personal development is sought rather than the learning of a body of material.

Masking

'Masking' is an approach which involves attempting to down out painful emotions by stimulating or amplifying other, more pleasurable emotions.

An Example

The designers of an accountancy programme intended for middle managers without a numerical background may suspect that for many people the whole field of calculations, figures, tables and financial matters is not only dry and unappealing but may also be a source of discomfort and anxiety. They may therefore try to make the course materials aesthetically pleasing, humorous and entertaining. Instead of written case studies, in which the bare financial information is set out alongside questions about possible financial and business strategy decisions, cases may be portrayed on videotape, episodes in which financial information is discussed being interpersed with moments of situational comedy, or even slapstick. The unfolding of events may be presented as a drama; other aspects of the functioning of the business, thought to have curiosity value, may be dwelt on at some length for light relief. The materials themselves may be attractively packaged, folding out neatly and conveniently on the learner's desk.

Limitations

There are inherent difficulties facing those who attempt a strategy of masking, or mixing education with entertainment.

This is because people differ not only in their tastes, but also in their reactions to such efforts. Some may conceive learning to be emphatically a serious process, and may be angered by what they see as gratuitious entertainment. Others, having made what for them has been a major step towards tackling something that they fear or have anxieties about, may wonder when the torture is going to start. Given the long build up within the programme, there must be something unpleasant about to happen! At the first sign of any real in-depth treatment of the subject, they may panic, switch off the set, or close the book. There is a risk that attention may wander away from the learning content toward elements of the entertainment, such as the incidental storyline. Even if the content is not simplified, people may feel patronised if they think it is coyly packaged.

Burkhardt et al. (1982) make the point that humour can become tiresome on second reading or hearing. This is a danger whenever education has been mixed with entertainment and learners have to review the material to revise the learning points.

Evaluating the Case

Masking can be attempted in a strong form, almost as a substitute for good entertainment, or in a mild form, a modest attempt to 'cheer up' the learner. Elton et al. (1984) advise designers to confine themselves to cheering up the learner, and for average learners this seems to be sound advice. Perhaps a strong form of masking could be made to work as a way of helping remedial learners to address educational content that they would otherwise find repulsive. As Mitchell (1979) points out, however, research must be done to reveal the effects of borrowing techniques from the world of entertainment and using them in educational programmes. Further research is also needed on whether strong masking (because it may help open up otherwise taboo subject areas) encourages learners to become self-motivated by learning, or whether (because it may make learners dependent upon the seduction of entertainment) it discourages ongoing learning and development.

In mild masking, humour and entertainment can be used to illustrate a serious point or raise issues for reflection (Koestler 1975). The style of some recent journal articles involves linking interesting plots or humorous punchlines with serious perspectives and insights (see, for example, Casey 1985, and Grafton-Small and Linstead 1985). The effectiveness of such attempts does not depend on disguising the content, but rather on bringing out the joy in the learning material. As is implied by Wilson (1980), the temptation to dress learning up as something else stems from a pessimistic view of human 'imprisonment,' in the world. It is equally possible to celebrate the learning process as a vehicle for power over ones own existence.

Soothing

What is sought by 'soothing' is the gentle edging out of painful or uncomfortable feelings such as anguish, despair, suffering, anxiety, and boredom, and their replacement by feelings of solace, calmness and relaxation. It is a strategy that some learners choose for themselves, seeking solace from partners or close friends.

Examples

Study guides may include techniques for relaxation among ways of coping with anxiety about or discomfort with the material. 'Soothing' comments may appear in the early part of a main study text, alluding to the need not to worry if the material is difficult to absorb at times, and suggesting frequent breaks from study. They may also be inserted just before the passages which the designers believe to be potentially the most difficult, confronting or threatening.

Computer-based programmes may have a more flexible soothing facility, which does not involve the designer in guessing when the learner may need soothing. They may simply offer, on pressing a Help button, a menu of straightforward, non-educational computer games to choose from, with the intention of allowing the learner to take a break without switching off the machine.

A counsellor trying to soothe, would simply listen sympathetically as learners shared their frustrations, aired their anxiety or complained about boredom. Such a form of counselling support may be thought to offer a facility for catharsis where ill-feelings about the programme are concerned.

Attempts may be made to encourage peer support on an informal basis among networks of learners. During the setting-up phase of a programme, for example, cohorts of distance learners may be brought together for 'community building' exercises, and phone numbers and addresses exchanged.

Limitations

Study guidelines, passages written into the text, or computer facilities designed to soothe may not necessarily be interpreted or felt to be supportive. It is possible, instead, that learners will feel that they are being treated in a patronizing manner.

Whether soothing support is sought from working colleagues and fellow learners, and whether such support is provided sympathetically or provided at all, depends on the climate of working relationships within the organisation or the learning group. In some cultures, such as that of the police, where a 'macho' image is still predominant, support may not be sought at all. To seek support could be taken as a sign of weakness and ineptitude, people may not know how to ask for support or how to handle requests or invitations to provide support. Study counsellors may not be visited because of connotations of 'loss of face,' or because of doubts about confidentiality.

Evaluating the Case

Experimentation may reveal whether there are any promising approaches to soothing without relying on human contact. If attempts to provide a social soothing facility are to get off the ground at all, then designers and deliverers need to pay special attention to the learning climate of the learner's work organisation and/or home setting. If these are not conducive to moments of relaxation or to the expression of feelings, then some other learning centre may need to be created or deliberate and full-scale interventions may need to be made into the culture of the organisation. If it can be made to happen, soothing can be helpful. If used on its own without any other strategy, however, it is severely limited in that it makes the learner adjust to the learning task and not the learning task suit the learner's needs.

Working With and Through Feelings

Working with and through emotional pain or discomfort involves using such feelings constructively as a guide to further learning and development.

Examples

I have not yet found any study guides written to help learners to interpret the meaning of their feelings and work out how to act on them. But I think they could include a section setting forth some of the reasons why learners feel bad during study: association with school days or other learning situations which were unpleasant; getting stuck because of ambiguous instructions or explanations, or because of 'bugs' in the programme; 'feedback' that is provided in an offensive manner; failure to meet one's own standards of achievement; feeling one's own values are being discounted; coming face to face with conclusions about one's work and one's life that are difficult to come to terms with; or coming across sexism, racism, etc. in the programme. Provided that the range of possibilities is sufficiently comprehensive, it can be suggested that learners identify the reasons that seem to lie at the roots of what is troubling them. Depending on what is identified, there may be a particular piece of advice or information to refer to concerning what to do next. If, for example, learners conclude that they feel bad because of some unpalatable piece of self-discovery, there may be a reference to particular literature available from certain addresses or sources. Literature subsequently sent off for may catalogue self-help groups, organisations which run self-development workshops at a reasonable price, even self-development books or packages which learners may now decide are suitable for the new 'needs' they have identified. If the reason identified is the discounting of one's own values or perspectives, whilst it is unlikely that designers would wish to identify competitors' programmes which might take a different slant, there may be at least an offer of a visit from someone (perhaps the author of a particular part of the programme) to discuss the learner's own views.

It may be possible to build auto-counselling sub-routines into computer-based programmes. These would pose questions about how learners are feeling, about possible ways in which learners may deal with their feelings, and what the consequences might be, etc. There would be a facility to store and print out learner's responses, and suggestions as to how to go about making sense of the input/output, in *preparation* for dialogue with a human counsellor. One would not expect the computer to be a *replacement* for a human being in this context (see Vallee 1984).

A study counsellor may help learners to address emotional 'blocks to learning' (Stuart 1984) that lie at the root of their troubles. For example, learners may complain that they feel idle when 'just sitting with the programme' or feel impatient with having to pick out details from a videotape. In a sympathetic study counselling session, there would be an opportunity to explore whether this was symptomatic of a general reluctance to sit back and reflect, to analyse situations in detail, and to review experience. If this were agreed to be the case, learners then might be advised to persevere with the programme as a means of expanding their range of approaches to learning and developing. Discussions might range into matters of the learner's career aspirations, and possible alternative distance learning programmes may be identified in dialogue. The learners' pain or discomfort may stem from their over-harsh performance standards, and, through counselling, there would be an opportunity to explore issues of 'learning maturity' (Stuart and Holmes 1982) such as whether the learner has had sufficient practice in setting learning goals that are not only challenging but also achievable.

Similar functions to those performed by a counsellor can be attempted by a group of learners meeting together (see Robinson 1981). Possibly they could tackle the programme as a team and address issues of team and personal development and ways of helping one another work through emotions as they go through it (material could be provided to help them do so).

Limitations

Study guidelines and auto-counselling exercises intended to initiate the process of working with and through painful or uncomfortable emotions depend for their success upon the integrity of programme designers and managers. The latter need to be willing to enter, if necessary, into free dialogue (at least by correspondence) with disaffected learners, and to become part of a network of organisations providing services that learners may require. Otherwise, learners may be left with a sense of unfinished business that may add to their initial pain or discomfort. Skilled support from counselling specialists may be limited because of cost, and the effectiveness of counselling from peers depends on their levels of counselling skill.

Evaluating the Case

It seems that the strategies of prevention, masking and

soothing all have limitations borne out of the impossibility of predicting or controlling for any one learner where, when and how they will experience pain. Whatever is done, learners are likely to experience emotional pain and discomfort. By necessity therefore, we need seriously to consider ways of helping learners to work with and through feelings. I suggest that designers make it a priority to design and produce study guidelines or auto-counselling exercises that are of maximum possible help to learners in working with, and preparing to work through, emotional pain or discomfort towards constructive action. These facilities should help learners to get more from rare opportunities for peer or professional counselling, and alert them to opportunities beyond the direct scope of the programme. In many organisations it is perhaps over-optimistic to expect peer counselling sessions to be a major resource, unless there is a history of action learning (Revans 1979) or the learners have worked together on an intimate basis before.

Concluding Remarks

What is often achieved without prior contrivance or premeditation on residential programmes in addressing painful or uncomfortable feelings is heavily dependent on human relationships and on the facility to catch things as they happen. Designers of open and distance learning programmes who want to provide significant learning are faced with the problem of limited human contact.

Design teams can take positive steps to prevent pain by being sensitive in their writing and programming. A reasonably friendly tone of delivery may serve to mask discomfort. Beyond this, the temptation may be to try over-zealously to affect the learners' emotions, when it is more fruitful to provide materials and set up support systems which learners can use to suit their own particular emotional needs.

Within an open philosophy of learning, one important

intention would be to empower learners to address pain in ways which suit them. Learners would be subject to less risk of the pain which comes from being under constraint, and would be left with the risk of the pain inherent in learning.

COMMENTARY

Both chapters in this section are concerned with the attitude of teachers, diagnosticians and professionals towards the use of new technology in problem solving and in education when that technology threatens their previously indispensible roles. Both John Self and Dent Rhodes leave little doubt that for professional people the prospect of their human presence being replaced by a system of machines and software has limited appeal. And the cooperation of professionals which is vital if delivery systems or learning networks relying on new technology are to get off the ground, will not occur so long as assent implies redundancy.

Both chapters, however, range far beyond the traditional perception of new technology in open learning that is so threatening to teachers: i.e. an independent learner sitting at a terminal that provides instruction in expert knowledge. Indeed, John Self rules out the possibility of one kind of computer based system, the expert system, being used profitably to instruct novices in a body of specialist expertise. Self argues that no such system would be adequate for the infinity of circumstantial needs and purposes of novices, or match the intricacy and uniqueness of face to face dialogue between knower and novice. The practice of representing knowledge as sets of rules (upon which the design of an expert system relies) may do little justice to the complexity of the knowledge to be worked on.

Self-provides an alternative picture of the way in which expert systems may be used, suggesting that a cumulative body of rules in a given subject area may be built up and browsed through by a community of peer specialists and researchers. An example would be a body of educational principles expressed as rules, available on a computer system for consultation by educational researchers who could add to the system their latest findings. Such uses of new technology come close to Dent Rhodes' description of a transactive system: a network of professional peers readily accessible to one another and prepared to share their specialist knowledge with one another via telecommunications and by drawing on computerised data bases and catalogues.

A picture emerges of computer-supported development between and among professional peers, not of the educationally difficult and professionally threatening situation where computers instruct learners. In this way, the learner becomes 'peer' rather than 'pawn.' Dent Rhodes places a corresponding emphasis on control *by* the learner rather than *of* the learner, and on the definition of learning purposes *by* the learner rather than *for* the learner. The idea extends to that of the learner contributing thoughts and ideas through the network for the benefit of other learners.

Despite such possibilities, the question of the extent of openness in computer-aided education remains. Will access to such powerful co-learning networks remain restricted to members of particular professional organisations? Or will they be open to the ordinary home computer user? It is possible that the professionals concerned would find many reasons to prevent such openness, preferring instead to hold on to their expertise.

The conception of professional as 'expert' is particularly justified in some fields: in the pure sciences, for example, or medicine or engineering. There, a decision by the specialists to distance themselves from lay people might be excusable on the grounds that they know more rules which appear to work most of the time. Reluctant to extend access to a transactive network to lay people, the professionals in such fields might prefer to mete out understanding on their own terms, using new technology as a support rather than a replacement for the traditional teacher.

A case for the traditional conception of expertise and dissemination is, however, barely tenable in the social sciences, in management or in the humanities. Many specialists realise that the epistemological paradigms in those fields are built up on a web of ethical and moral presuppositions as well as on conjectures about the nature of reality which are unprovable. The process of teaching is itself such a field of expertise. Attempts to build up an expert system of rules to prescribe good practice, as exemplified by Self, may not be the most fruitful avenue of advance in these areas. A new conception of expertise is needed, perhaps where specialists are respected as advisors on and questioners of strands of argument, ways of seeing and states of the art, but the non-specialist is not treated as a blank-slated novice. Lay people could be regarded as co-inquirers into the social world to which we all belong and which we all play a part in constructing.

Here we return to the transactive system. It would be possible, for example, to build a transactive system around a learning community of 'teaching' staff who see their roles as advisers and questioners and non-specialist learners whose role is one of co-inquiry. Each group could draw on, and be linked to one another through, various telecommunication and computer networks. They might also benefit from meeting together from time to time! If in the social sciences and humanities we can begin to acknowledge the intellectual wealth as well as the frailties of the non-specialist, then we might begin to approach a kind of de-schooled, open, computer-aided society beyond the dreams even of Ivan Illich. If, on the other hand, computer-aided learning networks were to become the sole prerogative of groups of professionals, then a massive underclass of people would run the risk of being confined to exclusion, alienation and isolation.

11

TEACHING FOR THE OPEN UNIVERSITY

The Teaching Package

The Open University student's tuition takes many forms. The major element is the series of correspondence units, despatched at regular intervals to the student's home. Much of the working material is designed to help him to learn for himself. The correspondence units are closely related to radio and television broadcasts and the whole teaching package of written and broadcast material is produced by a course team which is composed of central and regional academic staff, members of the BBC and educational technologists. The student must respond to this teaching material in an active way, by carrying out experiments, writing essays, working through problems, projects, etc., and while some of this work may be used for self-assessment, the majority is assessed in written form either by a tutor (tutor-marked assignments) or by the computer (computer-marked assignments). Ultimately the best of the student's assignments together with the final examination determine the award and standard of a credit.

Study Centres

Although the Open University student works mainly at home, the University has established, usually in other educational institutions, some 260 study centres sited throughout the country in areas of high population or where transport links are good. Attendance at the study centre is voluntary. They offer students a range of facilities which can supplement some of those available at home but above all they enable students to meet each other and to learn from each other in discussion groups. The study centre is also the focal point for the undergraduate students' meetings with tutor-counsellors. These meetings are an important element of the programme at foundation level where numbers normally allow provision for local contact.

The main purpose of this contact is to remedy in tutorial sessions any academic weaknesses or deficiencies of understanding and to support in counselling sessions the individual student's overall progress.

The range of correspondence units and broadcasts provides the student with information and guidance in a standard package. It is through the tuition and counselling system, however, that this standard package is interpreted according to the student's individual needs and ability.

Local Support

When they begin their studies undergraduate students are assigned to a tutor-counsellor at their local study centre. The tutor-counsellor will normally be responsible for all tuition and counselling in the foundation year, although in some instances, e.g. for the science foundation course, specialists may be brought in for particular tuition and assessment. The tutor-counsellor is available on a fairly regular basis at the study centre and may discuss strictly academic matters associated with the course or may deal with study skills on a much wider basis as well as reviewing and assisting with his students' progress in the University's unique and complex teaching system. As a supplement to these meetings, and as a substitute in cases where students cannot or choose not to attend the study centre, contact between the tutor-counsellor and student is maintained by other means, including correspondence and telephone. In addition the tutor-counsellor is responsible for marking and commenting on scripts sent to him by individual students. When the undergraduate student advances to post-foundation level courses the correspondence tuition is provided by a specialist course tutor who may in addition meet his students for tutorials or, increasingly, contact his students by other more flexible means. However, the tutor-counsellor continues to provide an element of stability and continuity in the life of the Open University student since he retains his board role as a general educational adviser at a local level throughout the student's educational career.

Correspondence Tuition

Correspondence tuition is the central and continuing teaching process in the Open University system. The techniques and approach of the correspondence tutor are not always immediately grasped by those who have successfully taught students in conventional full-time and part-time teaching. In the same way learning through correspondence does not always come easily to the adult student to whom such a system is generally new. At foundation level the tutor-counsellor has the responsibility for training and preparing undergraduate students for this novel method of learning. The student is asked to make a response from time to time to correspondence texts, broadcasts and other course material. This response is given in the form of an assignment. The assignment is graded and commented on by the tutor and these comments constitute the main part of the student's personal tuition. Even at foundation level, the assignment may be the only opportunity for regular communication between the student and the tutor.

It would be difficult to overstate the importance of the correspondence teaching function in the Open University context. In writing assignments students are reconstituting their newly received knowledge in terms of their previous experience and knowledge. The way in which they do this will depend to no small extent on the ways in which they perceive their relationship with their tutor. If they perceive the relationship as one of strict authority on the part of the tutor, their attempts to explore and to present ideas will be minimised and the educational value of the tutor-marked assignment will tend to become subservient to its role as a grading instrument. The students' initial estimation of the role of the tutor marked assignment is likely to be an enduring one. It is therefore of considerable importance that as foundation level students they should be directed to use assignments as a means of exploring knowledge within a particular framework and of receiving specific guidance which will help to improve their work.

Teaching by Correspondence

A university which aims to teach students who have homes and families, and perhaps a full-time job as well, and who may be relatively remote from centres of population, cannot expect to rely on the traditional lecture and tutorial method of teaching. Thus, in the Open University correspondence teaching is central and over-riding in importance. The main source of individual advice, guidance and constructive criticism for an Open University student on a particular course is his course tutor, who bases his teaching primarily on the student's written work in his 'tutor-marked assignments,' and his advice is primarily written advice. This implies that a tutor new to correspondence teaching may need to make a conscious adjustment to his new role: marking a script that is to be returned to a student by post, if it is to be a helpful and constructive process, is not at all the same as marking an examination paper or making notes on an essay that will be discussed in a conventional tutorial.

General Principles

What, then is it like to teach at a distance, by correspondence? It is perhaps surprising, though gratifying, at first to realise the depth of involvement that can develop and the sense one has of getting to know the student, at a personal level, through his written work, even when one never sees the student at all Much depends on previous teaching experience. After that, an ability to put oneself in the student's position and thus assess the relevance and clarity of one's own comments make on the script is the single most important factor. Naturally, the work varies between levels and between faculties. However, what follows will attempt to discuss, with examples, the common features underlying all correspondence teaching work.

In commenting on assignments the tutor (or tutor-counsellor — we shall not distinguish between the two in the correspondence teaching role) must seek to adapt the course material to individual needs as best he may. By evaluating the work and offering criticism, he may suggest to his student ways in which he might improve. This requires two things from the tutor: the ability to convey, through his comments, advice for further study and the ability to perceive his student's present state of knowledge and conceptual framework so that the advice may be relevant. How this works out in practice may be seen in the following example. A social science tutor had to award an 'F' grade on assignments 1. He wrote the following explanation on the PT3 from (the form accompanying each written assignments, copies of which are kept for reference by the tutor, the student and the University), in the space provided for overall assessment:

> I am sorry that the mark is so disappointing, and I hope I do not seem over-critical. The essay was not a catastrophic fail, but I do not feel that it merits higher than 'F' for the following reasons:
>
> 1. The wording of the question means that main focus must be on the contemporary situation — major portions of your essay were essentially historical.
> 2. The concepts I have just outlined need to be matched with relevant evidence — too often your discussion was at too general a level — you could, e.g. have

> drawn on Sec. 62 and 63 of Unit 3, TV 2 on Ibadan, or several authors in Breese. It is early days yet, and this block and questions were difficult — don't let the failure to hit the target this time worry you unduly.

The key features of this comment are that it is humane, and not destructive of the student's self-esteem, and that it is both constructive and supportive. It also underlines an important restriction placed on tutors by the framework of the Open University. Part-time staff must use, in some manner, the package of written material and broadcasts upon which the University centres its tuition, and in relation to it the responsible tutor must be at once critical and independent, yet knowledgeable and constructive. As in the example quoted, references to Open University course material in a tutor's actual correspondence comments seem an obvious means of helping the student to achieve a similar relationship. This is not, of course, to imply any kind of slavish dependence on the course material any more than on any other book (or on any other experience that one learns from). But specific references to particular passages in the texts should be a valuable and economical way of expanding advice — the student can then follow up the suggestions independently.

In some courses, assignment rubrics and tutor notes have been carefully 'escalated' to suggest a teaching strategy over the year's work — moving from the exercise of minor or basic skills to more sophisticated assignments requiring a more searching analysis and a more comprehensive synthesis of ideas by the student. The conscientious tutor will try to work within any such overall strategy, aiming to develop the individual student's distinctive abilities methodically and cumulatively. There is a tendency towards over-simplification among adult students (and tutors) working under pressure — each assignment or section may be seen in isolation so that the course becomes a mere succession of disconnected 'blocks' lacking any cumulative rhythm or dynamic. Such a danger may be especially real in inter-disciplinary courses and certainly in multi-disciplinary ones. Careful attention to assignment rubrics and tutor notes is likely to be especially important at foundation level when good habits need to be established. The assignment questions and rubrics are the University's main means of helping to develop powers of disciplined thought in its students. Accordingly Open University students have to be led to interpret assignment rubrics with scrupulous fidelity to the intentions behind them. Adult students have ideas of their own which they wish simply to substitute for those they are asked to consider, but while freshness or independence of mind is vital and not to be discouraged, discipline is also necessary.

A further point that we have already noted in the example of the social science tutor's comment was the manner in which criticism was offered. Much tutorial discussion at university level inevitably involves taking issue with a student's opinions, at times even in a robustly sharp manner. Open University correspondence work, however, may require a rather more circumspect or 'remedial' tutorial tone — 'nursing' the student (good nurses being cheerfully stimulating and sensibly practical rather than 'sympathic' in the sentimental sense). Written comments need to be very carefully phrased and considerate — the opportunity for a hasty aside or added explanation is not available when the student opens the envelope. More important, though, at foundation level a tutor-counsellor may need to be especially concerned not just to strike out errors or to debate with the student but to assist him to develop basic skills and form views that are worthy of debate. At higher levels, the balance may change, though in a multi-disciplinary context one cannot depend upon that.

Course tutors in the Open University system may find it helpful to remember that students taking the course that they tutor may have come from a very different kind of course, or even from a different faculty. Students are sometimes taken aback when the abilities expected of them, and painfully acquired, in one course seem to count for little in a subsequent one. If a student had done well beforehand, a sudden barrage of low grades, however well warranted, may upset him considerably. Indeed, all students given low grades — and certainly all given 'R' and 'F' grades — should be given careful, specific advice by Open University tutors. The temptation to comfort a student with higher grades than are strictly deserved must be denied. In such cases, a telephone call might be invited or a meeting at a tutorial or, at foundation leave, a special session for remedial tuition might well be arranged.

It is essential to do everything to forestall demoralisation and consequent 'drop out' in a 'distance teaching' system. To illustrate some of these matters, here is a PT3 comment (accompanying a 'D' grade) that may seem to be on the right lines, though the actual advice could, with advantage, be more specific.

> It's clear that you have spent a lot of time on this, and there are aspects in which it is good, but on the whole I felt that there were one or two areas needing attention. You have not, perhaps made the fullest use of Unit 6. Have another look especially, at Sections 20.4 and 20.5: this was where the crucial material for this assignment was covered.
>
> You write clearly, but not always in complete sentences. It is important to do this: as I've commented on the script, it is not advisable to write in note-form unless specifically asked to do so. Again, you answers, even though brief, needed rather more careful planning. You tend to set down your ideas rather as they occur to you, I think. Your answer to question 5, unfortunately, contained a great deal of material that wasn't really relevant, and you omitted to consider the second part of the

> question. But don't be disheartened: there's a lot to commend here too.

Thus tutors might take pains to avoid anything like an abrupt or curt style. It is not easy to write short comments that do not seem 'short' in the adverse sense. This is not to advocate unction, but a correspondence tutor has to study how to raise the issues with a largely unknown student on paper while conveying the air of companionable co-operation that is usually shown in a live tutorial by 'non-verbal gesture.' A correspondence tutor therefore has to acquire the knack of friendly 'verbal gesture.'

Even the new tutor-counsellor (perhaps especially the new tutor-counsellor) should not (and, indeed, cannot) depend on meeting the students to establish good relations. He ought to excel as a correspondence tutor first and foremost.

Admittedly, considered comment takes time to produce and part-time staff do not have excessive time at their disposal, but 'not too little, not too much' is a sensible rule of thumb in correspondence tuition as in other matters. A half dozen points of constructive criticism or positive advice on the PT3 form, related to half a dozen specific comments in the margins of the script itself (together with correction of factual errors) should normally suffice. There is a law of diminishing returns here, in that students may respondent more to a few well directed comments than to a large number of miscellaneous suggestions. This may be particularly true of weak students, who, faced with an overdose of criticism and correction, may pursue the less important at the expense of the more important, or even give up altogether in the face of so big a task. Certainly many students at foundation level seem to need to learn how to learn from written comment and may need some coaching in how to do so. But the hard-pressed tutor would also do well to remember that the *good* student deserves stimulus as much as the weaker one needs 'remedial' advice.

Not only should comments be specific to be effective, they must be clearly self-explanatory, even to the point of giving examples of what is meant. The PT3 comment should contain specific references making it concrete and comprehensible. If some of these can refer to points also commented on within the body of the script, so much the better (e.g. 'see your second paragraph, page 3' directs the student firmly and encourages him to follow up advice).

An example of phraseology on a foundation level social science script which reads well and which invites a student to pursue his argument further is:

> Yes ... though this in turn might reduce productivity, by keeping workers in low productivity jobs. This in turn would reduce wages which in turn ...?

Or, from a mathematics script:

> It is easier, and more elegant, to start by adding x to both sides of Y > x. Try it!

Then too, comments should be clear. For example, if a tutor criticises a student on the PT3 form for being 'repetitious,' then the repetitive passages should be clearly marked on the script.

Tutorial Teaching

We have seen that correspondence marking is the chief method by which a tutor teaches his students. But most courses offer a limited number and give. It must be realised that face-to-face tutorials which course tutors have to plan and give. It must be realised that face-to-face tuition within the Open University does not try to assume the function it has in most colleges, polytechnics and universities, where it is of prime importance. In the conventional teaching system, face-to-face tuition embraces both lecture (formal dissemination of information) and tutorials (opportunities for educative dialogue). In the Open University the former is executed through the medium of course units and broadcasts, and the latter for the most part through correspondence tuition.

The class tutorial in the Open University does have an important, if restricted part to play in the teaching system. Its original intention was that it should be remedial and supportive in nature. The main role of the tutor here is not to develop new themes and ideas, but to ensure that students understand the ideas and arguments in the course units and broadcasts, and to remedy students' academic weaknesses. This sounds a very narrow brief: many tutors and students believe strongly in the value of tutorials and one of the commonly heard questions is: why doesn't the Open University provide more opportunities for face-to-face contact? But there are some general points which the Open University tutor must bear in mind. Many students have so little spare time that they cannot afford to travel to a study centre even for a 'good' tutorial, because they feel the time spent on travelling and on the tutorial itself is better spent on the course materials. Some students are deterred by expenses while others are kept at home by family responsibilities or physical handicaps. This is summed up by a D101 student:

> It was a waste of time coming — it took an hour to get in an hour to get back, I spent two hours there, turned to page x, looked for answers to these questions. Honestly, I'd rather put in four hours' serious study at home ... I wanted it really to be just a correspondence course. I'd find it binding to *have* to go every week.

So it is clear that one cannot expect even the majority of one's group to attend tutorials. Moreover, it is clear that while class tutorials need not be narrowly 'remedial,' they are most likely to fill a definite need if they are distinctly different from a lecture, which could after all be broadcast or read. The essential feature of a face-to-face meeting is that the students can participate; perhaps it is not too much to say that if students are not active in the class, the tutor should ask himself what is the point of the meeting.

Of course, students may expect to be allowed to sit and listen while the tutor does the work, and they may even say that they expect to be 'taught.' Even arts students, at day schools, have been known to clamour for lectures, and to dismiss any idea of 'hearing each other talk.' Once a class has begun to think in this way (because only the more passive students are still attending?) It can be tempting to take the line of least resistance, but observations of class tutorials suggest that this is not the best solution. The alternative of stimulating the class to think in a new way about a few topics related to the units is likely to be much more profitable, and perhaps more true to the ideal of university education.

Use of Broadcasts

The broadcasts form a vital component of the teaching materials provided for Open University students. Increasingly, as the pattern of student performance becomes clearer, they are being more effectively integrated into the rest of the materials, and on some courses, such as the new mathematics foundation course, M101, they provide the only place where a particular topic is taught. To assist students to make effective use of broadcasts, tutors might consider arranging for their group as a whole to listen or watch, at home or at the study centre, and then to compare notes. (For some courses audio visual cassettes are available, and all radio broadcasts can be provided, on loan, recorded on tape cassettes). This note-taking can of itself be a useful skill for students to acquire, and the notes can be used as a point of departure for tutorial classes.

It may be that students do not obtain the maximum benefit from broadcasts at present. Research tends to show that the more successful students watch broadcasts more consistently, through there is no clear pattern of cause and effect. It seems very probable that some students on each course value broadcasts highly, while others do not. (In the same way, perhaps, some students value tutorials, while others do not). This may reflect a genuine difference between the preferred learning pattern of students, but it is also possible, or even probable, that more students could benefit from broadcasts if they were given more help to do so. It may be the case that broadcasts encountered resistance, from both students and tutors, because of the tendency to judge them solely on aesthetic criteria. If so, tutors can play a very useful part in encouraging the use of different criteria in judging programmes and in developing more positive attitudes to the broadcasts by making more use of them in their tutorials.

We shall not discuss regional day schools at length here, although some course teams lay down a programme of day schools. In some cases, when held at a major population centre, they offer a better use of restricted tutorial time for groups of students who live some distance from their tutor. Such day schools may offer a most fertile 'mix' of lectures, seminars, films and special exercises where the effect of the whole is more than the sum of its parts. For courses without summer schools, well planned and integrated day schools may be invaluable, and tutors should plan them carefully in consultation with their regional staff tutor.

Finally, what may one say about classroom manner? At the risk of labouring the obvious, it is important to point out that the tutor must avoid embarrassing the shy or less able student, some of whom hesitate to expose their (real or imaginary) weaknesses to their fellow students' scrutiny. It is easy for a tutor to appear very discouraging when a student makes a contribution that is not relevant or wrong; but ignoring contributions or dismissing them abruptly soon reduces the number of good contributions as well as the bad! Indeed, this aspect of tutoring needs careful cultivation: if one catches oneself being dismissive of a student's suggestion, it is often a good idea to apologise, to try to let him down lightly. According to Gibbs and Durbridge, the characteristics most often mentioned by staff tutors in discussion of Open University tutor's work were warmth and understanding. One assumes that competence in the subject was taken for granted, but even so it is a telling comment on the importance of a tutor's personality.

The framework for study

Continuity of Concern

By linking each undergraduate student at foundation level to a tutor-counsellor and by continuing this association beyond foundation level whatever possible the Open University has sought to meet a discerned need. It seeks to provide a continuous educational support which cuts across disciplines and across faculties. The frequent contact, whether by face-to-face or other methods, the subject link which is reinforced through the correspondence element and the provision of sympathetic help in planning a beneficial work pattern, all these generate a sound basis of mutual understanding between students and tutor-counsellors at foundation level which students may rely on throughout their later studies. It is this relationship which breaks down the isolation of the home-based student and begins to encourage and shape the effective dialogue which is the basis of education. There has always been a perspective which regards education as personal development rather than helping people to memorise information. The continuity of contact and concern which is the basis of the relationship between a tutor-counsellor and a student facilitates this personal development.

Support of Associate Students

The system of continuity of concern on the part of a tutor-counsellor for individual students from foundation level to course completion is, of course, particularly important for undergraduate students. Associate students enter the

University for a period of study which is of shorter duration than a degree. Often, however, such students remain with the University for longer than a year taking two or more courses which may or may not be recognised in themselves as a specific qualification. For them the same principles hold good, namely local support of a general academic nature and normally more distant support from a course tutor relating to the specific academic content of the course. However, because their registration as students is normally of a more transient nature, it is not always possible to establish the same relationship at a local level as for undergraduates. The University's response to the varying needs of associate students is to tailor support systems to the particular needs of associate students. Equality of consideration rather than equality of provision is the aim here.

Complexity and Flexibility

The Open University student probably has more freedom and more choice in his degree profile than any other student. This freedom, however, in turn demands of the individual student a number of important decisions. It is an interesting and sometimes infuriating paradox that this provision of flexibility to cater for individual needs tends to result in complicated administrative procedures which may in themselves present the student with problems. The tutor-counsellor must be able to help each student administratively, academically and vocationally. He must interpret and resolve with the student any divergence between the objectives of the course and any preconceptions with which the student might approach his work. But he must not merely deal with the various problems as they arise. He is not the deus ex machina of the crisis but rather a supportive and knowledgeable adviser who is closely involved with every aspect of his students' studies.

Personal Relationship

As we have seen the students in any one tutor-counsellor's

group can be and are likely to be diverse in their backgrounds; but they all have in common the fact that, as part-time students they can suffer from feeling isolated and are working within a very complex organisation which might tend to increase that isolation. The tutor-counsellor can best make his advice, knowledge and support available, if he develops a personal relationship with each one of them. Early individual contact with new students is clearly important for the establishment of this personal relationship. It is, however, difficult to say much about this in a general way, as so much depends on an individual's approach, but aspects are discussed throughout this booklet and in the *Handbook for Part-Time Tutorial and Counselling Staff.* Certainly a trusting and friendly relationship can be established only if the tutor-counsellor is in regular contact with his students. With many students particularly in their foundation year, this contact occurs at meetings at the local study centre; but such meetings are not an essential requisite for success; much counselling work may be carried out by correspondence and telephone, especially in the case of higher level students. Tutor-counsellors, like — course tutors, can develop a good relationship with students whom they seldom or perhaps never see.

12

INTERACTION AND INDEPENDENCE

Introduction

A major educational development over the last decade has been the creation and growth of remote learning systems in many countries of the world. This article is primarily concerned with multi-media distance study systems at the university level.

The conceptual and historical bases for this new mode of higher education have been discussed elsewhere. They can be summarised by observing that the long tradition of independent study has, with the aid of modern developments in the technology of education, been married to the more recent ideological trend of open learning to produce new types of educational enterprises which fulfil economic and political needs in both industrial and developing countries.

We wish to examine in particular the difficult synthesis which distance learning systems have to effect between those activities in which the student works alone and those which bring him into contact with other people. It is in this sense that the terms *interaction* and *independence* in the title of this paper are to be understood. However, since these words are used widely elsewhere with a variety of meanings, further clarification of their connotation in this context will be useful.

Interaction

In what is probably the most general theory of human learning to appear to date, Pask holds that all learning is based on conversations. However, these conversations are often internalised as when a solitary and silent student mulls over the 'knowables' in a text he is reading. Clearly in this sense all learning involves interaction.

In this article we shall use the term interaction in a more restricted manner to cover only those activities where the student is in two-way contact with another person (or persons) in such a way as to elicit from him reactions and responses which are specific to his own requests or contributions. Such contact need not imply face-to-face meetings, indeed we shall examine the role of interaction by telephone, nor do the reactions have to be immediate (e.g. the mail delay in correspondence tutoring). The modes of interaction we shall be studying are:

- counselling students before entry into the system and during their studies;
- tutoring students involved in courses and projects;
- contact about projects with tutors or *animateurs;*
- teaching over interactive telecommunications systems;
- bringing students together into discussion groups;
- residential gatherings of the 'summer school' type.

Independence

The term independence will be used broadly to denote those learning activities where there is no interaction as we have defined it. These include:

- study of written material;
- watching/listening to broadcasts (or audio-visual materials that can be played back at home);
- writing essays and assignments;

- working alone at a computer terminals;
- surveys and project work.

Placing essay writing and computing in the 'independent' category requires a word of justification. Clearly most essays or assignments are done with a view to later interaction with a tutor about their content. However, we shall consider that the interactive phase begins with the tutor's reply. We also class interactive computing as an independent activity, except where an electronic mail system is employed, because the replies which a student elicits, however appropriate they may be to his needs, are standard and pre-programmed.

Having divided students' activities in remote learning into these two categories, we shall now explain why we regard the balance which is maintained between them as the crucial issue facing distance study systems.

The Problems of Distance Education

Distance education already embraces a variety of approaches. In systems such as Britain's Open University centrally produced multi-media courses are taken by large numbers of students whereas in most US open learning projects the emphasis is placed on allowing students to define their own curricula. Naturally systems pursuing different aims will encounter different problems although all face the problem of apportioning resources between interactive and independent activities. In this article, we shall place greater emphasis on the problems encountered at the multi-media course end of the distance education spectrum, simply because this has been the approach espoused most commonly in Canada (e.g. Quebec's Tele-universite, Athabasca University, and the off-campus offerings of many other Canadian universities). For this reason, we shall refer frequently to articles in the excellent Journal *Teaching at a Distance* published by the Open University.

Problem 1 — Choice of Content: Authority vs Autonomy

Multi-media courses centrally produced for large student enrolments have an authoritarian flavour. Kirk talks of the creation of 'a large teaching proletariat and a small academic ruling class,' and Harrison says that 'part-time tutors and the students face similar problems as fellow travellers on the outside rim of the Open University wheel.'

Particularly among the part-time tutors at the Open University one detects a certain jealousy at the role of the central course teams which not only decide the content of the course but by all accounts have great fun doing it. In a sense the traditional university, in which a course is conceived in solitude in the lecturer's study and delivered inteactively in the classroom, has been stood on its head in the Open University approach where the course is conceived in interaction and studied (largely) in solitude.

In a sensitive article Parraton argues that the problem of who chooses the content is not a simple one. He suggests that the Americans are wrong in looking to greater individualisation of content choice as a cure for dissatisfaction with universities, for this may exacerbate the bittiness of curricula which he sees as the major fault of the existing system. Quoting Mao Tse Tung to the effect that the role of the educator is to 'teach the masses clearly what we have received form them confusedly,' Perraton suggests that the local tutor or animateur, who is present at the interface between the student and the centrally produced course, is best placed to ensure a happy medium between irrelevancies imposed by authority and bittiness chosen individually. Mentioning with approval Quebec's Tevec project, he insists that learning is a social activity and that local animateurs should provide a supportive artificial network which will enable the content to be gradually adapted to the existing natural network in which people are living. The animateur's task is thus to discover local needs and relate course materials to them so that knowledge can play its key role as an agent of change in society. Harrison concurs with this function of the tutor as the meeting point between 'popular culture' (the real and local life patterns of particular students) and 'educated knowledge' (the course texts, audio-visual materials, the tutor's academic background)

Problem 2—Economies of Scale

Among ten characteristics of open learning systems Wedemeyer includes the following:

> As an operating principle, the system is capable, after reaching a critical minimum of aggregation, of accommodating increased numbers of learners without a *commensurate* increase in the unit cost of the basic learning experiences: i.e. costs must not be directly and rigidly volume sensitive. After reaching the necessary level of aggregation, unit costs should show a diminishing relationship to total system costs.

This criterion is, for the most remote learning systems, the crucial issue in determining the blend of interaction and independence. Coming on the scene at the dusk of the golden era of university expansion of the 1960s, remote learning systems are expected to be more costs effective than traditional approaches. Broadly speaking, independent activities have great possibilities of economies of scale since the marginal costs of printing extra copies of texts or broadcasting to more students are low. However, the costs of interactive activities tend to increase in direct proportion to the number of students.

The choices forced upon remote learning systems by these simple facts are extremely painful. Most educators want high quality and a healthy degree of redundancy (so as to accommodate differences in learning styles) throughout the system. In the early days choices can be made consciously, but as the system grows and different departments are created to handle the various components of the learning experience, competition for resources can become severe, political and acrimonious. In our own institution, the Tele-universite, there is a particularly lively debate between the protagonists of more interactive support in the regions and those who would like the graphic presentation of the course texts to be immediately attractive.

Thus the economic problem requires choices to be made — but other problems have to be taken into account as well.

Problem 3 — Does the Activity Suit the Student?

Most remote learning systems recruit their students among working adults. Although such students are usually highly motivated, family and professional obligations compete with their studies for the little spare time they have available. Not surprisingly our students at the Tele-universite tell us that the flexibility in planning study time which our courses permit is one of the main reasons why they chose to enrol. This constraint of student availability is of such fundamental importance for a remote-learning system that it is worth discussing its impact on each of the activities listed earlier. We shall take the independent activities first.

> *Written Texts* Media buffs often criticize remote learning systems for what they see as their retrograde emphasis on the written word. Leaving aside claims, such as that of Turok, that correspondence is the best vehicle for degree-level distances study, we feel that such critics underestimate the remarkable flexibility of print. On other medium at present available can be carried around and consulted with the same ease.
>
> *Broadcasts/Audio visual materials* Broadcasting has tremendous possibilities for economies of scale. However, the very detailed studies that have been conducted at the Open University by Bates, and

which are probably applicable to most systems, show that only by broadcasting programmes twice a week at different times is it even theoretically possible for more than 90 per cent of students to view or hear them. Audio-visual materials (e.g. cassettes) which can be played back at home circumvent this problem to some extent, but with the penalty of losing economies of scale.

Essays and assignments Since students can plan essay and assignment writing to fit their own schedules this type of activity is inherently flexible. However, the value of assignments depends greatly on the quality of the later (interactive) marking phase. It is important to match the style of assignment to the student's background. The academic essay, for example, is not a natural form of expression to most entrants to a distant study system and some training is needed to attain the high level of written exchange between student and tutor reported, with examples, by Harrison. Similarly many of our students at the Tele-universite claim that our objective tests require unfamiliarly lucid and careful reasoning on their part.

Computing Remote learning systems working to less densely populated areas than Europe will have some difficulty placing 'interactive' computing facilities within the reach of all students in a cost-effective manner. Furthermore few students are accomplished typists and operation of even the simplest and most fool-proof terminal can pose problems for the adult who may have to work with it alone in the evening at his local centre.

Laboratory experiments The Open University home experiment kits are the object of worldwide admiration and provide a rich source of photogenic material for films on distance study. Since such kits are greatly appreciated by most students, it is a pity that only the largest institutions such as the Open University have large enough enrolments in science and technology courses to achieve economies of scale on the enormous costs of designing simple, safe and telling experiments and the equipment to go with them. Buying kits from the bit institutions is probably the only way for smaller systems to incorporate this element of remote learning.

Surveys and project work These are usually a form of assignment and once again there can easily be mismatch between the student's preparedness and the tacit assumptions of the course planners. Students almost invariably bite off more than they can chew and grossly underestimate the time a project will take. Henry argues that projects are best considered in the category of interactive activities because of the guidance needed at the three major stages of choosing the topic, collecting information, and writing up the results.

When we consider the interactive aspects of remote learning the difficulties we have enumerated for independent activities pale into insignificance, for interactive experiences, to the extent that they require the bringing together of people, submit the remote student to just those constraints of geography and time that he enrolled in the system to escape. Crucial to all remote learning systems is the scatter problem described by Turok and we shall return later in this article to the important role of telecommunications in overcoming the geographical difficulties.

The interactive piece de resistance is clearly the summer school type of gathering. The Open University planners incorporated summer schools into their programme after visiting Australian correspondence operations and their role has been a subject of heart searching ever since.

Woodley and McIntosh report that a quarter of those who decide not to apply to the Open University desist because they could not have attended summer school. In another article McIntosh examines the whole question of summer schools and highlights the essential problem: although summer schools are a hugely appreciated experience for most students their very existence prevents some students enrolling. However, were attendance made voluntary there is a fear that, in common with all optional extras, their 'mainline' role in the system would disappear.

Moreover, even the much more minor disturbance in the schedule of an adult student which is caused by the opportunity to meet tutors and counsellors or to attend discussion groups at other times during the course must not be underestimated. Since such interactive activities tend to be inconvenient for the student and expensive for the institution, all remote learning systems have a strong incentive to use them efficiently. This article includes a guide to good practice which we hope will be useful in this regard.

Problem 4 — To Pace or not to Pace?

Pacing is a question fraught with ideological issues and pregnant with practical administrative problems. Upon the decision of a remote learning system with regard to pacing will largely depend the sort of mixture it can achieve between interaction and independence.

The ideological issue is simply stated: if a system has, as its chief priority, respect for the freedom and autonomy of the individual students, it will allow him to begin a course of study whenever he chooses and to finish it at his convenience. The student paces himself and there are no external constraints although the good correspondence school, whose model this is, will have a system of written reminders, encouraging phone calls and even financial incentives to incite him to keep at it. Nevertheless the drop out, or non-completion rate, with such a free approach is usually horrendous (over 50 per cent) if the students are humans rather than angels. In the nineteenth century, when correspondence schools began, the idea of the survival of the fittest was more acceptable than it is today and most modern remote learning systems, knowing that many of their students join them with feelings of educational inadequacy, are concerned to do everything in their power to prevent the student dropping out with his sense of failure reinforced.

The usual way to encourage students to continue with a course is to provide some form of pacing, i.e. to introduce into the system a series of events taking place at fixed times which become deadlines for the students to meet. Several remarks about pacing can be made with reference to our two categories of activity.

> *Independent activities* Of the independent activities identified in an earlier paragraph, broadcasts and assignments are the most obvious means for pacing. The Open University has always regarded this as a major function of its television and radio programmes and practically all institutions which adopt pacing use assignments in this way by fixing 'cut-off' dates for each.
>
> *Interactive activities* Whilst individual contacts between a student and his counsellor or tutor are not a mechanism for pacing, and indeed should provide a safety net for the student who is having difficulty keeping pace, group interactions are usually impossible without pacing, simply because they are based on bringing together students who are at the same point in a course. Admittedly there are interesting exceptions; Athabasca University holds group meetings for students who have reached widely different points in a course and the Open

University, in response to the problems of residential gatherings already mentioned, now holds joint summer schools for several courses within the same discipline.

However, homogenous group meetings remain more common and at the Tele-universite, where we do not have access to broadcasting for most of our courses, the local meetings with an animateur, held at approximately three-week intervals, are our key pacing mechanism. We are sure that these meetings keep many students up to the mark and that without them our drop out rate would be higher.

Finally mention should be made of completely paced systems such as the Wisconsin Education Telephone Network where weekly interactive teleconferences are the major element of the courses.

To conclude this discussion of pacing it may be helpful to give a concrete example of how different mechanisms can be used. The Tele-universite offers to the adult population of Quebec, without academic prerequisites, a series of credit courses in a programme entitled *Connaissance de l'homme et du milieu* Table 12.1 indicates the pacing mechanism in each of the thirteen courses available to date.

The Tele-universite claims to run a paced system where courses are offered in periods corresponding roughly to regular university terms. Whilst we feel that some sort of pacing is essential and would not contemplate changing to the correspondence model, our present problems with pacing may be of interest. These are two; the start and the finish.

How do you administer a staggered start? Although we hopefully indicate starting dates, and even enrolment deadlines, in our publicity, the majority of students enrol after the deadlines, sometimes several weeks after. Admittedly we are in a phase of rapid growth (enrolments doubling every term) so that the ripples of our publicity reach potential students late, but we also have the impression that students like, and take advantage of, our image as an open university unconstipated by the usual bureaucratic rules about enrolment.

Although the Open University has the luxury of refusing applicants, the Tele-universite (in common with most North American remote learning systems working to the relatively small populations of individual states or provinces in an era when higher education is no longer the favourite of government) has good political and financial reasons for accepting as many applicants as possible.

Naturally late applicants pose problems for the pacing mechanism. In the case of broadcasts the obstacle is almost insuperable and even in the case of group meetings postponing the first course meeting in a particular region may displease and discourage the students who enrolled in good time.

Bringing in the Stragglers Other problems occur at the end of courses. Once the broadcasts and meetings are finished and the deadline date for the last assignment is past there usually remain a significant number of students who have not completed the course but who do not consider themselves to have dropped out. They intend to finish the assignments/ exams at a later date. In the Universite du Quebec network such students receive an 'I' (incomplete) grade which, if not converted within one term into a letter grade, results in failure. We are under pressure from our course teams to change this procedure and will probably do so. However, it is unlikely that simply extending from one term to

> one year the period of grace before the guillotine falls and puts a 'fail' on the student's record is going to cause many stragglers to complete — unless a mechanism is set up to help them do so. Remote learning systems must beware of the illusion of solving problems with flexible rules which make the staff feel liberal and warm inside but which do not of themselves help the student attain his goals.

Analysing these four live issues in distance education has shown us why it is important for remote learning systems to achieve a good mix between independent and interactive activities. Interaction with others can temper the otherwise authoritarian style of a course and motivate the student to persevere by providing psychological support and a degree of pacing. However, since interactive activities are expensive, especially if they require the maintenance of a network of study centres, and usually inconvenience the student to some degree, the effectiveness of each must be examined regularly. In their study of seventeen open systems around the world, MacKenzie et al recall that although the Open University allots nearly one third of its budget to ineractive student services a causal relationship between use of these services and success in gaining credits has yet to be established.

In the next section of this article, we shall try to provide a guide to good practice in the interactive components of remote learning. The functions of counselling, tutoring, and group meetings will be examined in turn.

TABLE 12.1

Course title	*Pacing mechanism*
Initiation a la cooperation	3-weekly meetings (5); assignments
Initiation a l'economie du Quebec	3-weekly meetings (5); assignments
Histoire du Quebec d'aujourd'hui 1 et 2	3-weekly meetings (5); assignments

La gestion: un art meconnu	Meetings (2) at beginning and end of course; assignments
L'informatique, c'est pas sorcier	3 group meetings; schedule for work at computer terminal
L'environment : un bien collectif menace	4 group meetings
Action-environment (project)	None—except tutorial exhortation
L'individu, son affectivite, sa sexualite 1 et 2	6-7 group meetings; assignments
Francais pour tous, francais pour tout	Assignments only
La publicite au Quebec	Weekly broadcast TV programmes (30); assignments
Vieillir, c'est quoi?	Weekly meetings

Interactive activities: a guide to good practice

Counselling

In this context we shall denote by counselling the advice, help and support given to an adult of facilitate his progress in the remote learning system. Excluded by this definition are the tutoring function with respect to a particular course, which will be considered in the next section, and the advice and help an individual may need to solve various personal (e.g. family and financial) problems which may impinge on his studies but are not directly related to them. Nicholson distinguishes three stages in the relation between the adult student and the institution at which counselling is necessary: induction crisis, differential transit, and settled connection, a classification which we shall adopt.

> *Induction crisis* The adult student approaches remote learning with some anxiety and in this first period of contact, when his investment of effort is still small, he will be more likely to withdraw from the system in the face of difficulties or unexpected demands. MacKenzie et al insist on the importance of treating adults as adults, not simply in the design

of course materials but also in the wording of forms and letters and in answering enquiries. These authors suggest that the counsellor has three tasks at this stage:

- instilling self-confidence: the adult may have a sense of failure from his previous contact with formal education;
- helping the student cope with the freedom of open learning;
- helping the student improve his study habits.

In this context Redmond reminds us that the adult student may not consider the learning role to be part of adult life in the same way as his occupation and family obligations. If this role can be accepted and internalised the student will be likely to do better in his studies. Furthermore the adult is used to controlling his environment — limiting the number and type of unexpected things that can happen to him — and will feel vulnerable in unpredictable situations. The sensitive counsellor will realise that the new student is having to accommodate himself to a specialised and formalised pattern of interaction which may be foreign to his everyday habits. Those with the least formal education probably need the most help an encouragement.

The development of good study habits has been discussed by Gibbs and Northedge who suggest it is not enough simply to give the student a text on study skills. Since people change their existing habits and constructs on the basis of cautious negotiation, constantly relating the new to the old, these authors propose holding group sessions in which students are encouraged to develop a self-analytic attitude and to question their present study habits. We shall return later to the discussion technique used but a typical starting point would be for students to make notes on the same text, swap and criticize them in pairs, bring their conclusions on note-taking together in a group of four and so on. In a similar manner marking essays is urged as an excellent training for writing them. Experience with these techniques shows that a good counsellor can organise an intensive group session on study habits which leads students to continue to refine their study techniques independently thereafter.

Differential transit Nicholson suggests that rather different challenges face the counsellor once the student is fully integrated in the system, especially as the academic challenge increases on going from early general to later specialist courses. Family and colleagues may feel by then they have made enough allowances for the adult's studies. Good counselling on the choice of advanced courses is especially important.

Settled connection Even for those fortunate students who achieve a harmonious equilibrium between study and day-to-day life, the counsellor has a role to play. He should be ready to guide at the recurrent choice points and to help the student who finds job satisfaction decreasing or is faced by an unforeseen event which upsets his schedule. Simpson has compared the views of both Open University students and counsellors on counselling at the 'settled connection' stage. Counsellors were generally uncertain about their role but divided fairly easily into *interventionists* who initiated contact with students and *consultants* who waited for students to contact them. Naturally interventionists have more contact with students although both types had some reluctance to invade a student's

> privacy by making contact. All felt that continuity and knowing the students were essential to good counselling.
>
> Nearly all students expected their counsellor to take an interest in their progress and over three-quarters both wished to keep the same counsellor throughout their studies and wanted him to initiate contact at least every three months using the phone where possible.

What makes a good counsellor? This question has been addressed by Thomas, Northedge and Murgatroya. After a study based on the critical incident approach Thomas identified the following qualities and habits of good counsellors: enthusiasm, takes initiative, sympathetic, contacts students, helps with problems, uses the hierarchy, has a flexible programme, can manage group activities, competent academically, knows the system, liaises with others, shares management tasks. Northedge concentrates on the roles of counsellors and distinguishes the *caring supporter* and the *efficient manager* as the two key functions. Since caring and managing require different skills the counsellor must make a conscious effort to balance the two. Murgatroyd cities Carl Rogers' three conditions for personal development through face-to-face interactions, namely empathy, genuineness and an unconditional positive regard for the student.

In remote learning systems other than the Open University counselling is more often a case of guilty conscience than a help with problems since there are few systems where the function has been institutionalised. Although a counselling service is clearly desirable, the need for continuity in the counsellor-student relationship to make it effective is a refrain that runs through writings on the subject. Cook has discussed the administrative and organisational aspects of ensuring continuity.

Young institutions such as the Tele-universite which do not have, nor feel the need for, a counselling service may be living in a fool's paradise. Experience elsewhere shows that remote learning systems begin with a 'cream-skimming' stage when they attract students who have both higher motivation and greater experience than those who will provide the steady state clientele some years later. This gradual change in student profiles, together with the greater complexity and bureaucracy which occurs as an institution grows may create a real need for counselling.

Tutoring, Animating and Facilitating

By tutors, animateurs and facilitators we shall understand those people whose interaction with the students is based on a particular course. Since the word facilitator still sounds to the present authors like the name of a new brand of prophylactic we shall use the more expressive 'animateur' to cover this function. The difference in meaning between tutor and animateur was evoked in the first paragraphs.

As the next section will deal with group discussions we shall postpone consideration of the tutor-animateur's role in group meetings and concentrate here on the one-to-one relationship.

We can agree with Perraton that 'the thing which a live tutor can do which we can't mechanise and we can't mass-produce, is to enter into a dialogue with his students.' Beevers has described how this function was made operational in the early days of the Open University and emphasises how few of the University staff were experienced in what was to be the main mode of a dialogue, namely correspondence tuition. Official documents tell tutors that 'In this essentially home-based teaching system where attendance at the occasional tutorial is voluntary, your relationship with students in formed mainly through the exchange of assignments. ' In a revealing phrase Kirk, herself a tutor, after quoting this directive states, 'Thus, the part-timer's teaching duties are regarded *merely* as the assessment of, and support for, a centrally designed programme...' (our italics).

Naturally there is a tendency for tutors unused to dialogue by correspondence to attempt to pull the system towards more of the face-to-face contact which they find more familiar and fulfilling. The Open University seems to have successfully resisted this move, which would have imposed inconvenient and costly constraints on both students and the University, and indeed has developed impressive expertise in correspondence tuition. Harrison describes how essay marking should be an exercise in conversation rather than an issuing of directives. On the same theme MacKenzie discusses how to combat 'an established tendency, quite foreign to the way thought really develops; to see assignments as a series of paper hoops to burst through and discard.' Both tutors and students need to pay more attention to the progressive nature of the learning process. Occasional reviews of a series of assignments by a given student might be useful here.

Rhys suggests that the tutor, when marking assignments, should be balancing three types of consideration against each other; organisational requirements, communication with the student, and attention to the content. The balance will vary from essay to essay since the whole point of the dialogue is to avoid a mechanical process in which the tutor merely decides to what extent the student has followed the recipe for a good Open University essay.

The characteristics of Open University tutors have been studied by Gibbs and Durbridge. There was a broad agreement across faculties that the personal style of the tutor (understanding, systematic, informal, flexible, interesting) was the most important quality, followed by his teaching competence. Academic qualifications, as opposed to knowledge and handling of the subject matter, rated very low.

There is a parallel here with the experience of institutions using non-academic animateurs for dialogue with students. At the Tele-universite we are finding that animateurs are moving from one course to another in different subjects with greater versatility than we expected. Implicitly we are placing more emphasis on personal characteristics and less on academic respectability in selecting these staff. The animateur's own confidence in his ability to handle the subject matter is a sufficient guarantee in nearly all cases.

Since few other remote learning institutions place as much emphasis on written interaction as the Open University we would encourage them to examine the examples of student-tutor exchanges collected by Lewis and Tomlinson which show impressive maturity and thoughtfulness. Indeed, the main conclusion of our discussion of the tutoring functions is that remote learning systems would do well to place greater emphasis on written interaction. Not only would this reduce both time and travel constraints on students and part-time staff compared to face-to-face encounters, but it would also be more cost-effective.

Such a move would pose problems of training for part-time staff who, as already mentioned, are normally inexperienced in this function. However, this is only one aspect of the general issue of training and briefing of part-time staff, and we shall devote the rest of this section to this question.

We know of no remote learning system which is proud of the way it trains part-time staff. Macintyre has been one of few people to study needs in this area. He found that part-time staff most wanted training in grading and with face-to-face sessions. Interestingly most respondents held that meetings with other part-time staff were the most effective form of training. In view of our previous remarks it is perhaps surprising that few tutors felt the need of help with correspondence tuition. Macintyre is unable to decide whether this reflects cool competence or misplaced confidence.

Since personal characteristics have been shown to be so important in good counsellors and tutors, their selection should be uncomplicated. The articles we have reviewed suggest that their training should include information on the structure, organisation and methods of the remote learning system which is employing them and clear directives on their role in it—which may be counter-intuitive or at least very different to their regular job in another institution. Once the staff have been trained and are in the system, regular and loosely structured meetings with other part-timers may be a sufficient incentive to further development.

Group Meetings

Group sessions have become the pons asinorum of our time and this fad has taken root in adult education with infectious rapidity. This is not to suggest that group meetings have no place in adult learning, simply to recall that bringing people together does not automatically create a useful educational experience. Since students in a remote-learning system will be sceptical about any gathering which implies travel and time constraints, institutions have a duty to make group meetings effective. We shall first discuss face-to-face meetings and then examine the increasingly frequent use of telecommunications.

> *Face-to-face* Lewis reminds us that students dislike 'face-to-face aimlessness' and do not necessarily appreciate a sharp contrast between highly structured media packages and amorphous get-togethers. Watkins and Northedge have addressed themselves to the problem of making discussions useful to students. Both acknowledge their debt to Hill but suggest that his techniques need some modification in remote-learning systems.

Northedge has found that the pure Hill technique

is too introspective and places too much emphasis on the mastering of psychological concepts and the analysis of interaction with others. He proposed maintaining Hill's emphasis on an agreed agenda and reports on a technique which includes the following steps:

1. individual work (note making) (5 minutes)
2. work in pairs (comparing and consolidating) (10-15 minutes)
3. small group (4-6) (comparing and consolidating) (30-45 minutes)
4. report back to whole group (30-45 minutes)

Use of this technique, which he claims is 'robust enough, and simple enough to survive a wide range of conditions,' produced greater student enjoyment and increased the participation of quieter students whilst improving the quality of the argument considerably. In contrast to Hill's method this technique does not require the Group to cover all the content, thus respecting Watkins claim that the students themselves should control the pace and orientation of the discussion. Both Watkins and Northedge emphasise the importance of starting the meeting with a short period when students write preparatory notes. This helps to delay subjective reactions to the content until it has been objectively analysed.

So far we have implied that a part-time staffer is present to lead and guide discussions. However, remote learning systems are finding, in response to the scatter problem, that discussion groups with no tutor present can be found very useful by students. Sewart has reported on the formation of such study groups, of which there were over one thousand in the Open University in 1974, and

Whitlock, writing later, warns against the danger of stereotyping these groups into set paradigms. It appears that about one-third of students, many of them taking only one course and finding the going fairly tough, attend student study groups regularly. The groups met roughly every three weeks and often, particularly in mathematics, an informal network of telephone contact operates as a result. Whitlock urges that regional staff pay more attention to helping these groups get started and that courses suggest some group activities.

Telecommunications As lower enrolments in advanced courses scattered students further from each other and from potential tutors, the Open University turned to the teleconference to surmount the problem of maintaining groups meetings. Short reviewed available evidence to show that teaching by telephone is acceptable in to many cases and L'Henry-Evans has reported on how it feels to guide a group discussion by telephone. More recently Turok has summarised Open University experience with group telephony and concludes that it has an important future. Naturally similar developments are occurring in other remote-learning systems. The Tele-universite uses teleconferences to link animateurs to isolated students at their home pones in groups of five or six and has published guides for those involved with this medium. In other places, notably Wisconsin, dedicated educational telephone networks are used as the main vehicle for a whole series of adult courses. Those interested in the role of the telephone in education should consult the proceedings of two conferences on the subject. Telephony can make a very cost-effective contribution to remote learning and even in the densely populated UK it provides interaction at a lower cost than face-to-face meetings for advanced courses. Study groups without a tutor can of course meet by phone too although they will probably need help to set up the conference. Drop-out from telephone groups has been shown to be very small.

Conclusion Putting it all Together

We must disappoint the reader who, having persevered thus far, is expecting a recipe for the ideally cost-effective and educationally efficient remote-learning system. Such a recipe is impossible, simply because a system can only be conceived in relation to the country and context in which it is set. Barker reminds us that printing and publishing resources are rare in developing countries, let alone television and radio production facilities. MacKenzie et al point out that not all postal systems combine universality, reliability, uniformity, speed and low cost sufficiently to make them the basis for remote-learning.

Although the political, cultural and technological contest of a country will affect all components of a remote learning system it will have greater impact on what we have called the independent activities. This is partly why we have devoted most of this article to interactive activities, the other reason being that the costs of interactive activities are more rigidly volume-sensitive and hence can eat dangerously into the cost-effectiveness of a system. It is no doubt possible to write a guide to good practice for text-writing and electronic media production in remote learning, although for such common activities it is surprising how few systematic guidelines exist, but we shall leave that to others.

In building a remote-learning system from the components we have examined, we stress first that the adult student is a vehicle that can run well on a variety of mixtures of instructional fuel. Dubin and Taveggia, in their much quoted but little read comparative study on the effectiveness of various types of instruction, found no significant difference with dull regularity. This means that a remote-learning system has considerable room for manoeuvre with the purely instructional parts of its programme. However, the adult student is busy and pragmatic. His involvement with the remote-learning system is only a minor aspect of his life. Learning activities must be organised to provide maximum advantage for minimum inconvenience.

Within these limits there is great scope for diversity. Indeed, Baume and Hipwell, in an article about courses for workers on offshore oil rigs written with engaging verve, suggest the mixture should be changed constantly to maintain a permanent Hawthorne effect. At the Tele-universite we seem to have observed this maxim — although more by serendipity than by design!

Although some remote-learning systems operate without any personal contact we hope to have shown that the inclusion of properly planned interaction can be a help to the student. As well as socialising his learning it can provide an element of pacing and round off the authoritarian edges of the courses. However, interaction need not always mean face-to-face contact and most remote-learning systems would benefit by exploiting more fully written exchanges and teleconferences.

A second guideline is that the maxim 'nothing succeeds like excess' does not hold true in remote learning. Perhaps the major defect of the team approach to course design is the tendency to over do things. Partly because the team invariably underestimates the time an average student will take over a piece of work, and also because many 'nice to know' sections are given the benefit of the doubt when the team is faced with choices, the remote-learning course that requires less study time than advertised is a rare phenomenon. The adult student is usually very conscientious — over-conscientious perhaps — and it is only fair for the course designers to be equally thorough in ensuring that the credit given for a course is commensurate with the study time the student puts in.

Related to the question of workload is our third guideline, namely the need to combine complexity with clarity. The more complex the combination of activities in a course becomes, the more important is it for the student to have a map of the maze in the form of a well written study guide. The students are the only people who experience every aspect of a course and unless the designers realise this they may find that the course as a whole is greater only in confusion than the sum of the parts.

Oddly, for people whose profession is devoted to precise thought, many academics have great difficulty specifying exactly what they want a student to do. It seems to them childish to indicate the time a student should spend on an activity or the length his essay should be. In a rather similar way some feel that their profession requires them to include frequent bibliographies along with vague exhortations, even though they know the student has no means of consulting the references cited.

In conclusion then, the leader of a team putting together a course for a remote-learning system must first bring his people down to earth and then keep them there. He must ensure that the diversity of activities planned and the enthusiasm of his team does not lead to overkill and confusion. He must remember that he is working for a busy adult, who always has good reasons for putting study off until tomorrow, and when he must motivate, Pacing and interaction can be useful but it helps if the course is fun. The somewhat technocratic approach to course design used in distance education should not mean that the product is laundered of that zest for life and learning so necessary to the human spirit.

13

LEARNING TO READ

A great deal of time and thought has been given, over many years, to the question of trying to establish with some precision the mental processes by which children learn to read. It would be far from accurate to imply that teachers and researchers are still no nearer to identifying any convincing lines of advance than they were in the days before it was fashionable to give so much attention to the teaching of reading. There is now, for example, quite an impressive accumulation of evidence which suggests that children can be helped to look at the component parts of words and find clues, that help them in word recognition. This is an extremely important hypothesis, in terms of practical teaching, which seriously undermines the validity of the wholly 'look-and-say' approach that not so long ago was almost exclusively advocated—at least until children were considered to be sufficiently mature to dissect words or even sentences into smaller parts.

On the other hand evidence concerning cognitive processes, however carefully assembled, inevitably depends to some extent upon subjective interpretation; and in any case there is still much that is not conclusively known. There is more than one theory of how children learn, and certainly more than one view of the mechanisms by which they learn to read. The teacher must therefore weigh up the evidence available and the interpretations put upon it, and then determine upon a course of action which, it is hoped, will yield results. We obviously cannot wait to teach children to read until we are certain beyond doubt of the best way of doing so.

We must, however, try to take account of the probability that not all children may learn by precisely the same procedures. If teachers are to do this, they need to know some thing of current opinion concerning these learning procedures. They are then in a better position to allow, as far as in practice they can, for more than one possible way of learning. This assumption obviously cannot be carried too far. There are limits to the permutations which any presentation of material or fluidity of class organisation will permit, and in any case the teacher who is caused to worry so much about all the things she may not be doing could well be inhibited from being effective in the practice she already employs to some purpose. Nevertheless, familiarity with current opinion may enable her to extend the possibilities of learning within the practical framework of the conditions of her class.

Learning Theories

One theory is that learning is a process of conditioning. (The dog that learns to come for food when he hears his dinner bowl being rattled is responding to this principle.) By associating, for example, the word 'cat' with a picture of a cat, the child will in time be conditioned to making the association even when he sees the word without the picture. Taken a little further, the child is more likely to respond effectively to the conditioning if the material with which he is concerned has interest for him and is related to his daily life. On this assumption, it may be more likely that the child will be 'conditioned' to learn to read 'dog' because his Fido is a dog than to read 'jackal' since he does not ordinarily meet jackals as he walks down the road.

Reinforcement is an essential part of conditioning. A single experience of associating word and picture is unlikely to be enough. Repeated association is necessary (with more repetition for some children than for others); and since interest must be sustained a variety of ways in which identical word and picture situations can be presented must be devised. It is also important to recognise that conditioning will not be equally effective with every child.

The normal provision in an infant classroom will usually include material of this kind. Modern reading theory, however, suggests that there is more to it than straightforward whole word/picture association—that the child certainly seems to use more detailed clues to help his memory. (This will be further discussed later in the chapter.) It must be remembered, too, that words and pictures are not the only associations that provide for conditioning. Letter/sound associations may be made in the same way and so indeed may many others. It is the *principle* of conditioning that has theoretical significance for the teacher.

Another theory, primarily associated with the work of Piaget, is that learning is cumulative. It builds upon, and incorporates, past experience. A child's response to a particular situation will bring about certain results. The next time he meets a similar situation, he will meet it will certain expectations which arise as a consequence of his earlier experience—in other words, he learns to anticipate the result of his actions in known circumstances. The child assimilates the consequences of his experience as it accumulates, and in due course he *internalises* his actions and they become thoughts. He can then organise these thoughts so that he can adapt them in order to learn from the next situation.

In his earlier writings Piaget suggested that this process of adaptation operates more readily and with greater versatility as the child matures and develops. Indeed, he implied that at the beginning of the First School years most children are at the stage when, in effect, they believe the evidence of their eyes—their mental assumptions are largely based on imagery.

They do not have the power of interpreting differences they see by making intellectual deductions; that is to say, they may distinguish a long world from a short one when they meet it in a known context, but they distinguish it because it is clearly long and not for any reason which has been intellectually deduced.

At a later stage of intellectual maturity, the child would be able to use his experience of seeing and hearing words to abstract certain characteristics which were not entirely dependent upon imagery. For example, he could deduce that 'hop' becomes 'hope' because of the addition of the terminal 'e'. This hypothesis can hardly be at variance with the experience of the teacher of children who are learning to read. We all know that there is no point in talking about the 'magic e' to the child who has not made a start with even simple word recognition. The significance of the developmental theory, however, is the implication that progress is, in essence, a function of maturation. In recent years more weight has been attached to the view that *training* may play a greater part in precipitating learning than Piaget originally implied.

In practical terms, the developmental theory would lead the teacher to concentrate on giving the child as rich and varied an experience as possible in all the activities and materials which may help him to learn to read. She may also try to 'precipitate' his learning by helping him to make intellectual deductions which, without her positive help, might be unduly delayed.

All this would mean plenty of opportunity to use language, to see and compare word—and possibly letter—shapes (i.e. matching), to associate visual and auditory patterns and to perceive the mental connection between what the child hears described as 'reading' and the printed patterns he sees in the books and other materials which he handles; and the teacher provides for learning of this kind with the environment she establishes, the materials and activities she makes available, and the teaching which helps the child to move through a logical reading progression.

A third theory which may have an important bearing on learning to read is concerned with learning by 'insight'. When faced with a learning situation the child, on the basis of his knowledge existing at that time, considers for himself the nature of the problem and tries to find its solution. It would seem that there may be an element of trial and error before the solution is found, and the child may, for a number of reasons, jump to inaccurate conclusions before he comes to the right one. For example, in trying to read 'little' he may at first say 'kitten' because of the 'tt' in both words. He finds, perhaps by being told, perhaps from a piece of self-correcting apparatus, that he word is not 'kitten'. On a subsequent occasion, slight modification of his earlier insight may enable him to arrive at the new correct solution.

Lovell suggests that almost all children have some degree of insight, even though they may be dull. '...insightful behavior is possible at all levels of intelligence in children, provided the learning task is at the correct level of difficulty. On this view, the task of the teacher is to start from whatever insight his pupils possess and to direct them to new situations of the appropriate complexity which they can solve by insight.'

A range of matching activities (some of which might be self-correcting) would help the child who may learn in this way, as would those of the 'put a ring round the right word' variety, selecting the correct sound to attach to the beginning or end of the word, and other material of this nature. Since the success of insight learning depends to some extent on the insights a child already possesses, he would seem more likely to profit from it once he has made a beginning in recognising what reading means; but when this point comes, it is unlikely that special provision will be necessary. Materials which would help the child are generally to be found in most infant classrooms.

The Process of Learning to Read

Having considered briefly three of the learning theories which may be directly applicable to reading, we should now examine in more detail how the actual process of learning to read is thought to take place.

This learning undoubtedly calls upon a considerable range of abilities and skills, both innate and acquired, and there are in addition other factors (for example temperament) which appear to make a significant contribution. No useful attempt can be made to arrange all these elements in order of importance, partly because we do not know enough about it to establish such an order, and partly because some elements are likely to be more important than others according to individual differences in children. We do, however, need to be aware of what these elements are believed to be, and we should try to consider then directly in relation to classroom practice as far as it is possible to do this realistically in a book.

Eye Movement and Fixation Span

It is known that in reading, the eye (in our written language) travels from left to right in a series of movements and monetary pauses. It is during the pauses, often known as *fixations,* that reading takes place. Schonell explains that 'during each eye pause the [skilled] reader fully recognises two or three words in the material being read, and partially recognises a word or two on either side. The amount properly recognised at one pause is called the *span of recognition...'* (also called the *fixation span*).

The size of the fixation span is dependent upon the skill of the reader and the difficulty of the material. The beginner may well assimilate only two or three letters in one fixation. The fluent reader probably makes good use of the areas of partial recognition to comprehend what is being read and to anticipate the next words, but the extent to which the child just beginning to reach can make use of this assistance is doubtful. In his concentration on 'decoding' he tends to forget what he has already seen and so his eyes must repeatedly move back to re-register the earlier impression. It is therefore most important that the difficulty of the material should be matched to the child. Too many eye movements (particularly those which are regressive) will retard fluency and comprehension. The teacher's contribution here is to try to ensure that the reading material presented to the child is progressively graded so that it may lead him on and not hold him back.

We tend to assume that children will naturally move their eyes from left to right when learning to read, but Goodacre found that this is not necessarily so. The teacher may well need to help the child to form this habit. She could run her-finger unobtrusively along the word or phrase the child is trying to read, casually draw his attention to the direction in which she is writing for him while he watches, and help him to start at the left when he begins to write or trace his own name. It is doubtful whether this help would be necessary for long and once the habit is formed the child is unlikely to try to reverse it.

Unit of Recognition

There has long been some diversity of view as to whether the unit which children begin by recognising most easily is the letter, the word, or the phrase or 'sentence'. Schonell was emphatic that the child responds primarily 'to the total visual pattern of the whole word...it is the marked differences in the visual patterns of the words as wholes which enable him to recognise each word'. He stressed the importance of differences in length and of variations in shape caused by projecting letters. Hence the vogue among teachers for some time of outlining words in order to draw the child's attention to these differences in visual patterns. For example.

come   look

Despite his emphasis on the visual pattern of the whole word, however, Schonell did not exclude the child's use of other clues in word recognition. He noted the use of initial and final letters as clues, of known syllables, of double letters and of meaning. 'It would seem,' he said, 'that recognition of a word is based on a combination of the total shape of a word, of groups of letters (as in the double 't' in 'little') and of individual letters in it.'

Schonell's *Happy Venture* reading scheme was published in 1937. Later a determined movement towards being concerned with the 'whole child' developed. This resulted for a time in the widespread acceptance of the view that learning to read was a natural part of the child's total development; and that as long as the learning environment encouraged this, he would learn to read by a kind of 'absorption' process in which attention to detailed reading skills was out of place. This view is crystallised by Mellor: '...children will learn to read by listening and reading, as they learn to talk by listening and talking.'

The happy long-term result of this climate of opinion has been to give far greater attention to the variety of influences which affect a child's ability to learn, and to try to eliminate unnecessary conventions which inhibit or constrict. But the less fortunate effects were that the teacher was too often diverted from an examination of detailed learning process, and in teaching reading she was sometimes led to an almost exclusive concern with 'meaning' and 'fluency'. She was given to understand that anything more specific must inevitably result in 'barking at print'.

Teaching which directed attention to letters or individual sounds or even, at its extreme, to just one word, was therefore frowned upon. The sentence method, which admirably fitted this global view in its lack of concern with detail, was widely used. It was not easy, however, to escape the controlled vocabulary if the thing was to be kept within bounds. The result was a spate of reading schemes described by Dr. Margaret Peters as 'both boring and far removed from children's own idiom.... As vehicles of "meaning" they were a complete failure; as stimulants of literacy, they were disastrous.'

In the meantime, however, serious attention was again being given to trying to establish whether the unit of recognition to which the child was most likely to respond was not in fact something much more detailed than the phrase or sentence—or, indeed, than the whole word. It began to be whispered abroad that children *do* look at letter shapes, particularly those at the beginning and end of words, and at times appear to use them as clues.

This question of the clues which children seem to use to help them in word recognition has, in recent years, been much considered. There is growing evidence to support the view that the unit of recognition *is* the whole word but that letter shapes and sounds are among the most significant clues which help children to distinguish one word from another.

Daniels and Diack developed this theory in England and presented it in practical form in the *Royal Road Readers* published in 1954. Thy describe their approach as the 'phonic word method'. In differs from the strictly phonic method in that it begins with whole words and identifies the letter differences, both by sight and by sound, in order to distinguish one word from another; whereas the phonic method begins with the sounds of the letters and then fuses or synthesises them to build the word—hence the description of the phonic method as 'synthetic'.

Daniels and Diack are concerned not only with word recognition, but also with word meaning.

The phonic word method...whilst not rejecting modern theories of maturation based upon the child's interests and play activities, pays much greater attention to the training of visual perception and the teaching of letters than do methods based upon word-whole theories. The *Royal Road Readers* are based upon a scheme of graded phonics which, however, do not so concentrate on teaching letter meanings that word meanings are neglected. Indeed the main idea which gave the material its shape and design was that, at all times, the child should be looking through letter-meanings to word-meanings. The necessity for going beyond mere 'word recognition', beyond mere 'word-calling' to word-meanings is imposed upon the child by the design of the teaching materials.

In an extensive investigation Daniels and Diack found that both in word recognition and in comprehension children taught by the phonic word method were 'significantly superior' to those taught by mixed methods, in the tests by which their reading was measured.

A variation of this view formulated by Eleanor Gibson and her colleagues (1962) is that it is the letter group or phoneme pattern which is the critical unit of language and to which the child's attention should be drawn when he is learning to read. Roberts interprets this specifically.

Reading is now seen as decoding the phonemic or sound patterns of spoken language rather than decoding single letters...these letter/sound correspondences should be introduced in different contexts, so that the child can see them operating in many different words, and thereby learn and understand their invariant relationship. In this way the child will achieve more easily what he has to learn anyhow—to perceive as units the clusters of letters that represent the basic sounds of spoken language.

The significant for the teacher of these developments is

that they are founded on evidence which casts serious doubts on the effectiveness of the exclusive use of look-and-say methods, whether these are based on whole word or, perhaps especially, on sentence recognition. The widespread use of the sentence method was based on the belief that since children's thought and their language take place in sentences or phrases, it is logical that they should begin to read in the same way. The child was presented with short sentences associated with a picture, a major advantage being that there need be no restriction on relating the material very much to the learner's everyday life and activities. It was thought that at first the child would 'read' the sentence by memorising it in conjunction with the picture and eventually he would come to recognise the sentence without the help of the picture. In due course, he would isolate words which he could then read in the true sense, and finally he would break down the word into letters and sounds.

It was felt that this sequence was not only more natural to children but also that it gave them help from the context; and in emphasising primarily 'meaning' and fluency it discouraged the unprofitable habit of 'word-calling'. In practice, however, the sentence method frequently—perhaps nearly always—became a whole word method, partly because the component parts of a sentence are essential to the whole. It was often observed that less able children, in particular, really needed to reduce the sentence to a more manageable unit. And if, as now seems likely, children generally break down even the word in order to find clues which help them, then a large unit of recognition like a sentence would, in this context, be inappropriate.

However, we cannot really abolish the whole word as a tentative unit of recognition in the very early stags of learning to read. We cannot escape the fact that our written language includes not only words in which single letters and clusters of letters have a regular sound correspondence, but also words in which such correspondence is totally irregular. Leaving aside for the moment i.t.a. and other approaches which are based on the principle of eliminating this irregularity, we also find that an exclusively phonic approach is ineffective in the early stage of learning to read. In the circumstances, we must surely each the conclusion that neither the one nor the other provides, *by itself,* the whole answer.

The practical consequences of this dichotomy are not, however, as open-ended as they seem. In the first place, it should be made clear that the use of the component parts of a word to assist in its identification does not represent a return to the old phonic method of 'tne pig in a wig did a jig' variety. Daniels and Diack, for example, do not imply that their analytic phonic word approach is based on this principle.

The point at issue is that instead of eschewing, in word recognition, the help of the sound of appearance of certain letters or letter combinations, the teacher encourages the child to use them (when possible) as a positive means of identification. For example, when using the *Janet and John* scheme in a reception class some yeas ago, the teacher told the children a delightful story about a rude little man with his toes turned up and his tongue stuck out, who looked like this—'t'. Few children thereafter had any difficulty in distinguishing 'Janet' from 'John', because 'Janet' ended with a picture of the rude little man. The fact that 'toes' and 'tongue' also begin with the sound of the letter gave the teacher an admirable opportunity for introducing some early phonic training quite naturally and informally and very valuably.

At the beginning therefore words, and perhaps little phrases which have personal significance, such as 'my dog', will be presented in look-and-say form. It would be hard to find a leading authority on the initial teaching of reading who could not approve of this. But right from the start the importance of clues in the recognition of a word should be stressed. The clue may be a picture, the shape of the word, its length if this is a distinguishing feature, the presence of a double letter, the long tail at the beginning, the little man with his toes turned up. When letter/sound correspondence can be introduced informally and conversationally—without pressing it in any sense as a drill—there is no reason why the teacher should not make use of the opportunity.

This approach does not deny the contribution of look- and say as *one element*, probably a very important one, in the presentation of early reading material. It does, however, add another element and in this we may agree with Donald Moyle. 'While one would certainly not underestimate the difficulties involved in letter recognition, the evidence available seems to point to the conclusion that it cannot but be helpful to make the child aware, in some way, that words are composed of letters from the very beginning of instruction.' The children's attention should therefore be drawn to the *appearance* of certain letter forms, with or without their associated sounds according to whether this is appropriate.

Roberts goes even further:

> ...look-and-say should be regarded as part of the preparatory approach which should be clearly differentiated from word identification and learning to read in the true sense of the phrases. Indeed, where look-and-say persists beyond the necessary preparatory period the children will learn to read by other means, in that they will learn to make correspondences between letters and sounds for themselves. Later, when they have learned the fundamental skills of reading, then look-and-say techniques can be used to achieve a quicker, easier rate of reading.

Almost any look-and-say reading scheme can be adapted to make use of clues, including letters, in word recognition;

though it must be admitted that some schemes which are very resolutely based on the sentence method make this more difficult. However, if we accept that clues in words do help children, we must reduce the sentence to a unit which is small enough for the child to accommodate.

Visual and Auditory Discrimination

If children are to learn, or be trained, to see the differences in the written patterns of words and to recognise the correspondence between these patterns and the sounds that they hear, it is plain that in order to help them we must know something about their powers of visual and auditory discrimination. It is now thought that these abilities are partly innate and partly acquired. At one time it was thought that they depended almost entirely upon maturation and could not be appreciably hastened by training of any kind. More recent evidence, however, strongly suggests that this is not the case and that training, provided it is directed towards that part of the child's acquisition of these skills which may respond to it, may indeed play a significant part.

With regard to visual discrimination it used to be widely believed that before the age of about six children's eyes were not sufficiently developed physically and physiologically to enable them to make the fine visual distinctions that reading requires. It now seems fairly firmly established that this is not so. In studies which have been undertaken to investigate this question, children starting school have generally been found to be capable of seeing quite fine distinctions, though they may not immediately register some of the very small differences in letter shapes.

They have not, however, been found capable of remembering the *sequence* of letter shapes in a word and they do have difficulty in distinguishing, between inverted letters such as 'b' and 'd'. In these skills, maturation may well be significant but it is also possible that helping the child to look for similarities and differences in words, and for 'clues' (which is not the same thing as expecting him to memorise, at an early stage, all the letter shapes and their associated sounds), assisting him to form the habit of left/right sequence, giving him the opportunity of seeing and forming letters, and informally familiarising him, where this is appropriate, with the association between certain sounds and letters or groups of letters—that training of this kind will help to precipitate the learning which his degree of maturation makes possible. In a careful study of reading readiness Downing and Thackray say that the weight of evidence 'seems to favour the view that the perceptual activities of children should not be under-estimated, and more consideration must be given to the extent to which we can develop these various abilities through training'.

Concerning auditory discrimination, it is evident that this may not be fully developed before a mental age of about seven to seven and a half years. It has been found that the sounds which are heard in the middle and lower frequencies can be distinguished earlier than those in the high frequencies. It is not, therefore, a situation in which the discrimination of *all* sounds is more or less uniformly uncertain for the young child: *some* sounds can be distinguished at an earlier age and others cannot. Goodacre refers to some evidence which teachers may find very helpful here:

Work by Poole (1934) is often quoted which shows the *latest age* at which consonant sounds appear in normal children's speech.

'Age 3½ sounds mastered b-p-m-w-h

Age 4½ sounds mastered d-t—n-g-k-ng-y

Age 5½ sounds mastered f

Age 6½ sounds mastered v-th (as in then)-sh-zh-l

Age 7½ sounds mastered s-z-r-th (thin)-wh-ch-(j)'

What is important to note is that the sound acquisition in children's speech is progressive and that amongst normal children the particular speech sounds may not be correctly used until as late as seven or eight.

Dr. Goodacre goes on to reinforce this with recent evidence.

The conclusions reached from all the work done on auditory discrimination therefore support the view,

(i) that at five the normal child can distinguish between the sound patterns of whole words;

(ii) that the discrimination of the sounds of individual letters takes place progressive, until it is generally complete by a mental age of about seven and a half;

(iii) that the ability to beak down the whole word into the sounds of all its constituent letters, and to arrange them into correct sequence, is very much a maturational process. The ability to do this will clearly develop first with short, phonically regular words, and many children in the First School, given appropriate training, can analyse the sounds of words like 'but' and 'in' and arrange them in their correct order both in reading and in writing. But more complex arrangements of sounds will naturally be longer delayed and the teacher must judge this capacity very much in accordance with the ability and maturational level of individual children.

These conclusions have important implications for phonic teaching, and they suggest certain lines of approach:

(i) From the beginning of reading instruction, the teacher may informally draw the child's attention to the sounds of some of the letters and letter combinations, beginning with those that are thought to be within the child's auditory capacity at this stage.

(ii) As the child's auditory discrimination develops, this practice may be extended and undertaken by the teacher more systematically.

(iii) Help in establishing good left/right orientation is important.

(iv) Familiarity with the sounds of letters and letter combinations will be of great assistance to the child when he reaches the maturational level of being able to analyse the constituent sounds of words and assemble them in the correct sequence.

14

APPROACHES AND METHODS

Reference has already been made to the phonic, whole word and sentence methods of teaching reading. They will now be discussed a little further, as part of an examination of all the various methods and approaches that have been, or are being, employed to teach children to read.

Alphabetic Method

This was a spelling method, whereby children learned the alphabetic names of the letters and then spelt out and learned the words. Since, in addition to the difficulty this presented, the book from which children learned to read for much of the nineteenth century was the Bible, the modern infant teacher may flinch at the thought of this formidable task. It need hardly be added that this method has long since disappeared!

Phonic Method

The phonic method is based on word building according to the *sounds* of the letters and letter combinations, as opposed to then alphabetic names. It began to replace the alphabetic method in our schools something over a century ago and held sway until it declined in popularity thirty or forty years ago and finally disappeared as an initial method of teaching reading in most of our infant schools. It has since revived, in rather different form, in various approaches which are essentially based on phonic analysis, and these will be examined.

The overwhelming disadvantages of the early phonic method of teaching reading were:

(i) The inconsistency of English spelling. Exclusively phonic methods do not help children to read irregularly spelt words.

(ii) The suffocating boredom and irrelevance of reading material restricted to the limited number of sounds a child has learned.

(iii) The lack of distinguishing features in the short, phonically regular words in which only a few letter/ sound combinations can be used in the initial stages of learning to read.

(iv) The 'phonic drill', which, though not inherent in the method, was regarded as an essential part of teaching reading at a time when teaching generally was extremely formal.

It was partly because these disadvantages eventually came to be recognised. And partly because formal methods gave way in the 1930s and 1940s to techniques which were based on a strongly child-centred approach to infant teaching generally that the phonic method of teaching reading fell into disuse. Its shortcomings as an exclusive reading method and its association with the rigid attitudes which were being discarded ensured that no part of it could be assimilated into the more informal ideas.

Whole Word Method

Gestalt theories of psychology put forward the view that things were perceived in wholes rather than in parts of a whole and so it was believed that children would recognise words as wholes before they could break them down into smaller parts. It was therefore natural that the whole word method of 'look-and-say' should supplant the phonic method. It was theoretically convincing as a way of teaching reading, and the way in which the material could be presented was far more appropriate to the active child-centred classroom than the 'formal drilling' of the bad old phonic days.

One of the main problems which arose, however, was that the child had to know every word before he could read it. He could not make use of any self-help by building even simple phonic words; for indeed among the extreme supporters of the whole word method any overt reference to phonics, at least before the last year of the infant school, was regarded as pedagogically disgraceful and could not be countenanced. Many teachers, however, surreptitiously applied a little phonic prod now and then; and those who, while appreciating the virtues of look-and-say, were allowed to admit that there were a good many phonic words in the English language and to recognise that many children were quite capable of simple word building, long before they were promoted to the senior rank of 'top infant', openly used 'mixed methods'.

Mixed Methods

These were advocated as early as 1922 in the manual of the *Beacon Reading Scheme* published by Ginn. Its authors believed that children should learn to read by both phonic and look-and-say methods, uniting the two after they had made a start with each approach separately and were in due course ready to use both simultaneously. Schonell's *Happy Venture* reading scheme, published in 1937, renewed the mixed method approach but without the initial separation of phonic and whole word, as in *Beacon*. Simple regular words were first introduced in the text by look-and-say, and when children became familiar with them they began word-building and this increased as reading advanced. The anti-phonic school, however, continued for some time to rely exclusively upon look-and-say methods.

Phonic Word Method

Reference has already been made on page 27 to the more analytic phonic approach introduced by Daniels and Diack in the *Royal Road Readers.* Here children were taught to see letters and letter combinations, and to hear their corresponding sounds, *as part of a word*—not separately, in isolation, as the earlier phonic method required. Peters describes the *Royal Road Readers* as a scheme which 'for the first time really integrated an analytic approach with a progressive and excellently planned phonic system.'

It is, however, only in comparatively recent years that real interest has revived in integrating systematic phonic teaching with look-and-say methods; and teachers who use the phonic word approach tend to do so by adapting existing reading material to accommodate it. The current resurgence of interest in helping children to find clues of word recognition, and of introducing appropriate phonic teaching in order that they may not be hindered in reading phonically regular words, is likely to lead to greater emphasis being placed on this kind of approach than has been evident since look-and-say methods first gained the ascendancy.

Sentence Method

A look-and-say method based on the principle that the sentence or phrase is a more natural unit of recognition for the child than the word, the sentence method generally replaced the whole word method and many schemes based on it were published over the years. How for these were in fact used by teachers as sentence rather than whole word schemes one cannot say; and no look-and-say scheme could make incidental phonic teaching quite impossible, since the inclusion of regular phonic words in written English cannot be avoided. However, systematic phonic teaching really could not be undertaken nor, of course, was it intended that it should.

The Approach Using the Child's Own Writing

One development of the sentence method was the practice whereby the child was encouraged to learn to read, in the initial stages, entirely from his own words which the teacher wrote at this 'dictation' below a picture he had drawn of something that was of interest to him. This followed logically form the belief that thought and communication take place in sentence and if the sentences could come from the child and reflect his own personal interests and concerns he would be strongly motivated to try to read them. This approach also overcame the problem of the arid and remote nature of some of the sentences in introductory reading books, in which the controlled vocabulary and the need for repetition result in wording quite as absurd as anything to be found in the old-fashioned, wholly phonic reading schemes.

In many infant schools this practice was therefore adopted. The child's words .were written below his picture every day, comparisons made with the writings of previous days, the sentences discussed, similar words isolated. Again, it at times came very close to being used, in practice, as a 'whole word' method. However, in tits original form any phonic word-building was firmly excluded, in the belief that the child found his clues and any help he needed to develop his own word-building techniques entirely from the context.

Usually no reading scheme was used in addition to thsi approach, but many different books of the appropriate level were made available to the child as he progressed to the stage of being able to read them. Less frequently a scheme was used in parallel to provide 'check points' on the child's progress.

The use of the child's own writing as the basis for teaching him to read was pioneered by J.H. Jagger, an Inspector of Schools in London. Despite its widespread use, however, and its very evident merits it has not, over the years, proved wholly successful as a basic method of teaching children to read. Moyle puts his finger on the reason for this.

It must be faced...that Jagger really considered context a sufficient key to unlock the unknown word. This approach to word recognition is, at best intelligent guesswork and at worst sheer invention. However much we would like to think of reading as thinking inspired by communication through the printed word, we must acknowledge that children can only achieve fluency and confidence in reading if they have some facility in word building. Further, any method in which the child provides his own material brings its own difficulties. The teacher will be heavily taxed if she is to ensure a regular growth pattern in the child's attainment, for the vocabulary will lack control land the repetition ate necessary for memorisation will be difficult to achieve.

However, the practice of the teacher writing the child's own words under his picture continues, and for very good reasons. These are in part connected with providing the child with some of the necessary foundation for reading, such as showing him what words are, that they represent his spoken language, that they are written—and must be read—from left to right, and so on . But the teacher also does this in order to help the child to learn to write. However, as a method of teaching children to read, to the exclusion or even limitation of other methods, it no longer finds wholehearted support in modern studies of the teaching of reading.

The Language-Experience Approach

The use of children's own writing as part of their programme of learning to read has, however, recently returned to the scene in a slightly different form and has been given the name of the 'language-experience approach.' Just as Jagger over forty years ago expressed the view that children's own words in written form, provided the most valuable material from which they could learn to read, so the modern supporters of the language-experience approach attach great importance to the use of the child's language, inspired by his own activities, as the foundation on which his reading programme should be built. The approach has been defined as 'one in which the ideas born of intense interest of a child or a group of children are used as the material for reading. The interest-inspired ideas are stimulated by real or vicarious experiences. These experiences are then recorded to become the written material for reading. Reading, then, becomes part of an integrated language-arts plan.'

Basically many of the common practices, of which infant teachers have for years made extensive use, have reflected the language-experience approach. The captions and the writings beneath children's pictures described earlier; class and individual 'news' books, magazines or diaries; the writing that arises from projects, visits and other experiences; class, group and individual discussions which encourage children to use language, some of which will emerge in written form for them to read—all these activities which result in reading and writing based on children's own interests are founded on the languages-experience approach even though they were not in the past accorded the precise title.

Some exponents of this approach seem to support the integration within such a programme of a more structured development of the skills required in word recognition, others do not. The argument appears to have aroused more interest on the other side of the Atlantic, no doubt for the reason that the use of the child's own writing, in one form or another, is already deeply rooted in this country.

However, there may well be room in much of our own practice for making more direct connections between a child's own language and the materials and techniques which we use to teach him to read. This may be particularly true of our methods once reading skill begins to advance beyond the initial stage. A concise and helpful summary of the value, and the limitations, of this approach is given in the opening chapter of *Modern Innovations in the Teaching of Reading* by Donald and Louise M. Moyle, who conclude that 'for the greater success, the marriage of this approach to some more structural type of learning, say a linguistic approach, could draw together the best of both worlds during the early stages of reading development'.

The Uses and Limitations of a Reading Scheme

A reading scheme is not universally accepted as being an essential requirement in teaching children to read. Reading schemes or 'primers' have, however, been used continuously for a at least a century in the majority of infant schools and it is probably true to say that even today a scheme, or sometimes books from several schemes, are commonly found where children in school are learning to read. It is therefore worth asking ourselves why we so frequently make use of such materials.

The most important reason is probably that a reading scheme provides the teachers with a continuous line of structured or semi-structured leaning against which she can measure the reading progress of the children she is teaching. Without such a line of measurement it is much more difficult for her to be sure that systematic progress is being maintained, and it is also more difficult for her to feel confident that reading material is necessarily available to every child at the appropriate level to match his developing skill. With a reading scheme she knows that at least in one area of the reading programme the children can move forward in progressively graded steps. In addition, some teachers believe that reading schemes have value in giving children a goal, and a sense of achievement as they complete one book and set out upon the next. Furthermore, the controlled vocabulary of a reading scheme ensures that a child will always meet many familiar words when he embarks upon a new book and this helps him to feel confident that he is really learning to read. Teachers do, of course, see that the children have a good deal of other material in addition to the reading scheme.

Reading schemes, however, have their limitations. One of the main criticisms of many schemes is that the languages and subject matter are so far removed from the everyday lives of most children. The characters and their activities are frequently so depressingly uninspring and the content of the books is seldom rescued even by the fantasy in which the young child can find so much pleasure. It is therefore very difficult for children to be able to identify themselves with the characters and events, and the motivation of interest and personal concern is lacking. However, it must be added that this complaint is much more justified in some schemes than in others, and there are one or two notable exceptions which are well worth considering from this point of view.

Other criticisms of many reading schemes and their use are that in the early books the limitations imposed by the controlled vocabulary leave no room for anything other than uninspired repetitive wording; that to be tied to a scheme imposes an unwelcome restriction on the child's horizons; that children are inclined to look upon only these books as 'reading' and therefore attach insufficient value to other books; that they can become dominated by the objective of reaching the last book in the scheme, when they then believe that they can read and no further effort is necessary; that with a scheme children can measure their progress against each other and the slower readers become discouraged because everyone else can see they are falling behind; and that once a school is equipped with a scheme, it may be years before there is enough money to replace it if a better scheme comes on the market. For this same reason teacher shave, in fact, little or no choice about the scheme with which they teach.

All these criticisms are valid to a greater or lesser degree, though the effects of some of them can be mitigated by the way in which the teacher uses the scheme and the attitudes she encourages in the children. Some schools try to overcome these problems by having more than one scheme running parallel, using a limited number of books from each. Others use no scheme as a foundation and rely entirely upon children's own writing augmented by a variety of carefully selected books at the correct levels of difficulty.

This has a good deal to commend it, but it would be unrealistic to underestimate the difficulties it presents. The teacher must have a very accurate understanding of the stage of intellectual growth of each child in her class in order to be sure that his reading material is appropriately progressive. She must keep extremely careful records, to be certain that every child at some time reads the kind of book he should be reading at his stage. She must ensure that without a controlled vocabulary the child's confidence is not submerged under the weight of too many new words which he meets in too many different contexts. And she must have very considerable powers of organisation if, with a large class, the pitfalls really are to be avoided. It may be partly because of these enormous demands that reading schemes remain in use and are still found to be of practical help when children are learning to read.

Criteria for Judging Reading Schemes

Although financial and other considerations in a school rarely make it possible for a teacher to choose her reading scheme, occasionally she does have the opportunity to do so. In any case it is helpful for her to have certain criteria by which to judge the suitability of a scheme for her class. This may enable her to go some way towards compensating for its shortcomings, to modify its application, where possible, according to her judgement, and to extract the maximum value from it. A summary is therefore given in Appendix A of the points that should be considered in assessing the suitability of a scheme.

In order to judge the relative merits of reading schemes and to make comparisons between them, there is really no substitute for a teacher seeing them. Fortunately this is becoming a little easier nowadays. Some teachers' centres, and reading centres, hold a range for teachers to examine at their leisure and publishers will always send inspection copies to a school on request.

A selection of reading schemes is listed in Appendix B, with the name of the publisher, the date of publication, and a comment. This may help teachers to make an initial selection of schemes they would like to see, in order that they may themselves arrive at a considered judgement of the one most suitable for the children they are teaching.

15

'WHY HASN'T IT WORKED?'

In the 1978 Primary Survey, the Inspectorate presented a bleak picture of primary science. In their view, serious and effective work was achieved in only 10 per cent of schools. Elsewhere, much of the effort was superficial and the teaching in science was less well matched to the capabilities of pupils than in any other curriculum area. Few headteachers appeared to recognise that science could make a significant contribution to the development of young children.

This contrasts sadly with the hopes of curriculum reform in the 190s. Primary science teaching was due for reform having resisted criticism over many years: in 1913 Henry Armstrong had said of nature study that 'Nature too seldom comes into the work and too often study is the last thing thought of'.

The Nuffield Junior Science Project expressed the following belief in the natural power of children to learn: 'Children's practical problem solving is essentially a scientific way of working, so that the task in school is not one of teaching science to children, but rather of utilising the children's own scientific way of working as a potent educational tool' and '...their own questions seem to be the most significant and to result most often in careful investigations'. So the project's books gave general advice on how to follow children's leads and how to provide resources to support this strategy; facts, concepts, content were ruled out of order.

The project's successor, Science 5-13, built on this work, but differed in giving teachers a definite framework in the form of a set of over 150 behavioural objectives, divided into three neo-Piagetian levels. This was not to determine a syllabus—the child's motivation and the need for learning to be rooted in experience were still paramount. The objectives were to guide the provision of opportunities for learning and to form a basis for monitoring individual's progress. The project also provided a set of more than 25 books, each giving guidance, and examples of children's work, on a particular theme. This material was interpreted and analysed throughout in terms of the detailed objectives which the proposed activities might serve.

Both of these projects were based on the view that the essentials of scientific work lay in the processes of careful observation, perception of patterns, formation of hypotheses and design of experimental tests. Scientific concepts were inappropriate as a framework for curriculum design because they were too abstract and too little related to children's interests. At the same time, it was emphasised that science is a unique source of intellectual stimulus, being the area in which observation and thinking skills have to be based on direct experience. It was hoped that such work could play a distinctive part in an integrated curriculum where any one pupil investigation could lead to activity in science, art, writing, craft and other skills.

Two further projects succeeded these. Progress in Learning Science concentrated on the appraisal of the progress of individual children by a scheme based on the developmental objectives of Science 5-13. The other Learning Through Science is still in progress.

These four major projects, added to many smaller and local initiatives and to the normal efforts of authors and publishers, have influenced only a minority of schools. Yet if the materials produced have failed, it seems that they fell at the first hurdle—that of convincing teachers to take them seriously. A survey has shown that Science 5-13 has only been studied seriously in 30 per cent of schools and is being used by 22 per cent while the corresponding figures for Nuffield Junior Science are 20 per cent and 7 per cent respectively.

Primary teachers almost certainly lack confidence to take up the new philosophy. Muriel Whittaker has pointed out (in the *School Science Review,* March 1980) that most primary teachers probably have a strong aversion to physical sciences, which they last experienced in secondary schools where the didactic and factual approach left them with no experience of the type of work now required. Open-ended activity in which a teacher has to encourage particular skills by careful guidance of the pupils' own interests requires some knowledge, or confidence to learn, about many topics and some first-hand experience of the skills involved. Most primary teachers have neither. When the schemes of work they are offered have a complex rationale, offer a wealth of materials, but leave choice of the specific activities, and decisions about level and pace to them, it may not be surprising if the challenge is refused.

While it is clear that active help for primary teachers is a first priority, it cannot be assumed that the only problem is to help them to use the ideas and materials that exist. These materials themselves raise several problems.

One such problem concerns the view that science is organised common sense, arriving at its theories by intelligent induction. The practitioner works within and through a complex framework of concepts and it took the genius of Galileo and Newton, in defiance of the common sense of generations, to establish such concepts for mechanics.

It is, of course, true that these abstract concepts are beyond the powers of young children and that to channel work towards them risks loss of enthusiasm and meaningless rote learning. But the problems illustrated by the mechanics example will not go away: research with children is now establishing in this area, as in many others, that they construct their own conceptual schemes to cope with the problems of understanding nature and that these, like those of every scientist up to the sixteenth century, are a real barrier to the scientific understanding.

What then is to be made of the plea to encourage children to develop and rely on their own ideas? It is not now obvious, *a priori,* that the best route for developing understanding of science up to age 11 is to concentrate exclusively on the process skills of concept-free science.

Arguments for adjusting the policy about content in primary science were put forward recently by several authors, notably Professor Kerr (reprinted as 'Reading 1.3' in this volume), in the Spring number of *Education 3-13.* Norman Booth recalled another project of the sixties, the Oxford Primary Science Project. This offered a scheme which, although based on children's activities, wanted these planned to serve four broad themes—Energy, Structure, Chance and Life. This too failed, and perhaps one reason was the gap between the grand conceptual design and activities of which children were capable. Wynne Harlen, writing in the *School Science Review* in June 1978, proposed a more modest list of content drawing on her experience in the Science 5-13 and Progress in Learning Science projects. Her article reviewed the arguments for and against some content aims, and concluded that while the process aims must come first, the children's activity had to be about something and it might as well be arranged to cover some common broad themes.

Others have argued that children ought to begin to have access to those ideas which have helped scientists to make sense of the natural world. It is also evident that if children's own interests have to be a prime source for activity, then some interests, such as space travel on nuclear energy, may need a degree of reliance on secondary evidence that is fully acceptable in other areas (such as history) for 10 year olds.

If these various arguments have force, they would lead to a strategy in which children's interests and their needs for first hand experiences are still given first priority, but which also organise problems and materials to channel interest and to ensure that some of the experiences provide a helpful challenge in a few particular concept areas.

Such a strategy would have an effect on another aspect which also needs consideration, that of providing materials for pupils and more and more direct guidance for teachers. The experience of the superb work which can be produced when children's own initiatives are guided by the best teachers has led many to the view that any planned provision will be an obstacle to excellence. However, without such provision, teachers can only be given vague advice, and the demands, for decision, anticipation and preparation, become too great.

The recently published series on Teaching Primary Science (produced by the College Curriculum Science Studies Project under John Bird) has tried to provide firmer guidance, giving advice and samples on producing work cards for children and clearer background information for teachers with each of its themes, while also providing a short list of objectives to guide the activity, chosen from the schedule of Science 5-13.

Such designed activity can make the teaching task more manageable, partly because contrived experience raises problems which can more easily be guided to fruitful work than many that appear in the complex world of the natural environment. However, the strategy for choosing such activities will have to take account of a further factor that has been largely ignored hitherto. The science of most successful primary teachers has been pure science. If it had been technology, their philosophy and emphasis might have been different and the work of mechanical and electrical construction might have invaded the classroom.

Many and strenuous efforts are now being made to support and promote primary science. But those tending the feeble plant face the dilemma: does it need just light, air and water, does it need artificial fertiliser, or should we put it up again and have another look at the roots?

16

A PROMETHEAN FAITH

One of the most interesting plays of Ancient Greece is *Prometheus Bound* by Aeschylus. As a play it presents some special problems to a director. There is no formal introduction. It assumes that the audience is familiar with the whole story. It is, in fact, as if we were beginning with the second act. Again there is very little dramatic action and there is no change of scenery. There is nothing contemporary about it. It is clearly a play from a distant time. It does not deal with ordinary people. The language is far from ordinary, with an almost liturgical quality, and with the sweetest music in the words.

Zeus is discouraged with the race of men. He determines to destroy mankind and try something better. Thus he withholds certain gifts more appropriate for divinity than wretched and weak creatures like men. Among these is the gift of fire.

Moved by pity for man, Prometheus steals some embers, and man, with this new help from heaven, discovers art after art, lifting his status until even Zeus sees that man is too strong to be destroyed.

Zeus is checkmated. Prometheus, however, must pay the penalty. In challenging the power and will of Zeus, he has threatened the whole moral and religious base of society. Excuse him if you will, but he is guilty of unbridled self-assertion (hubris). Moreover, he is unwilling to repent. He must, therefore, pay the price.

As punishment, Prometheus is to be chained to a rock by Hephaestus and consigned to Hades. Nor is this all. Hermes, bringing a message from Zeus, tells him that he will be tortured daily by an eagle feasting on his liver. The liver will grow by night as fast as the eagle consumes it by day. Thus the torture will continue until some god voluntarily takes the place of Prometheus in Hades.

The play ends with a thunderbolt from heaven which strikes the rock to which Prometheus is chained and sinks it to Hades.

The name of Prometheus is honoured as the founder and savior of human civilisation. It is the Promethean spirit of challenge, invention, creativity, and courage that explains the glory of man and the wonders of human progress.

> Prometheus tells the story in these words:
> ...let me speak
> Of the miseries of men, helpless children till
> I gave them sense and ways to think...
> Though I do not mention man through any blame
> But only to unfold the love with which I gave.
> Those first had eyes to see, but never saw;
> Ears for hearing, but they never heard.
> Like huddled shapes in dreams, they used to drag
> Their long lives through, confusing all:
> Knew no brick-built homes to front the sun,
> No woodwork, but beneath the soil
> They lived like tiny ants recessed in sunless holes;
> No measured sign for winter, flowery spring,
> Nor summer full of fruit;

Without a clue they practiced everything,
Until I showed the stars to them,
Their rising and their set—
So difficult to calculate.
And numbers, too, I found them,
The key to sciences;
And letters in their synthesis—
Secret of all memory, sweet mother of the arts.
I was the first to break beasts to the yoke
And bring them to the collar and the saddle,
So make them take on mankind's heaviest work.
I fixed the horse submissively to carriages:
Golden symbol of luxury and state.
And I was the one—none other—to invent
The seaman's ocean-roaming chariots with linen wings....
...Ah! Listen to the rest; be more amazed
At all the arts I found, and all the ways,
The greatest: than when a man fell ill
There was no remedy at all,
No diet, liniment or draught. So men decayed.
To skeletons for lack of drugs,
Until I showed them how to mix emollient recipes,
So keep away from all disease.
...So much for these.
Now come to human blessings hidden in the earth:
Brass, iron, silver, gold....
Who claims he uncovered these before me?
...The whole truth in a sentence, if you want it short,
Is: Every art to man Prometheus brought. (440-506)

Schools and colleges are Promethean institutions. They too have brought every art to man. They have the Promethean faith in man. They have the Promethean courage and hope. Like Prometheus they look forward to the distant future, sustained by their vision of what some day mankind can be. They are not afraid of the human mind. They are not afraid of the new discoveries of science. They are determined to discover more. They are not afraid of change. They welcome it. They are not afraid of freedom. In their accent on intellectual inquiry, nothing is immune from investigation and study. There are no forbidden subjects, no forbidden books. If this is a dangerous course, so be it. Schools and colleges will face the danger and assume the risks.

This Promethean faith is far from universally shared. It runs counter to the mood of many of our leading writers. It is in conflict with the pessimism of the neo-orthodox in theology. Its view of man and society is unlike the fashionable slogans of fear and anxiety. It is at variance with the spirit of self-distrust which has been so characteristic of the twentieth-century intellectual. It proclaims a faith in man lost for almost a generation; a faith which must be reaffirmed if we are to cure the world of its present malaise.

As we enter the third century of the American Dream there are many who no longer believe in our economic growth and would check it if they could. They do not understand that without it half the world will remain poor, sick, and hungry. Again many of the people who speak so feelingly of improving the lot of the little man by more governmental spending appear to regard all business growth as evil. They would kill the goose that lays the golden eggs of jobs and dollars that are taxed.

Is it not a paradox that with every achievement of man critics are still so pessimistic about him? And has not the time come to balance accounts and take a more Promethean view? One of the most important problems of both philosophy and religion is to frame a more adequate view of man and the world.

We desire no oversimplified view of the world or of man and his problems. This is indeed an imperfect world. It is, however, a world that has come a long way. And it is a world for which we still have hope.

The late Anton Carlson of the University of Chicago took what I think is a balanced view and still preserved his faith in man.

> As I see it, ours is not an age of science. Men are still driven by greed and confused by guile, rather than guided by reason based on our expanding knowledge.... Whether science and the scientific method, whether understanding, honesty, reason, and justice can contrive survival values equal, if not superior, to the blind forces of nature which shaped man's past is as yet in the laps of the gods. Still, we cannot deny the possibility, and we will nurse the hope that the hairy ape who somehow lost his tail, grew a brain worth having, built speech and song out of a hiss and a roar, and stepped out of the cave to explore and master the universe may some day conquer his own irrational and myopic behavior toward his kin.

Albert Einstein had a simple but inelegant way of describing the problem of learning. He said: "You can't scratch if you don't itch."

To define education as the business of making people uncomfortable leaves many important things unsaid. Nevertheless, it is true that we learn most readily and quickly when we are made uncomfortable, when we are forced to use our mind. We begin to think and to learn when we are bothered by a problem we have not solved, a question we have not been able to answer, a mystery we would like to understand, a compelling need we desire to meet.

What complicates the problem of education in our time is that it must be education for change. The kind of world in which we will have our careers may differ in important respects from the world as it is today. A course of study deals only with the knowledge now available, with the transmission of existing knowledge. We can only speculate about what will be discovered and taught tomorrow. Where the future bears a close resemblance to the present, instruction in current knowledge is remarkably useful. But where the future differs in essential respects from the present, current knowledge is of less and less value except as a foundation for future learning.

The rapid obsolescence of knowledge forces more emphasis on habits of thinking, habits of reading, habits of seeing and hearing. We must go to school, in the sense of serious learning, as long as we live. We must learn only to find that what we have learned is not adequate. Life will be a constant adjustment to new conditions, new knowledge, new opportunities, new challenges, and new responsibilities. As Rosemary Park once remarked: "The one certain element about our future is surprise. The unexpected event may be more important than the certain and the fixed."

For a rapidly changing world we need the broadest possible educational programme. We should delay specialisation until we are grounded in fundamentals. The prospective journalist needs a wide background of science, social science, and the humanities as a preparation for the study of his own field. The prospective geologist needs mathematics, physics, chemistry, and biology as a condition to progress in his own specialty. How far he can go in geology depends particularly on his background in mathematics and physics. So it goes.

We are in the kind of world that requires a knowledge of the sciences and the humanities, and perhaps the region between them, which is the history and philosophy of science. The Baccalaureate degree given to a chemistry major should not be a certificate indicating ignorance of the humanities. The same degree awarded to a major in philosophy or history should not mean, as it of often has, a near absence of mathematical and scientific knowledge.

Education should deal with the whole man. Our Promethean faith is not in the mind alone but in man as a child of God, a creature with divine qualities, knowing good and evil.

Schools and colleges should minister as best they can to the needs of the whole man. They should try to inculcate integrity and honor. They should try to build character. They should attempt to protect our health. They should attempt to keep us sensitive to religious and moral values. They should try to give us concern for beauty as well as truth and goodness. And finally, they are conscious of the unmet needs of the world. They should try to teach us to be good citizens and to be socially useful.

Pericles said it in words that are as timely as they are timeless:

> Unlike other cities, Athens expects every citizen to take an interest in public affairs; and, as a matter of fact, most Athenians have some understanding of public affairs. We do believe in knowledge as a guide to action; we have a power of thinking before we act, and of acting too, whereas many people can be full of energy if they do not think, but when they reflect they begin to hesitate. We like to make friends abroad by doing good and giving help to our neighbors; and we do this not from some calculation of self-interest but in the confidence of

freedom in a frank and fearless spirit. I would have you fix your eyes upon Athens day by day, contemplate her potentiality—not merely what she is but what she has the power to be, until you become her lovers. Reflect that her glory has been built up by men who knew their duty, and had the courage to do it. Make them your examples and learn from them that the secret of happiness is freedom, and the secret of freedom, courage.

17

THE UNCOMMON LIFE

We have been told for a long time that this is the age of the common man. Perhaps we need to remind ourselves that the age of the common man was made possible by uncommon men. The age of the common man can be lifted out of cheapness and conformity only by uncommon men. Whatever our role in life we can all aspire to be uncommon in the quality of our minds, our character, and our service.

What expectations do we have a right to hold as the consequences of education? What image of outcomes ought we to envision? First, *education should lead to emotional maturity.* In its most comprehensive sense education represents man's permanent struggle for maturity. It is the process by which he grows up into freedom, and only the mature can be free.

Walter Lippman in his *Preface to Morals* says:

> We grow older, but it is by no means certain that we grow up. The human character is a complicated thing, and its elements do not necessarily march in step. It is possible to be a sage in some things and a child in others, to be at once precocious and retarded, to be shrewd and foolish, serene and irritable. For some parts of our personalities may well be more mature than others, not infrequently we participate in the enterprise of an adult with the mood and manners of a child.

> The successful passage into maturity depends, therefore, on a breaking up and reconstruction of those habits which were appropriate only to our earliest experience.
>
> In a certain larger sense, this is the essence of education. For unless a man has acquired the character of an adult, he is a lost soul no matter how good his technical equipment. The world unhappily contains many such lost souls. They are often in high places, men trained to manipulate the machinery of civilisation but utterly incapable of handling their own purposes in any civilised fashion, for their purposes are merely the relics of an infancy when their wishes were law, and they knew neither necessity nor change.

Education is man's attempt to know what he is by knowing both what he can achieve and on what he ultimately depends. This self-awareness means a consciousness of both psychological strengths and weaknesses; awareness of social roles as parent and citizen; awareness of the interrelations of the governments and labor unions and business and industry; awareness of the forces that make for productivity or self-development or moral virtue; awareness of the nature of culture. Impulsive reactions to an environment ought, with the achievement of emotional maturity, to give way to informed, accurate, and deliberate actions. Sensitivity to more than merely rhythm should characterise one's sympathy for music. The eye should be a gate for more than photographic reality in the presence of the visual arts. And loyalty to institutions and persons should be one's personal responsiveness in love and generosity.

A second outcome of education, as we have said, should be a continual involvement with books. The intelligent and habitual use of books provides an access to facts, ideas, and aesthetic experiences available in no other way. Certainly this involvement with books should not eliminate other aesthetic experiences communicated by sight and sound in the arts. Nevertheless books remain the basic tools of the educated man. They are his special concern as substance for the life of the mind.

A third outcome should be the habit of accuracy. Whether one is trained as an engineer, architect, historian, or poet, accuracy is an essential quality. It begins with the simplicities of spelling, pronunciation, and the use of numbers. It continues to the selection of appropriate words and on to the more profound problem of the psychological orientation to expressing the truth. If there be anything of good report, if there be any virtue, any praise in studies for the Ph.D., it is just at this point. At the graduate level, if no other, it is an education in accuracy.

Emotional maturity, continual involvement with books, and the habit of accuracy point toward two other qualities that educated men and women should possess.

One is a reflective mind. It was Pascal who said, "Thought makes the whole dignity of man; therefore endeavor to think well." To follow Pascal's counsel and "think well" requires a clear sense of importance, meaning, or value. It does matter, in terms of personal and social development, whether we learn to think in relation to subjects that have greater or less intrinsic significance.

The reflective mind, given to deliberation, will look for the premises as weil as at the structure of the argument. It will entertain opposing theses with calm dispassion. It will evaluate the interrelationships of means and ends, aware that forms of procedure do not necessarily determine ends and certainly are not to be confused with them.

The reflective mind is eager to be well informed, to have all the facts, not just those that lie on the surface. The reflective mind has respect for the knowledge of the past because it is aware of the great lesson of history, that those who do not know the blunders of the past are condemned to repeat them. The reflective mind, however, looks forward as well as backward. In a rapidly changing world it is deeply concerned with foresight and the emerging shape of the future.

And finally, the reflective mind is concerned with decision and action. "The art of life," said Mr. Justice Holmes, "consists in making correct decisions on insufficient evidence." Life does not permit perpetually suspended judgment. Werner Jaeger made a great advance in Aristotelian study by establishing the originality of that philosopher in his distinction of the practical intellect (phronesis) and the contemplative intellect (sophia) or wisdom. The reflective mind, although akin to Aristotle's contemplative intellect, is not one that cannot be made up. Indeed free men must act. A slave is a being who habitually submits to having his choices made for him by some other man. They very nature of a dynamic society is such that if a man does not decide himself, history will decide for him. For the educated man action or decision is preceded, not prevented, by thought. All too often people forget to engage the gears of the mind before stepping on the gap both figuratively and physically. There are times when one feels like crying out as did Demosthenes to the Athenians, "In God's name, I beg of you to think!"

A fifth outcome of education should be an ever-widening range of curiosity. The specialist is only half educated if he is only a specialist. The old box camera without a lens provided a rather narrow limit of focus. The 35 mm camera was a vast improvement upon this. The educated man should look on life with a collection of refined lenses ranging from the close-up portrait to the extended telephoto but especially the wide angle. His universe of concern should be an expanding universe, as is that in which he lives.

These five outcomes suggest an old Greek definition of

happiness as one suitable to describe education: "The exercise of vital powers along lines of excellence in a life affording them scope."

Now these five—emotional maturity, continual involvement with books, the habit of accuracy, a reflective mind, and widening range of curiosity—point one step further. Alfred North Whitehead reminds us that "apart from some transcendent aim the civilised life either wallows in pleasure or elapses into a barren repetition with waning intensities of feeling." This is what was meant by the ancient proverb in Scripture: "Where there is no vision the people perish."

Certain periods of human history, quite apart from favorable political or economic circumstances, indeed sometimes amid the most apparently unfavorable conditions, turn out to be times of enormous cultural productivity. Other times are arid and poor. Close scrutiny has not yet revealed the mystery of this grace of productivity beyond disclosing that at each such time there were individuals possessed of a deeper vision of ultimate reality than most of their fellows, persons consequently of new faith and stronger wings for action.

Athens presents such a case. Edith Hamilton opens her volume *The Greek Way* with these words:

> Five hundred years before Christ in a little town on the far western border of the settled and civilised world, a strange new power was at work. Something had awakened in the minds and spirits of the men there, which was so to influence the world that the slow passage of long time, of century upon century, and the shattering changes they brought would be powerless to wear away that deep impress. Athens had entered upon her belief and magnificent flowering of genius. The Greeks were the first intellectualists. In a world where the irrational had

> played the chief role, they came forward as the protagonists of the mind.... Men were thinking for themselves.

The vital element in civilisation is this quality that cannot itself be learned—"inspiration," "vision", "a transcendent aim." Call it what we will, but find it we must if we aspire to the uncommon life.

18

NO ORDINARY BIRD

The Book Jonathan Livingston Seagull begins with these words:

> It was morning and the new sun sparkled gold across the ripples of a gentle sea......
>
> Way off alone, out by himself beyond boat and shore Jonathan Livingston Seagull was practicing. A hundred feet in the sky he lowered his webbed feet, lifted his beak and strained to hold a painful twisting curve through his wings. The curve meant that he would fly slowly, and now he slowed until the wind was a whisper in his face, until the ocean stood still beneath him. He narrowed his eyes in fierce concentration, held his breath, forced one-single-more-inch of curve. Then his feathers ruffled, he stalled and fell.
>
> Seagulls, as you know, never falter, never stall. To stall in the air is for them disgrace and it is dishonor.
>
> But Jonathan Livingston Seagull—unashamed, stretching his wings again in that trembling hard curve slowing, slowing, and stalling once more—was no ordinary bird.

Like Jonathan Livingston Seagull, people deeply interested in the pursuit of learning are no ordinary birds. We pay no ordinary price in effort, practice, study, and self-denial. The pursuit of learning is not easy.

William James used to say that if he could preach only one sermon he would choose the text from the Second Chapter of Ezekiel: "Son of Man, stand upon they feet and I will speak to thee."

James believed that the proper posture for man was to stand erect, to stand with pride, resolved to do his full part in life. He believed that God helps most those who help themselves.

I like the text William James chose—but if I had a similar choice my text would be from the Seventh Chapter of St. Matthew: 'Strait is the gate and narrow is the way which leadeth unto life and few there be that find it."

There is an old saying of the Greeks that the beautiful is hard. Good workmanship is rare; perfection in art is rarer still. The beautiful is hard to create, hard to judge, and hard to preserve. A cathedral that required three hundred years to build can be destroyed in an instant by a nuclear bomb. One of the many tragedies of war and the acts of terrorist groups is the destruction of irreplaceable art—the accumulation of centuries.

Truth is also hard. It, too, is difficult to discover, difficult to judge, difficult to keep. Painfully made discoveries in the arts and sciences were lost in the decline and fall of early civilisations. Many arts and technical processes known to earlier cultures are still unknown to us today.

Truth is as elusive as mercury. Much that passed as science yesterday is fiction today. Much that was called truth is now regarded as superstition. Many of the things that seemed most certain are now but old wives' tales.

In some fields truth is particularly hard to find. The discussion of justice in Plato's *Republic* illustrates the difficulty of the quest for truth in the field of political science and human relations. We make constant use of abstract ideas like justice, goodness, and wisdom. How many conflicting definitions there are! Who among us can define them in terms that would win universal assent?

The New Testament suggests that there is also nothing easy about goodness. It, too, is difficult to define. It is difficult to judge, difficult to win, and difficult to keep. "It is a strait gate and a narrow way."

L.P. Jacks reminds us:

> when we examine the mysterious thing called "Life" there is one deeply interesting and significant fact which can hardly fail to provoke our wonder. All the activities of life operated in the face of opposition and cannot operate otherwise. Whether a government can be carried on without an opposition, remains to be seen, but life without opposition is not to be found anywhere. All of life's activities, physical, mental, moral and spiritual, and the last no less than the first, do their work in a resisting medium, and need it if they are to go on at all.
>
> Every living thing is an example of this. The bird needs the resisting medium of the air to fly; the fish of the water to swim; and man when he stands upright is resisting a tendency to fall, though he may be unconscious of it. Standing upright might be defined as successful resistance to the force of gravitation.
>
> So, too, when we turn to the sphere of our moral activities and study the man who is standing upright in the moral sense. He, too, is resisting a tendency to fall in another way, though he may be doing so unconsciously.
>
> Morality always functions in a resisting medium. The "good life," takes what form it may, is never a

> "walk over," never an operation performed in a vacuum.
>
> Whatever aspect of human life we examine, from the physical to the spiritual, the same conditions confront us. Every form of it represents a victory won over a resisting medium of one kind or another. Our common habits of decency are victories won over corresponding indecencies; our civilisation is a victory won over error, and our logic is a weapon for fighting our tendency to make mistakes.

James Hinton reminds us that "little inconveniences, exertions, pains,—there are the only things in which we rightly feel our life at all. If these be not there, existence becomes worthless, or worse; success in putting them all away is fatal. So it is men engage in athletic sports, spend their holidays in climbing up mountains, and find nothing so enjoyable as that which taxes their endurance and their energy. This is the way we are made, I say. It may or may not be a mystery or a paradox; it is a fact."

The good is hard in every field of knowledge. Whether our goal is music, art, literature, or science, we succeed only by exceptional dedication and effort. Paderewski practiced every day and every evening until late at night and did hours of stretching exercises for his short fingers that could barely reach an octave. He lived in stark poverty. His only son was a cripple, never able to walk. He lost his deeply beloved wife. But as the hero of his nation and greatest musician of his time he could still say: "You must accept your suffering in order to be urged on toward your ascent."

Paderewski tells us in his autobiography:

> It took half of my life, to realise that there are two ways of using the piano. The one is to play, the other is to work. If you use the one, you will never achieve anything. You are carried away with your

> own emotions and with the emotion of the contents of the work you are playing. And you might spend the whole of your life in playing without learning anything. *You can be drunk in any art on your own emotions.* And, alas, a great many people are wasting their time that way, arriving at no results at all. While working of course, you suffer, because you have absolutely no pleasure, only effort and pain.

Malvina Hoffman, whose "Hall of Man" in the Field Museum at Chicago is one of America's important contributions to art, echoes the same sentiment in her book, *Heads and Tales.* She is too modest to do any boasting but we learn that before she became a sculptor she spent years perfecting her accuracy in drawing and modeling, studied human anatomy by dissection, studied carpentry, learned to make and repair her own tools, learned how to build wood and iron armatures, and how to cast her own bronzes. She forced herself to master half a dozen trades. It was typical of her thoroughness that she was unwilling to make a frieze of Pavlowa's "Autumn Bacchanale" until she herself had learned this dance from start to finish. She had made at least a hundred drawings of Pavlowa at rehearsals and had been watching the Russian dancers for months, but it was only when she herself had experienced the full ecstasy of the dance that she felt ready to depict it on bas-relief.

In her autobiography *Yesterday is Tomorrow,* she refers to a winter of uninterrupted work on eight pieces of sculpture and then observes: "People don't understand that you have to work so hard and there are no short cuts. If there are, although I've lived rather long, I have never found any. I have to work my way to knowledge, and there never seems any other way to get it."

As we turn our attention to our future, the all-important question is our continuing growth and, as we grow older, our self-renewal. Our formal schooling is designed to help us become all that we are capable of becoming. In the years after school we should continue to grow. Life is the art of becoming.

Don M. Wolfe notes that "each new experience of high school or college opportunities represents an investment in perhaps the most fundamental of all unproved assumptions on the American scene; that children and adults are more plastic and malleable in their response to books, teachers, and ideas than any scientist has yet suspected." This does not mean, however, that education will make us equal. Animals are not equal. Men are not equal. Equality of educational opportunity simply gives all the same opportunity.

The productivity of men differs even more than the productivity of cows. Genetic differences are enormous in the same family. The Parable of the Talents recognises the inequality of men, but we pretend that we would all be equal if we had the same advantages. Christopher Jencks has made himself unpopular by reporting the evidence to the contrary.

We know more about genetic differences in farm animals than of genetic differences in farmers. We apply more sense to the breeding of animals than we do to the marriage selection process of men. It is important to know the ways in which animals and men are alike. It is even more important, however, to know the ways in which they are different.

The first difference is that man is unfinished at birth. As Professor William Ernest Hocking says, "Of all beings it is man in whom heredity counts for least and conscious building forces for most—other creatures nature could largely finish the human creature must finish himself."

Man is the most helpless of newborn animals. He has the longest infancy. He is less dependent on instincts, more dependent on the use of his mind and with unique powers of habit-making and habit-changing. It takes him longer to mature physically. Even when his legs begin to grow old and he has passed the peak of his physical powers, he is still unfinished in the development of his mental and spiritual powers. We should note, however, that the aging of the body and the decay of spirit and mind are closely related to their care, their exercise, their use. What is not developed is slowly but surely lost. Nature takes away whatever we do not use. Regardless of age, however, we are remarkably free to continue our learning and self-realisation.

The second difference is that man is a citizen of two world: the world of body and the world of mind, the world of matter and the world of spirit, the world of necessity and the world of freedom. In a more limited sense this may also be true of some animals. We should be slow to belittle intelligence and instinct in animals.

I remember a summer in Canada when I had purchased fifty green frogs and brought them to our camp in Georgian Bay. They were in a large bucket, and before going to beg I had put the bucket in the kitchen at the back of the cottage. In the middle of the night I was awakened by a curious scratching sound against the screens on the front porch. The frogs had escaped and, following their instincts, were trying to make their way through the cottage toward the world of water the cottage faced. They were demonstrating that they are citizens of two world—the world of land and the world of water.

Man too depends on instinct, but he is also moved by words and ideas. They can run in his head life a fever. He is influenced by hopes, dreams, ideas, ambitions and aspirations. He lives by values and by faith.

The third difference between man and animals grows out of the first two. Man is an unfinished animals with the capacity to learn as long as he lives. As a citizen of two worlds, we cannot put a ceiling on his development. Nor can we limit the degree of control he has over his future. In the world of nature man is unique in his ability to increase his mental, physical and spiritual powers.

To be sure, much is predetermined by heredity. Much, too, depends on diet, health, and care. The greatest difference, however, is man's response to opportunity for learning, his response to the influence of books and teachers, and his capacity for self-motivation, self-discipline, and self-direction.

There is an old saying, "Young man, be very careful about what you want from life, for almost certainly you will get it." The saying is true. The goal we build our life about, we are likely to get, whether it is money, political influence, eminence in a profession, or a life of unselfish service. We must choose carefully, for we may not like what we get.

To a surprising degree, assuming an opportunity for education, we can write our own travel ticket. What we want most, work hard for, and make substantial sacrifices to achieve is seldom beyond reach. Man is the only animal with the ability to choose his own goals and with the power to move toward them. He confounds all he skeptics about the limits of growth and development. Even with equal opportunity we are not equal; however, we are all malleable. We are all capable of astonishing growth in skills, knowledge, and power if we will pay the price in self-discipline and toil. Some of us come closer than others in realising our potential, but all of us have a higher ceiling than we reach. In the process from *posse* to *esse,* what is actual is but a part of what was and is possible.

One of the problems of Western society is its low view of man. It is a view of man as an animal, amoral and without faith. It is in incomplete view, an inadequate view. And a large part of it is because of the kind of models we have chosen to emulate. To achieve excellence we must have a vision of excellence. To achieve greatness we must have models of greatness.

Not too long ago there was a widely syndicated newspaper and radio series under the title, "Man is What He Eats." It had a high view of food and a low view of man. Food will make us fat. It will also keep us alive, but we are more than what we eat.

Perhaps a better thesis would have been, "Man is What He Reads." Certainly few things make so great a difference. The habit of reading widely gives life new dimensions and ensures growth and self-renewal. The diet of the mind either arrests or accelerates our mental development. It is clear that man is shaped by what he sees, what he hears, what he does, what he thinks, and what he aspires to be. "As a man thinketh in his heart, so is he."

Everyone who has spent his life with students should be an optimist about human nature and, with a few crossed fingers, about human society. Each year we witness the miracle of change and growth. Each year reinforces our faith in the value and importance of the learning experience.

There is much truth in the dreams of youth. We do need to aim high, to hitch our wagons to a star. In all the studies of bright young people that follow them through life, what appears to make the greatest difference is the level of their aspiration.

In his poem "The Road Not Taken," Robert Frost said,

> Two roads diverged in a wood and I took
> the one less travelled by and that has
> made all the difference.

Browning put it in his own inspiring words: "The aim, if reached or not, makes great the life," and again, "And a man's reach should exceed his grasp, or what's a heaven for?"

We can become what we want to become. We have enormous freedom and power in the art of becoming.

We began with the opening words of *Jonathan Livingston Seagull.* Let us close with the final paragraph: "And though he tried to look properly severe for his students, Fletcher Seagull suddenly saw them all as they really were, just for a moment, and he more than liked, he loved what he saw. No limits, Jonathan? He thought, and he smiled. His race to learn had begun."

Let each of us resolve that our race to learn has begun. Life is learning. Learning is the art of becoming.

19

KNOWLEDGE CROWNS THOSE WHO SEEK HER

At its highest and best, education is the intellectual and moral development of the perfect prince. It is the training of the wise and good ruler, be his name Caesar, King, or citizen in a country truly free.

As Plato remarks in the fifth book of the *Republic:* "Until philosophers are kings, or the kings and princes of this world have the spirit and power of philosophers, and political greatness and wisdom meet in one,....cities will never have rest from their evils." Plato was not successful in his efforts in ancient Syracuse as tutor to Dionysius II, who at the age of thirty had become the reigning tyrant. Nor are we likely to be successful as we attempt to improve city, state, and federal government. Nevertheless, this is what we should try to do. Plato was right. The goal of the American school and college is the education of the perfect prince or princess. We accept this as the goal for all the people, since all hold royal power, all are both citizens and rulers. How well we succeed determines the level of our culture, the strength of our nation, and the organisation of the world for prosperity and peace: *Suos Cultores Scientia Coronat.*

The classical revival made a deep mark on Upstate New York. Its villages and cities bear such names as Homer, Rome, Tully, Utica, Apulia, Troy, Hector, Cicero, Marcellus, Marathon, and Syracuse. Where communities bear such names there was nothing incongruous about a university motto that borrows the image of a prince not yet crowned. It was characteristic in that age of faith to understand that education is the key to power and that there is no royal crown more significant than the crown of knowledge. Those who selected the motto of Syracuse University were ambitious, but they were nonetheless simple, old-fashioned, God-fearing people. They selected a dead language because that was the language of the learned man. They liked the imagery of kings and crowned heads, but they betrayed their agricultural origins by using the word *cultors.* To be sure they did not use the term "agriculture"--the culture of the fields—but the meaning is the same. It is the figure of the man with a plough turning over the soil, a man drenched with sweat from the hardest kind of toil. Even when translated into the labor of a student it is work such as Goethe had in mind when he wrote that no one knows the meaning of work "whose bread hath ne'er been steeped in tears." *Suos Cultores"* is not a dilettante phrase. It is earthy, honest, and straight from the farm.

Scientia is a more modern and more controversial word. One wonders why it was chosen rather than *sophia*—wisdom, or *veritas*—truth. Its selection is something of a surprise. In general the world has been critical of *scientia.* This is the theoretical and philosophical knowledge of the intellect. This is the book-knowledge of the classroom and study, the product of the library and the science laboratory. It is the life of the mind. This is the peculiar business of a school or college. This is what distinguishes an educational institution from a church, a reform school, a hospital, a country club, a YMCA or a YWCA. There is a no point in being defensive about it. Whether a college succeeds or not depends on what it does about *scientia.*

Suous Cultores Scientia Coronat. To those who toil at this business—to those who work hard enough, to those who never cease to seek *scientia*—the reward is like the coronation of a king or of a queen. Commencement exercises are a kind of coronation. They are the democratic counterpart of an honors list at court. The work that earns an Associate degree, a Baccalaureate, a Master's, or a Doctorate is a progressive honors list, with varying degrees of nobility like the range from baronet to duke.

This, however, is a time of change. Even royal families are now insecure. The laurel of Apollo no longer guards the gates of the Caesars. Heredity alone no longer insures a throne. The right to rule must be earned again in each generation. This is true even in the democracies of the citizen rulers.

In knowledge, too, this is a new world, and the explosion of new knowledge is under way. We wonder how the members of a graduating class would react if the commencement speaker said " I regret to inform you that what you have learned is now obsolete."

It is not completely true, but there is too much truth in it for comfort. Moreover there is nothing any of us can do about it but to continue to update our education. Generations before could think of themselves as heirs of a magnificent past with enough intellectual capital so all could live on the income of it. Not so today. The past is still important, but it is no longer enough. The rate of change is too rapid. Tomorrow's demands will be very different from today's. Only with tomorrow's knowledge can we understand tomorrow's world.

Thus, the all-important questions are: will we keep on learning? Will we keep on seeking *scientia?* Can we still be described as *suos cultores?* In the world of tomorrow we will go to school in some sense as long as we live. There are some forty million Americans taking adult education courses of one kind or another, and the number grows greater each year. More than 50 per cent of those taking Baccalaureate degrees will go on to graduate or professional schools. Graduate work is already more common than undergraduate work was a generation ago.

The great emphasis of our time is on vocational or professional development. The young engineer knows that in order to keep up with his field he must continue his studies. The scientist, the teacher, the lawyer, and the doctor feel the same pressures. And now the young business executive is learning that what applies to the professional man applies also to him.

The pressures of a competitive society may take care of continuing education in our chosen vocation or profession. There is, however, no evidence of any like pressure to cultivate our private intellectual life. This will not be cultivated unless we feel strongly about it and continue to feel that way. This is a period when all of our communication media and our cultural influences tend to make us more and more alike. There is increasing homogeneity of attitudes, opinions, tastes, and consumption patterns. Yet if education has taught us anything it is that each of us is an individual, with his or her unique image. Moreover, if we do our own thinking we shall not think alike."

So the pressures of our day are to be resisted. Thinking is rare. Even the habit of reading good books is rare. The late Henry Mencken in a particularly cynical mood once declared: "Most men don't think thirty minutes in their whole lifetime. Any man who can think two minutes at a stretch is a genius."

Most of us will hear good music, will go to the theatre and enjoy it, will visit museums and keep up in some degree with changes in art. We shall probably also do our share of travel. What is more doubtful is how much poetry we will read, how much philosophy, how much science, how many forgotten classics, how much fiction and nonfiction not on the list of best sellers.

Will we read regularly and with enjoyment books that

feed the mind, that open new doors of understanding that throw light on complex issues, that rub away our prejudices and compel us to revise our views? Will we continue the building of our personal library with increasing discrimination and pleasure?

Richard Jeffries reminds us, "It is the peculiarity of knowledge that those who really thirst for it always get it." This makes it sound easy. The truth, however, is that everything in our busy Western life conspires against the cultivation of the private intellectual life.

Even among the literate there is a preoccupation with the latest fashions in thought and a singular unwillingness to challenge what Mill calls "the received opinions." Howard Mumford Jones reminds us that if one should inquire, as Crevecoeur did in 1832, "who is this new man in America," the answer would often be "he is a lonely soul lost in the wilderness of neo-Calvinism and midnight melancholy." But there is also the emptiness of life bounded by bridge and golf games, soap operas, and comic books. If there is a cure, we should find it in a wider and a deeper intellectual life. The life of the mind must be fed and exercised. It also needs a balanced diet. The mind does not continue to grow when left to itself.

In *Philosopher's Holiday* Irwin Edman tells of his experience over a period of years with a young sailor named Jewell. Professor Edman had introduced the sailor to Wagner's Meistersinger. In attempting to describe the music, the sailor referred to the Gospel of St. John: "Remember what he says about the Word become Flesh? It's a wonderful phrase and it tells a lot about writing. The Word became Flesh. Some writing is that. Touched with flame, certain writing is. The spirit become incarnate. You can tell at once the real thing from the fake. That Wagner music has it: touched with flame."

Professor Edman had his failures as well as his successes

with students. At the close of his essay he notes with sadness: "Jewell has been married some years now. There is a little boy who bears the writer's name. Jewell seems happy, though less exuberantly than of old, and he finds it difficult, he tells me when I see him, to keep up with ideas now. `And philosophical ideas don't seem such cures for the world as I used to think,' he said, not the world I see around me on shore and read about in the papers.'"

"I gathered," concludes Professor Edman, "that on a milkman's wages and with a wife to support and a child to bring up, things in general are not touched with flame, nor is ecstasy as obvious any more."

That is the problem, whether we are milkmen or housewives or business or professional people. What do we do about our education when things in general are not touched with flame, and ecstasy is not obvious any more?

The quality of our culture is revealed by the things we honor by our interests, our dollars, and our energies. If we are mindful of professional development and the private intellectual life, what about the duties of the citizen, the sense of social responsibility of the educated man? If education is the training of a prince, is not this of the highest importance?

The beautiful words of the Athenian Oath remind us, "We will ever strive for the ideals and sacred things of the City, both alone and with many. We will increasingly seek to quicken the sense of public duty; we will revere and obey the city's laws; we will transmit this City not only less, but greater, better and more beautiful than it was transmitted to us."

In a democracy the education of a prince is the education of the citizen. The mission of the school, the college, and the university is in part the education of the future ruler. If we really understood this, it is inconceivable that the course of study would be science alone or humanities alone. The study of public affairs, the understanding of our legal and political system, the complex issues of domestic and foreign policy, are central and continuing interests. Because we are citizen-rulers we cannot plead indifference or flee from responsibility. Because we are responsible we must keep ourselves informed.

One of the watchwords of our time is freedom. We should like all men to be free. It is not simply freedom, however, that has made the United States great. It is freedom with responsibility. We cannot divorce the two. The college graduate who has not taken seriously his duties as a citizen should begin now. There is much to learn. There is no time to wait. Yet, we should remember the caveat of Woodrow Wilson, "The fault of our age is the fault of hasty action, of premature judgments, or of a preference for ill-considered action over no action at all.... We see an error, and we hastily correct it by a greater error and then go on to cry that the age is corrupt."

Education for public affairs appears to be that part of the mind where logic and common sense count least. The saddest feature of American democracy is the failure of its citizens to understand what government cannot do even with all the money in this world. The future of democratic government is bleak indeed without better education for individual responsibility and governmental accountability.

To those who weigh and consider, to those who reflect and reason, life is a seamless robe in which both values and facts are threads. Character and scholarship are not two things. Rightly conceived they are one. Good scholarship demands honesty and reverence for truth. Our approach to knowledge must have the integrity of the scientist and the scholar.

We are conservators of a tradition that goes back to Homer. What do we conserve? Certainly it is not the answers, though the trail blazed in a wilderness of conflicting counsel is one all wise men will follow. Certainly it is not beliefs, though some have held the world together. Certainly it is not the findings of science, important as it is to keep the record of man's scientific inquiry.

We are conservators of the spirit of learning, of the place of freedom, of respect for reason, and of reverence for the search for truth. The question is whether we are strong enough to continue our learning without the lure of degrees, without the requirement of credits, without the supervision of teachers, without the paternalism and fraternalism of deans and professors and fellow students.

The late Charles C. Noble, Dean of Hendricks Chapel at Syracuse University, defined education as a love affair with truth; a love affair with knowledge and wisdom. It is a good definition—and Dean Noble gave it deeper meaning by reminding us that we cannot take such a love affair for granted. We must continue the courtship, continue the wooing.

Plato in one of his letters expresses some doubts as to whether we can explain what we mean by the word *philosophy*. "There does not exist, and there never shall, any treatise by myself on these matters. The subject does not admit as the sciences do, of exposition." Then follow these luminous words, which describe the meaning of education as well as philosophy. "It is only after long association in the great business itself and a shared life that a light breaks out in the soul, kindled, so to say, by a leaping flame, and thereafter feels itself."

Has a light been kindled in the soul? Will the leaping flame continue to be fed by the soul's hungers and ambitions? Will we commit ourselves to service beyond self, to magnanimity and brotherhood, and to search for goodness and truth that leads us to the Divine Source? Is this love affair with knowledge one that will endure?

In our active seeking for new knowledge we do not cease to be the conservators of the age-old quest for righteousness and wisdom. New answers do not halt the search for knowledge. New insights, broader views, fresh discoveries are welcome despite the havoc to prejudice and the conventional wisdom.

We cannot tell what we shall become. We do not know whether we can do all that is expected of us. All we know is that it is not beyond our reach. It is not impossible. It is, in fact, what we must take as our clear objective, our announced goal. Knowledge gives the laurel wreath to those who seek her. This is the crown we should resolve to win!